Preparing to Lead
Principles of Self-Leadership and Organizational Dynamics

Eighth Edition

Contributing Editors
Arthur Gibb, III, Ph.D. CDR, USN
Bridget Seymour, LT, USN

Pearson Learning Solutions, 501 Boylston Street, Suite 900, Boston, MA 02116
A Pearson Education Company
www.pearsoned.com

Printed in the United States of America

6 7 8 9 10 0BRV 17 16 15 14

000200010271805985

MM/GS

ISBN 10: 1-269-43200-1
ISBN 13: 978-1-269-43200-9

Eighth Edition Contributing Editors

Commander David Smith, USN, Ph.D.
LCDR Siddhartha Herdegen, USN
LCDR Kelly Welsh, USN
LT Mike Misch, USN
LT Bridget Seymour, USN
LT Brian Rutledge, USN
LT Niko Sidiropoulos, USN

Copyright Acknowledgments

Contents

Part 1: Self-Knowledge   1

    Chapter 1: On Building Combat Leaders   3

    Chapter 2: Critical Thinking   11

    Chapter 3: The Nature of Strengths   31

    Chapter 4: Personality Types   39

    Chapter 5: Values   45

    Chapter 6: Reflection   61

Part 2: Self-Leadership   65

    Chapter 7: Personal Mission Development   67

    Chapter 8: Motivation and Goals   83

    Chapter 9: Staying on Track   89

Part 3: Leading Others   105

    Chapter 10: Civility   107

    Chapter 11: Active Listening   115

    Chapter 12: Social Influence   121

Chapter 13: Group Dynamics   145

Chapter 14: Brigade Leader Seminar: Peer Leadership   159

Chapter 15: Ownership   167

Chapter 16: Moral Leadership   175

Chapter 17: Leadership Case Study   181

Course
Introduction

"Never doubt that a small group of thoughtful, committed citizens can change the world. Indeed, it is the only thing that ever has."

Margaret Mead
US anthropologist (1901–1978)

Leaders change the world! When you strip away all of the "buzz words" and slogans that's what it comes down to. As leaders we are responsible for making the world a better place. No Lieutenant ever sat down with his Commanding Officer for his fitness report debrief and proudly pronounced, "Sir, I am a great leader! My unit is not any better than when I took over; not even a little. I can maintain the status quo better than anyone!"

John Kotter (1996) puts it this way, "Leadership defines what the future should look like, aligns people with that vision, and inspires them to make it happen despite the obstacles." (p. 25) He goes on to say, "...successful transformation is 70 to 90 percent leadership," and, "...this leadership often begins with just one or two people." (p. 26, 30)

You are going to become an officer in the Navy or Marine Corps. As such, you will define what the future will look like for yourself, the people you lead, your service, and the world around you, but will the future you define be as good as it should be? Will the person you become be a result of choice or circumstance? Will you be able to align your own actions with the future you desire? What about the actions of others? Will you be able to overcome obstacles? Will you be able to inspire others? Will you be able to lead yourself as well as others? In other words, will you be one of the few that change the world?

Becoming a world-changing leader does not happen overnight. It doesn't happen the instant you climb Herndon, put your Naval Academy ring on, or when you throw your cover up in the air at graduation. It is a process that takes place every day of your life. That process starts with self-knowledge. It continues with self-leadership and culminates in team leadership.

Self-knowledge is a lifelong pursuit that all leaders must undertake. It involves finding out our values and their priority, what type of personality we have, our strengths, and how our own perceptions may disguise reality. The better we know ourselves, the better we can control the will that drives our actions. The closer we can get to the core of who we are, the more our actions will originate from that core instead of originating from the opinions of others. It is only when we act from our core that we can effectively lead others towards something better.

Imagine if someone knew the cure for cancer, but chose not to tell anyone. What good are they? Any knowledge that is not used in some way to serve others is useless. Self-knowledge is no exception. You can know everything about who you are and how you work. However if you do not use that knowledge to better your life and the lives of those around you then what good are you? Knowledge has never changed the world; only applied knowledge changes things. If you want to be a world-changing leader then you have to know how to apply the knowledge you have.

When we choose to apply our self-knowledge we call that self-leadership. We apply the knowledge of our values by using them to govern the way we act. We apply the knowledge of our strengths by using them to define and accomplish goals. We apply the knowledge of our personality type by using it to find out how we best work with others to accomplish tasks. It is only when we apply the knowledge we have of ourselves, when we start practicing self-leadership, that we can truthfully say that we are living our own life instead of living the life others think we should. The last stanza of William Earnest Henley's poem Invictus states:

> *It matters not how strait the gate,*
> *How charged with punishments the scroll,*
> *I am the master of my fate:*
> *I am the captain of my soul.*

Are you the master of your fate? Are you leading yourself or being led by the wishes and expectations of others? Do you not only choose what you want to do with your life, but stick by those choices when it is hard to do so? It is only when we practice self-leadership that we can even hope to effectively lead others, *and* know what we are leading them towards.

A few years ago I saw a movie called Gladiator. At the beginning of the movie, the Roman general Maximus leads his army against the barbaric hoards in battle. In the middle of the chaos of war Maximus' men instantly obey his commands and are willing to sacrifice their lives for him. The battle scene is filled with fiery arrows and epic fight scenes that are incredibly exciting, but that is not what I liked best about it. What I liked best happened just before the battle began. Maximus walked among his troops, greeting many by name, checking to make sure they were prepared for the battle, and giving encouragement to those that seemed to need it. You see Maximus remembered something that a lot of modern leaders do not; that leading others is about *relationships* more than anything else.

Instant obedience and the willingness to sacrifice for a leader is not born on a battlefield, it is born and nurtured in the day-to-day relationships we have with those we lead. If you want to effectively lead others you must know yourself, you must practice self-leadership, and then you must understand, create, and maintain relationships between yourself and others as well as groups of people.

> *"True leaders have strong identification with the mission, projects, and job at hand. They are true believers full of enthusiasm coupled with honest concern for and with people and their families, and, to the extent possible, are familiar with their people's personal histories. Tell people what is to be done and why. Invite limited discussion. Identify the group as a team. Keep all informed. Be quick to publicly praise worthy performance, and do most of necessary personal criticism in private."*
>
> CDR Lloyd Bucher
> *Former captain of U.S.S. Pueblo*

The purpose of this book is to help you start the process of becoming a world-changing leader. It is divided into three major sections. The first is "Self-Knowledge" and it will help you understand how you think, what values you have, what kind of personality you have, and what your natural strengths are. The second section is "Self-Leadership." In this section you will develop a mission for your life, learn how to effectively set goals, and how you can stay disciplined and motivated enough to accomplish those goals. The final section is "Leading Others." In this section you will learn techniques that will help you build relationships with others, understand group dynamics, and use social influence to your advantage instead of your detriment.

If you take it seriously and put in time and effort, this book will help you start the process of becoming a world-changer! The steps in this process do not take place one right after the other. You will probably be working on all three of them throughout your entire life. However it is important to know that the three steps are mutually supportive. You cannot become an effective leader of others unless you can lead yourself, and you cannot lead yourself unless you know how you are made.

The only question left is whether or not you truly want to be a leader that changes the world around you. Sadly, most people in our society do not. Mediocrity is the standard in the world, and those that wish to become great are often pulled down by those that are comfortable with being average. They do this with sarcasm, cynicism, and sometimes outright hostility. Are you going to give in to mediocrity or pursue greatness? We hope you choose greatness.

Part
One

Self-Knowledge

1 *On Building Combat Leaders*

Learning Objectives:

- Describe the concept of a Leadership Continuum and explain why one's position on the continuum is fluid.
- Identify the three common leadership myths and critique their validity.

Written by Dr. Brad Johnson
Professor, United States Naval Academy

Reprinted from Johnson, W. B., & Harper, G. P. (2005). *Becoming a Leader the Annapolis Way: 12 Combat Lessons from the Navy's Leadership Laboratory.* The McGraw Hill Companies.

The scene is a crowded seminar room at the famed Wharton Business School at the University of Pennsylvania. The speaker, an esteemed professor of leadership and management at Wharton, is launching into a summer lecture to leaders from a range of organizations and businesses. To kick things off, the professor inquires of the audience: "I wonder whether most of you think leaders are born or whether they are made? Those who think leaders are born, raise your hands."

The vast majority of the audience members send their arms skyward. There are nods and smiles all around and emphatic murmurs of agreement as it becomes apparent that most in this group concur—excellent leadership is innate. Undeterred, the professor continues, "And does anyone feel that leaders are primarily made?"

In the front row of the hall, several white-sleeved arms shoot up. The crowd gawks in surprise, but these front-row occupants keep their hands aloft. Each arm belongs to a uniformed naval officer—a leadership instructor from the Naval Academy's Department of Leadership, Ethics, and Law. The group has come to glean the latest in leadership research and practice. They are accomplished junior officers who spend their days teaching midshipmen the mechanics of good leadership. Most of them are graduates of USNA themselves and all of them have seen midshipmen with apparently low aptitude for leading become outstanding leaders in the fleet. Their experiences at USNA and beyond have convinced them that, given the right mix of ability and aptitude, excellent leadership can be dramatically shaped and developed.

This true story from a recent Wharton seminar highlights an important assumption undergirding all that we do at USNA. The assumption goes something like this: Aptitude is important but it's not enough. Becoming an excellent leader requires hard work, intensive training, careful coaching, and deliberate feedback from seasoned leaders. Yes, certain traits seem to make leader-development easier for some, but traits alone will never make a leader.

The classic trait approach to leadership assumes that some people are simply natural born leaders. Unfortunately, massive research efforts in psychology and management have failed to elucidate these crucial personality characteristics—traits that reliably predict success in the leader role. Although personality features may make leadership somewhat more comfortable and effective, there are other important questions to ask about potential leaders than "What are they like?" For example, what do these people actually do in different situations? How do they spend their time? What are their priorities? How do they gain and use power? What are their interpersonal relationships like? How do various situations and contexts influence their leader behaviors? These are important variables and we have observed them at play in a vast number of naval leaders over the course of our careers.

Of course, we do not mean to ignore the importance of ability and aptitude when selecting leaders. Requiring one of the nation's most arduous collegiate application procedures, USNA enjoys the profound luxury of selecting only a small percentage of applicants from among a wide pool of remarkably bright and multitalented students. One cannot ignore the importance of choosing leaders who are intellectually bright, highly motivated, and imbued with positive personality traits. Still, these characteristics do not ensure excellent leadership. It takes more than capacity.

First, Forget What You've Been Told About Leaders

In this chapter we debunk a few common leadership myths often propagated as common sense or "givens" whenever leadership is discussed. The worst of these myths include:

- Leaders are born, not made.
- Good leadership is all common sense.
- The only school that teaches leadership is the school of hard knocks.

Before becoming an effective leader in the military or anywhere else, you had better work at recognizing these statements as mythical and as antithetical to the hard work required to rise in the ranks of outstanding leaders. In the balance of this chapter we dispatch each of these pernicious myths.

Leaders Are Made (Though Aptitude Sure Doesn't Hurt)

A particularly ridiculous yet maddeningly enduring leadership myth is that excellent leaders are simply born that way. Although most of us have heard this statement so many times that we tend to believe it on some level, it is actually quite a laughable idea. The statement that leaders are born implies that the world is full of leaders and nonleaders, that you either "have it" or don't in the leadership area. The fact is that each of us has a unique blend of emotional, intellectual, and behavioral talents and proclivities that place us somewhere on the continuum from poor to excellent leadership. And most important, one's location on the continuum is not static but fluid; leadership is responsive to a range of factors such as motivation, new learning, maturity, and experience. People often become more effective leaders. One alumnus shared with us an experience that we think illustrates this point very well. Robert Niewoehner, Class of '81 recalled

> Fall of my 3/c [second] year, I was a struggling member of the Lightweight Crew team. Because the team was not comprised of an even multiple of eight, several guys were left at the boat house every day to train by themselves. It seemed my number came up 2–3 times per week to stay behind. It was pretty discouraging, and I really wrestled with sticking it out.
>
> Thursday afternoons, after practice, the coach would pull four upperclassmen aside to pick boats for Friday's practice, an hour-long race from USNA around Holiday Island and back. This process was much like picking teams for sandlot baseball or soccer in elementary school. One Thursday after boats were picked, one second class took me aside and told me,

Continuum:
a) A continuous series or whole, no part of which is noticeably different from its adjacent parts, although the ends or extremes of it are very different from each other; b) Anything that goes through a gradual transition from one condition, to a different condition, without any abrupt changes

"Rob, I think you're the most underrated member of the team. I specifically wanted you in my boat, and I want to see you make big puddles for me tomorrow." All the discouragement from the previous weeks was lifted by that one remark. He could certainly not have known the extent of my discouragement.

I exhausted myself the next day on the end of that oar, determined not to disappoint his trust. I was staunchly his supporter when he was elected Team Captain the following year, for in my eyes he could do no wrong.

His remark set the tone and the path for my entire Naval Academy experience.

I committed to crew and resolved that I was going to letter by graduation.

Though I finished second in my class, held five stripes, and finished a Master's in Electrical Engineering before graduation, I am far more proud of my "N" (varsity letter) for it came at a far greater price. Encouragement is a very powerful thing. Make a point to notice the quiet ones standing in the back, tentative about whether they can fit in or contribute. It may not take much to move them.

But what about personality? Don't people with specific personality traits make better leaders? The answer appears to be: Certain traits help, but they are not enough. Positive personality features assist excellent leadership but don't guarantee it (later in this chapter we highlight some of the primary personality characteristics among those who lead well). For evidence that innate personality features do not alone predict leadership success, one only needs to consider the case of two famously successful World War II admirals.

We refer, of course, to Vice Admiral William F. "Bull" Halsey and Rear Admiral Raymond Spruance. Following the Japanese attack on Pearl Harbor and a series of Japanese naval victories, morale in the service was at low ebb. With the Japanese planning a bold attack on the U.S. naval base at Midway Island, America's ability to survive in the Pacific depended upon the success of an aircraft carrier task force led by the notoriously charismatic and outgoing VADM Halsey. A gung-ho leader who personified extroversion and was fond of large informal meetings, Halsey was interpersonally affable and prone to intuitive decision making. He was inspirational and popular among the enlisted ranks. Halsey was also a "brown shoe," a naval aviator, who was outgoing, bold, and sometimes maybe even a little too daring.

When Halsey became seriously ill shortly before the Midway battle, he was ordered hospitalized by Admiral Chester Nimitz and was quickly replaced by RADM Spruance. Now, Spruance was a "black shoe," a surface warfare officer. "Black shoes" traditionally have been quite different in their view of fleet operations when compared to their "brown shoe" brethren. "Black shoe" officers had long clung to the doctrine that battleships were the capital ships of the Navy and the carriers and naval aviators were only to be used to scout out the enemy for the battleships. The "black shoes" would then engage in the classic surface action in the tradition of the Battle of Jutland. "Black shoes" sailed at 30 knots, whereas "brown shoes" flew at 300 knots. Of course Pearl Harbor changed all of that.

Differences in the personality constellations between Halsey and Spruance were immediately noticeable. In fact, the two men appeared to be polar opposites on many dimensions of personality. In contrast to his predecessor, Spruance was quiet, reserved, and preferred reflection over constant interaction. More comfortable with small meetings and individual conversations, he was notorious for sifting through facts and analytical decision making. Officers in the carrier task force must have wondered how this introverted surface warfare officer could possibly succeed in replacing one of the most popular and admired naval aviators in history just before the most important battle of the war. Could Spruance possibly be as effective a leader? Sure enough, the wardroom had great difficulty adjusting to Spruance. Halsey had been outgoing; Spruance preferred quiet channels. Halsey paid minimal attention to detail; Spruance was compulsively focused on details and facts. Halsey was a free spirit; Spruance was deliberate and methodical.

In the end, Spruance led Carrier Task Force 16 to one of the greatest naval war victories of all time. It marked the crucial turning point in American resolve and morale in the Pacific theater. History shows that Spruance was a superb combat leader, as was his predecessor VADM Halsey.

It appears that nondescript introverts can lead as effectively as gregarious extroverts. This is a lesson learned over and over at USNA and in the Navy at large. Although certain personality traits may fit certain tasks and contexts better than others, personality will always be secondary to leader knowledge, skill, and attitude.

Have you seen good leadership from people with very different styles and personalities?

Excellent Leadership Requires More Than Common Sense

Related to the myth that leaders are born is the equally unsupportable notion that leadership is a matter of common sense. Translation: Anyone who is not a total flake can lead well because the keys to good leadership are self-evident. Again, we disagree. If leadership were common sense, it is unlikely that there would be so many problems with ineffective leadership in everyday life. Even the Navy suffers from its share of less than sterling leadership.

When USNA graduate CDR Michael Abrashoff, USN, became the commanding officer of the guided missile destroyer USS *Benfold,* he immediately set to work reading exit interviews from crewmembers who had recently departed the ship. He wondered why so many had been departing this ship and the Navy prematurely. What he found appalled him.

> I assumed that low pay would be the first reason, but in fact it was the fifth. The top reason was not being treated with respect or dignity; second was being prevented from making an impact on the organization; third, not being listened to; and fourth, not being rewarded with more responsibility.

Either Abrashoff's predecessor had no common sense or good leadership is more complex and demanding than most realize. As he set about listening to his sailors and seeking creative means to inspire and motivate them to turn the *Benfold* into a fighting community defined by high morale, Commander Abrashoff employed more than common sense. Aware of Gallup poll research showing that 65 percent of those who leave their companies are actually seeking to escape their direct managers, Abrashoff drew from science-based principles of reinforcement, organizational models of team building, and four years of intensive practice for leadership at the Naval Academy.

What things do Midshipmen do that are considered "common sense" that could require some more critical thinking?

Commonsense leadership is rooted in the erroneous assumption that *if most people believe it, it must be right.* Of course, throughout history, the majority of military leaders have at times held to clearly false beliefs such as: "Unless your men fear you, they won't respect you," and "Good leaders know when to break some china!" Further, many forms of common sense are clearly incompatible. For example, if counseling a sailor about going to sea and leaving his girlfriend behind, which common sense advice would you give: "Absence makes the heart grow fonder," or "Out of sight, out of mind"?

It comes as no surprise that research in psychology and business consistently shows that people (including would-be leaders) frequently assume they know more than they actually do; we overestimate our understanding of how to lead. When students enter the Naval Academy, many are immediately thrust into leadership roles in their company, in their classes, and in the larger brigade of midshipmen.

The School of Hard Knocks is Not the Best Way to Learn Leadership

A final myth bearing on leadership training holds that the best way to train a naval leader is to send him or her directly to sea where leadership will be inculcated in the raw and unforgiving school of hard knocks.

Academic preparation accelerates learning in the fleet. Midshipmen learn models of leadership and behavioral principles for motivating and influencing others and then apply them in the context of pervasive feedback—both around the yard and during summer assignments with the Navy and Marine Corps.

John McCain recently recounted his first class cruise and some of the lessons he learned:

> I boarded the USS *Hunt* to begin my first class cruise to Rio de Janeiro in June 1957. The *Hunt* was an old destroyer. It had seen better days. It seemed to me a barely floating rust bucket that should have been scrapped years before, unfit even for mothballing. I spent most of the cruise on the bridge, where the skipper would order me to take the conn. There is a real mental challenge to running a ship of that size, and I had little practical experience for the job. But I truly enjoyed it. I made more than a few mistakes, and every time I screwed up, the skipper would explode, letting loose an impressive blast of profane derision. "Dammit, McCain, you useless bastard. Give up the conn right now. Get the hell off my bridge. I mean it, goddammit; I won't have a worthless S.O.B. at the helm of my ship. You've really screwed up this time McCain. Get the hell out of here." As I began to skulk off the bridge, he would call me back. "Hold on a second, come on back here, Mister. Get over here and take the conn." And then he would begin, more calmly, to explain what I had done wrong and how the task was done properly. We would go along pleasantly until I committed my next unpardonable error, when he would unleash another string of salty oaths in despair over my unfitness for service, only to beckon me back for a last chance to prove myself worthy of his fine ship. One beautiful afternoon, the flagship of the Destroyer Division to which the *Hunt* was attached, flying the ensign of the commanding Admiral, approached us for the purpose of replenishing the *Hunt*'s depleted stores. The skipper gave me the conn, and without a trace of apprehension, made me bring her alongside the Admiral's flagship. He told me to bring her up slowly, but offered no rebuke when I ordered, "All engines ahead two-thirds." At precisely the right moment I ordered, "All engines back full." A few moments later, again well timed, I ordered, "All engines ahead one-third." Thrillingly and to my great relief, the *Hunt* slipped into place so gracefully that any observer would have thought the skipper himself, master shiphandler that

he was, had the conn. The skipper was proud of me, and I was much indebted to him. He had given me his trust, and I had had the good fortune to avoid letting him down. After the two ships were tied up, he sent a message to the Admiral. "Midshipman McCain had the conn." The impressed Admiral sent a message to the Superintendent of the Naval Academy informing him of my accomplishment.

Deliberate training and education equip new officers for the range of leadership challenges they will certainly encounter in the fleet. The school of hard knocks has proven inadequate as a leadership laboratory. More than 230 years of American naval experience has taught us this lesson: If you want great leaders, prepare them to lead. And never assume that hard knocks alone produce leadership skills.

If leadership is more than personality, common sense, and experience born of hard knocks then what do leaders need to learn? Our answer is lots. But here is a summary of some key things leaders learn to do—not just as students, but also as a way of life.

- Manage time effectively.
- Make commitments to tasks and organizations and be faithful.
- Recognize that following well is a prerequisite to outstanding leadership.
- Actively seek out opportunities for leadership.
- Observe and critically evaluate one's own leadership performance. Reflect on outcomes and explore alternatives for use in future situations.
- Understand that character matters; leadership requires virtue.
- Correctly diagnose leadership situations and select the most appropriate leader style for the situation.
- Constantly and tenaciously work at increasing both technical and interpersonal expertise and competence.
- Become inoculated to stress and capable of maintaining emotional equanimity during difficult situations; maintain focus without disturbance.
- Develop interpersonal skills and communication savvy; heighten emotional intelligence.
- Empower and praise always.
- Be an intentional model; lead by example.
- Take care of your people first.

Questions for review:

1. How does the "leadership laboratory" at USNA help mold you into a leader? Can you use this system of leadership to help debunk the three common leadership myths?

2. Think about your leadership roles in the past and those to come during your time at the Academy. What events could change your place on the leadership continuum?

2 *Critical Thinking*

Learning Objectives:

- Explain why the concept of critical thinking is essential to your role as a future Naval or Marine Corps officer.
- Analyze the consequences of egocentric thinking.
- Apply the Universal Intellectual Standards to a given argument.
- Identify and describe the eight Elements of Thought.
- Critique an article or situation using the eight Elements of Thought.

I: Critical Thinking

Introduction by LT Mitch Eliason, USN

Having recently returned from the Fleet as a now very salty submarine officer, I come bearing the gift of a phenomenon I call "Junior Officer Ping-Pong."

As officer candidates or midshipmen we are taught to always seek out the Chief or Gunny as our go-to for almost every answer. It turns out, that is pretty good gouge. So when I was a fresh Ensign and my Captain asked me if my division had completed the maintenance on the radar system, I looked him right in the eye, and with every intention of running straight to my Chief for the answer, confidently said, "I'll find out, sir."

Moments later I found the aforementioned ETC(SS) Rieger and inquired, "Good morning, Chief. Where do we stand with the radar maintenance?"

"Is it a good morning? I hadn't noticed I've been so dang busy" he said without looking up. "Sir, it is not 'maintenance'—we just have to grease the radar. We are not scheduled to get underway for another hour and will have it done before then."

"Roger that Chief. Thanks for the info. I will let Cap'n know," I said trying to sound like I was serving a purpose in these critical minutes before the underway.

A minute later in the Captain's stateroom I was teaching him that the he was incorrect in his use of the term 'maintenance' and that the work to be done was just a quick greasing. We would have it done before we pulled away from the pier in just under an hour.

After allowing me to educate him on how his submarine worked, the Captain responded, "Ensign, I have been driving submarines since before you were born. I know about the greasing and I know that it takes 30 seconds to do. Why hasn't it been done yet?"

Back to the Chief for an answer.

"Chief, sorry to bug you again, but it turns out this greasing only takes 30 seconds. Why isn't it done yet?"

"Sir, Ensign, sir," with no sarcasm at all I am sure, "we have to gather the parts for the maintenance, get the right personnel, follow the procedure, and test the radar after we are done. It takes much more than 30 seconds. More like five minutes. We will get it done."

Back to the Captain for some explaining.

"Captain, sir, it turns out that greasing the radar takes more like five minutes after you gather all the parts. I explained the urgency to the division's Chief and he assured me he is getting the troops working on it."

"Ensign, this is getting ridiculous. There must be something going on here. Go and personally ensure the maintenance gets done."

Back to the Chief... That morning, in the hour before we got underway, I walked between the Captain's stateroom and my Chief's workplace approximately 331 times. Each time I bounced between the two, like a ping-pong ball going back and forth across the table, I learned a little bit more about greasing the radar. More importantly I learned that I was wasting a lot of time and not doing my job as a Division Officer as effectively as I could.

If during the first meeting, I had thought to ask ETC(SS) Rieger questions like "Why hasn't the maintenance been done yet?" or "Is there another issue that is preventing us from doing a relatively small task?" or "What can I do to make sure this gets done as soon as possible?" – I could have avoided bouncing around the boat like I did. If I dug a little deeper and offered to search for a solution, rather than just serve as a conduit for passing information, I actually could have helped in the process.

One of the Naval Academy's required attributes for all graduates is to be *critical thinkers and creative decision makers with a bias for action*. As officers we need to do more than just follow orders or pass word. We need to question our assumptions, dig for more information, think outside our innate conclusions, and be the activators for appropriate action. Unfortunately, junior officer ping-pong happens way too often for fresh Ensigns and Second Lieutenants.

In this chapter you will learn a model that will aid you in thinking critically. You will learn that this is not natural for most humans. Use this model and the intellectual standards that follow it to develop yourself into an effective thinker. Use this critical thinking model to think about your thinking *with the goal of improving it*.

The Problem of Egocentric Thinking[1]

Egocentric thinking results from the unfortunate fact that humans do not naturally consider the rights and needs of others. They do not naturally appreciate the point of view of others nor the limitations in their own point of view. They become explicitly aware of their egocentric thinking only if trained to do so. They do not naturally recognize their egocentric assumptions, the egocentric way they use information, the egocentric way they interpret data, the source of their egocentric concepts and ideas, the implications of their egocentric thought. They do not naturally recognize their self-serving perspective.

As humans they live with the unrealistic but confident sense that they have fundamentally figured out the way things actually are, and that they have done this objectively. They naturally believe in their intuitive perceptions—however inaccurate. Instead of using intellectual standards in thinking, they often use self-centered psychological standards to determine what to believe and what to reject. Here are the most commonly used psychological standards in human thinking.

"IT'S TRUE BECAUSE I BELIEVE IT." Innate egocentrism: I assume that what I believe is true even though I have never questioned the basis for many of my beliefs.

"IT'S TRUE BECAUSE WE BELIEVE IT." Innate sociocentrism: I assume that the dominant beliefs within the groups to which I belong are true even though I have never questioned the basis for many of these beliefs.

---

[1] Reprinted from Elder, L. (2006). *The Thinker's Guide to Critical Thinking: Concepts and Tools*. Dillon Beach, CA: The Foundation for Critical Thinking.

"IT'S TRUE BECAUSE I WANT TO BELIEVE IT." Innate wish fulfillment: I believe in, for example, accounts of behavior that put me (or the groups to which I belong) in a positive rather than a negative light even though I have not seriously considered the evidence for the more negative account. I believe what "feels good," what supports my other beliefs, what does not require me to change my thinking in any significant way, what does not require me to admit I have been wrong.

"IT'S TRUE BECAUSE I HAVE ALWAYS BELIEVED IT." Innate self-validation: I have a strong desire to maintain beliefs that I have long held, even though I have not seriously considered the extent to which those beliefs are justified, given the evidence.

"IT'S TRUE BECAUSE IT IS IN MY SELFISH INTEREST TO BELIEVE IT." Innate selfishness: I hold fast to beliefs that justify my getting more power, money, or personal advantage even though these beliefs are not grounded in sound reasoning or evidence.

Think of a time you were in an argument. What happens when you realize you are wrong? Do you admit it, or fall back on egocentric thinking?

Because humans are naturally prone to assess thinking in keeping with the above criteria, it is not surprising that we, as a species, have not developed a significant interest in establishing and teaching legitimate intellectual standards. It is not surprising that our thinking is often flawed. We are truly the "self-deceived animal."

A Definition: Critical thinking is the art of analyzing and evaluating thinking with a view to improving it.

The Result: A well cultivated critical thinker has these traits:

- @ raises vital questions and problems, formulating them clearly and precisely;

- @ gathers and assesses relevant information, using abstract ideas to interpret it effectively;

- @ comes to well-reasoned conclusions and solutions, testing them against relevant criteria and standards;

- @ thinks openmindedly within alternative systems of thought, recognizing and assessing, as need be, their assumptions, implications, and practical consequences; and

- @ communicates effectively with others in figuring out solutions to complex problems.

Critical thinking is, in short, self-directed, self-disciplined, self-monitored, and self-corrective thinking. It requires rigorous standards of excellence and mindful command of their use. It entails effective communication and problem solving abilities and a commitment to overcome our native egocentrism and sociocentrism.

Questions Using the Elements of Thought (in a paper, an activity, a reading assignment...)[2]

Purpose:	What am I trying to accomplish?
	What is my central aim? My purpose?
Questions:	What question am I raising?
	What question am I addressing?
	Am I considering the complexities in the question?

[2] Reprinted from Elder, L. & Paul, R. (2006). *The Thinker's Guide to Analytic Thinking*. Dillon Beach, CA: The Foundation for Critical Thinking.

Information:	What information am I using in coming to that conclusion?
	What experience have I had to support this claim?
	What information do I need to settle the question?
Inferences/	How did I reach this conclusion?
Conclusions:	Is there another way to interpret the information?
Concepts:	What is the main idea here?
	Can I explain this idea?
Assumptions:	What am I taking for granted?
	What assumption has led me to that conclusion?
Implications/	If someone accepted my position, what would be the implications?
Consequences:	
	What am I implying?
Points of View:	From what point of view am I looking at this issue?
	Is there another point of view I should consider?

The Elements of Thought

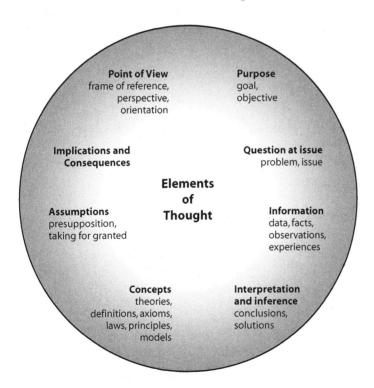

Point of View
frame of reference,
perspective,
orientation

Purpose
goal,
objective

Implications and Consequences

Question at issue
problem, issue

**Elements
of
Thought**

Assumptions
presupposition,
taking for granted

Information
data, facts,
observations,
experiences

Concepts
theories,
definitions, axioms,
laws, principles,
models

**Interpretation
and inference**
conclusions,
solutions

Used With Sensitivity to Universal Intellectual Standards

Clarity ⟶ Accuracy ⟶ Depth ⟶ Breadth ⟶ Significance
Precision
Relevance

Think About Purpose

Your purpose is your goal, your objective, what you are trying to accomplish. We also use the term to include functions, motives, and intentions.

You should be clear about your purpose, and your purpose should be justifiable.

▣ Questions Which Target Purpose:

- ❷ What is your, my, their purpose in doing _____?
- ❷ What is the objective of this assignment (task, job, experiment, policy, strategy, etc.)?
- ❷ Should we question, refine, modify our purpose (goal, objective, etc.)?
- ❷ Why did you say...?
- ❷ What is your central aim in this line of thought?
- ❷ What is the purpose of this meeting (chapter, relationship, action)?
- ❷ What is the purpose of education?
- ❷ What is the function of this _____ (bodily system, machine, tool, economic policy, plant, ecosystem)?

Be aware: All of what we do is guided by our purposes or goals. We are aware of only some of our goals. When our goals reflect our greed or possessiveness, or such, we deny them as goals. We then describe our actions in such a way as to hide purposes to which we cannot admit.

State the Question

The question lays out the problem or issue and guides our thinking. When the question is vague, our thinking will lack clarity and distinctness.

The question should be clear and precise enough to productively guide our thinking.

▣ Questions Which Target the Question:

- ❷ What is the question I am trying to answer?
- ❷ What important questions are embedded in the issue?
- ❷ Is there a better way to put the question?
- ❷ Is this question clear? Is it complex?
- ❷ I am not sure exactly what question you are asking. Could you explain it?
- ❷ The question in my mind is this: How do you see the question?
- ❷ What kind of question is this? Historical? Scientific? Ethical? Political? Economic? Or...?
- ❷ What important questions does this discipline address?
- ❷ What would we have to do to settle this question?

Be aware: Often the real question or problem is hidden or obscure. People resist admitting problems that cast them in a negative light. We need intellectual courage to bring the real problems and issues to the surface.

Gather Information

Information includes the facts, data, evidence, or experiences we use to figure things out. It does not necessarily imply accuracy or correctness.

The information you use should be accurate and relevant to the question or issue you are addressing.

Questions which target information:

- What information do I need to answer this question?
- What data are relevant to this problem?
- Do we need to gather more information?
- Is this information relevant to our purpose or goal?
- On what information are you basing that comment?
- What experience convinced you of this? Could your experience be distorted?
- How do we know this information (data, testimony) is accurate?
- Have we left out any important information that we need to consider?

Will you always have all the necessary information in the fleet? How can you go about improving the information you have?

Be aware: of missing information, especially information that reveals contradictions, hypocrisy, and self-deception on our part. Most people seek only information that supports what they already believe. They ignore or discount the rest. Critical thinking requires intellectual integrity.

Watch Your Inferences

Inferences are interpretations or conclusions you come to. Inferring is what the mind does in figuring something out.

Inferences should logically follow from the evidence. Infer no more or less than what is implied in the situation.

Questions you can ask to check your inferences:

- What conclusions am I coming to?
- Is my inference logical?
- Are there other conclusions I should consider?
- Does this interpretation make sense?
- Does our solution necessarily follow from our data?
- How did you reach that conclusion?
- What are you basing your reasoning on?
- Is there an alternative plausible conclusion?
- Given all the facts what is the best possible conclusion?
- How shall we interpret these data?

Be aware: Our conclusions are often distorted by our self-serving interests, which disengage our sense of justice. Make sure that your conclusions are based on all the relevant information and that you haven't excluded information that does not support your preconceptions.

Check Your Assumptions

Assumptions are beliefs you take for granted. They usually operate at the subconscious or unconscious level of thought.

Make sure that you are clear about your assumptions and they are justified by sound evidence.

If assumptions are often unconscious, what are some ways you can check them?

Questions you can ask about your assumptions:

- What am I taking for granted?
- Am I assuming something I shouldn't?
- What assumption is leading me to this conclusion?
- What is... (this policy, strategy, explanation) assuming?
- What exactly do sociologists (historians, mathematicians, etc.) take for granted?
- Why are you assuming...?
- What is being presupposed in this theory?
- What are some important assumptions I make about my roommate, my friends, my parents, my instructors, my country?

Be aware: The root of problems in thinking often lies with false assumptions. Because assumptions are usually unconscious, they often embody prejudices, biases, stereotypes, and one-sided or false beliefs. Practice explicitly identifying assumptions and checking them for justifiability.

Clarify Your Concepts

Concepts are ideas, theories, laws, principles, or hypotheses we use in thinking to make sense of things.

Be clear about the concepts you are using and use them justifiably.

Questions you can ask about concepts:

- What idea am I using in my thinking? Is this idea causing problems for me or for others?
- I think this is a good theory, but could you explain it more fully?
- What is the main hypothesis you are using in your reasoning?
- Are you using this term in keeping with established usage?
- What main distinctions should we draw in reasoning through this problem?
- What idea is this author using in his or her thinking? Is there a problem with it?
- Can you name and explain some of the basic principles of physics (chemistry, sociology, etc.)?

Be aware: The ways in which we think about the world are determined by our ideas or concepts. Yet these concepts are often twisted in self-serving ways by the mind. We often use concepts to manipulate people or to pursue vested interests. Use language with care, precision, and fairness.

Understand Your <u>Point of View</u>

Point of view is literally "the place" from which you view something. It includes what you are looking at and the way you are seeing it.

Your point of view or perspective can easily distort the way you see situations and issues. Make sure you understand the limitations of your point of view and that you fully consider other relevant viewpoints.

Questions you can ask to check your point of view:

- How am I looking at this situation? Is there another way to look at it that I should consider?

- What exactly am I focused on? And how am I seeing it?

- Is my view the only reasonable view? What does my point of view ignore?

- Have you ever considered the way Germans (Japanese, Muslims, South Americans, etc.) view this?

- Which of these possible viewpoints makes the most sense given the situation?

- How often have you studied viewpoints that seriously challenge your personal beliefs?

- What is the point of view of the author of this story?

- Am I having difficulty looking at this situation from a viewpoint with which I disagree?

- Am I uncritically assuming that the point of view of my government is justified?

What are your feelings about the value of "Pro-Quizzes"? What point of view are you looking at this from? How does your training staff or Company Officer feel about this topic?

> Be aware: All of reasoning is couched within a point of view. We often fail to consider viewpoints with which we disagree. Why? Because to consider those viewpoints might require us to change our own viewpoint, to give up some beliefs or goals we want to maintain. Realize that one of the hallmarks of the critical thinker is a willingness to enter sympathetically into any and every viewpoint, and then to change one's views when the evidence warrants a change.

Think Through the <u>Implications</u>

Implications are the things that *might* happen if you decide to do something. Consequences are the things that *do* happen when you act.

You should think through the possible and probable implications in a situation before acting.

Questions you can ask about implications:

- If I decide to do "X", what things might happen?

- If I decide not to do "X", what things might happen?

- What are you implying when you say that?

- What is likely to happen if we do this versus that?

◉ Are you implying that...?

◉ How significant are the implications of this decision?

◉ What, if anything, is implied by the fact that a much higher percentage of poor people are in jail than wealthy people?

Be aware: Thinking through the implications of one's thought prior to acting requires discipline and the ability to think at multiple levels. Every action we take has implications. What is more, we should be aware that once we identify important implications of an act, we should also identify important implications of those implications. Implications are like the concentric circles that radiate outward when a stone is dropped in a pond.

Universal Intellectual Standards: And questions that can be used to apply them[3]

Universal intellectual standards are standards which must be applied to thinking whenever one is interested in checking the quality of reasoning about a problem, issue, or situation. To think critically entails having command of these standards. To help students learn them, teachers should pose questions which require students to apply them, questions which hold students accountable for them, questions which, through consistent use by the teacher in the classroom, help students internalize them.

The ultimate goal, then, is for these standards to become infused in the thinking of students, forming part of their inner voice, which then guides them to better and better reasoning. While there are a number of universal standards, we have elected to comment on the following:

Clarity: Could you elaborate further on that point? Could you express that point in another way? Could you give me an illustration? Could you give me an example?

Clarity is a gateway standard. If a statement is unclear, we cannot determine whether it is accurate or relevant. In fact, we cannot tell anything about it because we don't yet know what it is saying. For example, the question "What can be done about the education system in America?" is unclear. In order to adequately address the question, we would need to have a clearer understanding of what the person asking the question is considering the "problem" to be. A clearer question might be "What can educators do to ensure that students learn the skills and abilities which help them function successfully on the job and in their daily decision-making?"

Accuracy: Is that really true? How could we check that? How could we find out if that is true? A statement can be clear but not accurate, as in "Most dogs are over 300 pounds in weight."

[3] Reprinted from Elder, L. & Paul, R. (2006). *The Thinker's Guide to Intellectual Standards.* Dillon Beach, CA: The Foundation for Critical Thinking.

Precision: Could you give me more details? Could you be more specific? A statement can be both clear and accurate, but not precise, as in "Jack is overweight." (We don't know how overweight Jack is, one pound or 500 pounds.)

Relevance: How is that connected to the question? How does that bear on the issue? A statement can be clear, accurate, and precise, but not relevant to the question at issue. For example, students often think that the amount of effort they put into a course should be used in raising their grade in a course. Often, however, "effort" does not measure the quality of student learning, and when that is so, effort is irrelevant to their appropriate grade.

Depth: How does your answer address the complexities in the question? How are you taking into account the problems in the question? Is that dealing with the most significant factors?

A statement can be clear, accurate, precise, and relevant, but superficial (that is, lack depth). For example, the statement "Just Say No", which is often used to discourage children and teens from using drugs, is clear, accurate, precise, and relevant. Nevertheless, it lacks depth because it treats an extremely complex issue, the pervasive problem of drug use among young people, superficially. It fails to deal with the complexities of the issue.

Breadth: Do we need to consider another point of view? Is there another way to look at this question? What would this look like from a conservative standpoint? What would this look like from the point of view of...?

A line of reasoning may be clear, accurate, precise, relevant, and deep, but lack breadth (as in an argument from either the conservative or liberal standpoints which gets deeply into an issue, but only recognizes the insights of one side of the question).

Logic: Does this really make sense? Does that follow from what you said? How does that follow? Before you implied this and now you are saying that, I don't see how both can be true.

When we think, we bring a variety of thoughts together into some order. When the combination of thoughts are mutually supporting and make sense in combination, the thinking is "logical." When the combination is not mutually supporting, is contradictory in some sense, or does not "make sense," the combination is "not logical."

Significance: Is this the most important problem to consider? Which of these facts are most important? I understand this point but I don't think it is the root of the issue.

Significance examines whether the effort of the argument is invested in the right area. While the statement may make sense, it could be nothing more than a supporting argument or sidebar to a larger issue at hand. One must look at the whole problem in order to put the issue into context.

Fairness: Do I have any vested interest in this issue? Am I sympathetically representing the viewpoints of others?

The biases that one possesses when examining an argument must be considered just as much as those of the framer. Critical thinking is about questioning but also about being open-minded in order to examine all arguments justly. Because of our own individual biases, the standard of fairness must always be kept in mind when making decisions about an argument.

If you chose an opinion piece at random from a major news source, how do you think it would do in terms of fairness and breadth?

Clarity	Could you elaborate further?
	Could you give me an example?
	Could you illustrate what you mean?
Accuracy	How could we check on that?
	How could we find out if that is true?
	How could we verify or test that?
Precision	Could you be more specific?
	Could you give me more details?
	Could you be more exact?
Relevance	How does that relate to the problem?
	How does that bear on the question?
	How does that help us with the issue?

The Logic of Love

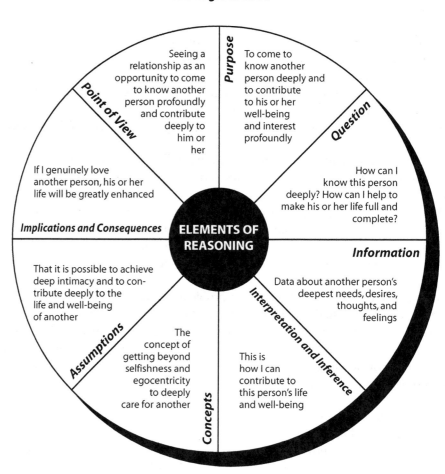

Be aware: Even emotionally powerful states of mind have a logic to them. All emotions have a cognitive content.

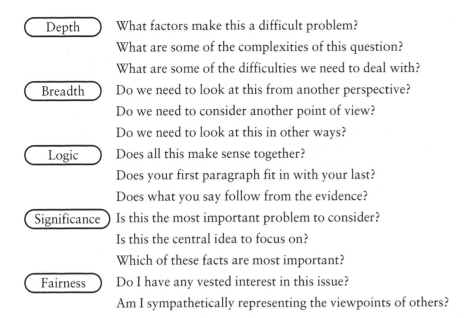

Depth	What factors make this a difficult problem?
	What are some of the complexities of this question?
	What are some of the difficulties we need to deal with?
Breadth	Do we need to look at this from another perspective?
	Do we need to consider another point of view?
	Do we need to look at this in other ways?
Logic	Does all this make sense together?
	Does your first paragraph fit in with your last?
	Does what you say follow from the evidence?
Significance	Is this the most important problem to consider?
	Is this the central idea to focus on?
	Which of these facts are most important?
Fairness	Do I have any vested interest in this issue?
	Am I sympathetically representing the viewpoints of others?

The Logic of Fear

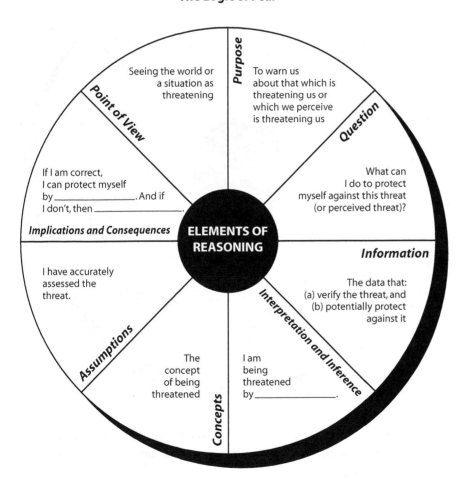

Be aware: Understanding the logic of fear is the key to dealing with fear in a reasonable way. Some fears are justified. Some are not.

Analyzing Problems[4]

Identify some problem you need to reason through. Then complete the following:

What exactly is the problem? (Study the problem to make clear the kind of problem you are dealing with. Figure out, for example, what sorts of things you are going to have to do to solve it. Distinguish problems over which you have some control from problems over which you have no control. Pay special attention to controversial issues in which it is essential to consider multiple points of view.)

The key <u>question</u> that emerges from the problem is... (State the question as clearly and precisely as you can. Details are very important.)

My <u>purpose</u> in addressing the problem is... (Know exactly what you are after. Make sure you are not operating with a hidden agenda and that your announced and real purposes are the same.)

The Logic of Anger

Purpose
To redress some perceived injury or mistreatment

Question
How can I best right the wrong that has been done?

Information
The facts, experiences, data that convince me that I (or others) have been wronged.

Interpretation and Inference
I (or others) have been wronged and I need to take action against those responsible for these injustices.

Concepts
The concept of being unjustifiably wronged

Assumptions
I have a right to take action against those who have wronged me (or others).

Implications and Consequences
If I successfully redress this wrong, this negative feeling will subside.

Point of View
Looking at someone else as having caused unjust harm and feeling strong disapproval in the light of this injustice.

ELEMENTS OF REASONING

Be aware: Anger can be intensified or diminished depending on how we cognitively relate to it. It is possible to take charge of our emotions. Emotions are the driving force in human life.

[4] Reprinted from Elder, L. & Paul, R. (2006). *The Thinker's Guide to Analytic Thinking*. Dillon Beach, CA: The Foundation for Critical Thinking.

Actively seek the <u>information</u> most relevant to the question. (Include in that information options for action, both short-term and long-term. Recognize limitations in terms of money, time, and power.)

Some important <u>assumptions</u> I am using in my thinking are... (Figure out what you are taking for granted. Watch out for self-serving or unjustified assumptions.)

If we solve this problem, some important implications are... If we fail to solve this problem, some important implications are... (Evaluate options, taking into account the advantages and disadvantages of possible decisions before acting. What consequences are likely to follow from this or that decision?)

The most important <u>concepts</u>, theories, or ideas I need to use in my thinking are... (Figure out all significant ideas needed to understand and solve the problem. You may need to analyze these concepts. Use a good dictionary.)

The <u>point(s) of view</u> is/are as follows: (Know the point of view from which your thinking begins. Be especially careful to determine whether multiple points of view are relevant.)

After reasoning through the parts of thinking above, the best <u>solution</u> (conclusion) to the problem is... (If the problem involves multiple conflicting points of view, you will have to assess which solution is the **best**. If the problem is one-dimensional, there may be just one "correct" solution.)

Analyzing Problems

The Problem of Pollution as an Example

What is the problem? The problem is pollution and the fact that because people are not doing enough to reduce it, a host of negative consequences are occurring (e.g. increased medical problems, loss of animal and plant life, increased contamination of the earth's water sources).

<u>Questions</u> that emerges from the problem are... What can I personally do to reduce pollution? A related question is: What can we collectively do to reduce pollution?

My <u>purpose</u> in addressing the problem is to increase the things I do to contribute to a more healthy biosphere.

The important <u>information</u> relevant to the question is information about what I am currently doing to increase pollution (such as generating trash that could be recycled, driving a car, etc.), information about what I could do to reduce the amount of pollution I contribute to (such as locating recycling centers, pursuing alternative forms of transportation, etc.), information about environmental groups I might support, etc.

Some important <u>assumptions</u> I am using in my thinking are that pollution is causing significant damage to the biosphere, that everyone can help reduce pollution, that I, and everyone else, have an obligation to make a significant effort to help reduce pollution.

If many people were to reason well through this issue, some <u>implications</u> are that there would be a longer and higher quality of life for millions of people. Additionally, plant and animal species and ecosystems would be protected. A host of other positive implications would follow as well, implications for the atmosphere, the waterways, the forests, etc.

If I, and many others, fail to reason well through this issue, the <u>implications</u> are that we will unnecessarily contribute to pollution's many harmful effects.

The most important <u>concepts</u>, or ideas, I need to use in my thinking are the concepts of pollution, and that of a healthy biosphere. Each of these concepts lead to a host of further technical, ecological, and ethical concepts required to understand the multiple dimensions of pollution and the ethical responsibilities that knowledge of its many harmful effects entails.

My <u>point of view</u> is as follows: I am looking at pollution. I am seeing it as something I can help reduce through many means.

After reasoning through the parts of thinking above, the best <u>solution</u> (conclusion) to the problem will be to put into action the various options that my research has revealed.

Analyzing the Logic of an Article, Essay or Chapter

One important way to understand an essay, article or chapter is through the analysis of the parts of the author's reasoning. Once you have done this, you can evaluate the author's reasoning using intellectual standards. Here is a template to follow:

1) The main **purpose** of this article is ＿＿＿＿＿＿＿＿. (Here you are trying to state, as accurately as possible, the author's intent in writing the article. What was the author trying to accomplish?)

2) The key **question** that the author is addressing is ＿＿＿＿＿. (Your goal is to figure out the key question that was in the mind of the author when he/she wrote the article. What was the key question addressed in the article?)

3) The most important **information** in this article is ＿＿＿＿＿. (You want to identify the key information the author used, or presupposed, in the article to support his/her main arguments. Here you are looking for facts, experiences, and/or data the author is using to support his/her conclusions.)

4) The main **inferences** in this article are ＿＿＿＿＿＿＿＿＿. (You want to identify the most important conclusions the author comes to and presents in the article).

5) The key **concept**(s) we need to understand in this article is (are) ＿＿＿＿＿＿. By these concepts the author means ＿＿＿＿＿. (To identify these ideas, ask yourself: What are the most important ideas that you would have to know to understand the author's line of reasoning? Then briefly elaborate what the author means by these ideas.)

6) The main **assumption**(s) underlying the author's thinking is (are) ＿＿＿＿＿＿＿ (Ask yourself: What is the author taking for granted [that might be questioned]? The assumptions are generalizations that the author does not think he/she has to defend in the context of writing the article, and they are usually unstated. This is where the author's thinking logically begins.)

7) a) If we take this line of reasoning seriously, the **implications** are ＿＿＿＿＿＿＿＿＿＿. (What consequences are likely to follow if people take the author's line of reasoning seriously? Here you are to pursue the logical implications of the author's position. You should include implications that the author states, and also those that the author does not state.)

7) b) If we fail to take this line of reasoning seriously, the <u>implications</u> are
_____. (What consequences are
likely to follow if people ignore the author's reasoning?)

8) The main <u>point(s) of view</u> presented in this article is (are) _____.
(The main question you are trying to answer here is: What is the author looking
at, and how is he/she seeing it? For example, in this mini-guide we are looking
at "analysis" and seeing it "as requiring one to understand" and routinely
apply the elements of reasoning when thinking through problems, issues,
subjects, etc.).

If you truly understand these structures as they interrelate in an article, essay or
chapter, you should be able to empathically role-play the thinking of the author.
These are the eight basic structures that define all reasoning. They are the essential
elements of thought.

> Be aware: It is possible to use the basic structures of thinking to analyze arti-
> cles, essays, and chapters. This analysis will deepen one's insight into the author's
> reasoning.

Analyzing the Logic of an Article: An Example

On the next page you will find an analysis of the following brief article (see pages
28–29 for the analysis template).

Is it Possible for the News Media to Reform?

To provide their publics with non-biased writing, journalists around the world
would have to, first, enter empathically into world views to which they are not at
present sympathetic. They would have to imagine writing for audiences that hold
views antithetical to the ones they hold. They would have to develop insights into
their own sociocentrism. They would have to do the things done by critical con-
sumers of the news. The most significant problem is that, were they to do so, their
readers would perceive their articles as "biased" and "slanted," as "propaganda."
These reporters would be seen as irresponsible, as allowing their personal point of
view to bias their journalistic writings. Imagine Israeli journalists writing articles
that present the Palestinian point of view sympathetically. Imagine Pakistani journalists writing articles that present the Indian point of view sympathetically.

The most basic point is this: journalists do not determine the nature and demands
of their job. They do not determine what their readers want or think or hate or fear.
The nature and demands of their job are determined by the broader nature of societies themselves and the beliefs, values and world views of its members. It is human
nature to see the world, in the first instance, in egocentric and sociocentric terms.
Most people are not interested in having their minds broadened. They want their
present beliefs and values extolled and confirmed. Like football fans, they want the
home team to win, and when it wins to triumph gloriously. If they lose, they want to
be told that the game wasn't important, or that the other side cheated, or that the
officials were biased against them.

As long as the overwhelming mass of persons in the broader society are drawn to news articles that reinforce, and do not question, their fundamental views or passions, the economic imperatives will remain the same. The logic is parallel to that of reforming a nation's eating habits. As long as the mass of people want high fat processed foods, the market will sell high fat and processed foods to them. And as long as the mass of people want simplistic news articles that reinforce egocentric and sociocentric thinking, that present the world in sweeping terms of good and evil (with the reader's views and passions treated as good and those of the reader's conceived enemies as evil), the news media will generate such articles for them. The profit and ratings of news sources that routinely reinforce the passions and prejudices of their readers will continue to soar.

The main <u>purpose</u> of this article is to show why the news media are not likely to alter their traditional practices of slanting the news in keeping with audience preconceptions.

The key <u>question</u> that the author is addressing is: "Why is it not possible for the news media to reform?"

The most important <u>information</u> in this article is:

1. information about how and why the news media currently operates:
   a. that the news media slant stories to fit the viewpoint of their audience. "Most people are not interested in having their views broadened...Like football fans they want the home team to win... The overwhelming mass of persons in the broader society are drawn to news articles that reinforce, and do not question, their fundamental views or passions."
   b. that the fundamental purpose of the mainstream news media is to make money. "As long as the mass of people want simplistic news articles...the news media will generate such articles for them. The profit and ratings of news sources that routinely reinforce the passions and prejudices of their readers will continue to soar."
2. information about how the news media would have to change to be more intellectually responsible:
   a. that the news media would have to actively enter differing world views "Imagine Israeli journalists writing articles that present the Palestinian point of view sympathetically. Imagine Pakistani journalists writing articles that present the Indian point of view sympathetically."
   b. That the news media would have to "develop insights into their own sociocentrism."

The main <u>inferences</u> in this article are: "As long as the overwhelming mass of persons in the broader society are drawn to news articles that reinforce, and do not question, their fundamental views or passions," the news will be presented in a biased way. Because the fundamental purpose of the media is to make money, and the only way people will buy papers is if their sociocentric views are reinforced and not questioned, the media will continue to distort events in accordance with audience views.

The key <u>concepts</u> that guide the author's reasoning in this article are: biased and unbiased journalism, egocentrism and sociocentrism, propaganda. (Each of these concepts should be elaborated.)

The main <u>assumptions</u> underlying the author's thinking are: The driving force behind the news media is vested interest—i.e. making money; that the news media therefore pander to their readers' views so as to sell more papers; but that, at the same time, the news media must appear to function objectively and fairly.

If this line of reasoning is justified, the <u>implications</u> are: Citizens need to think critically about the news media and how they systematically distort stories in accordance with reader bias. They need to notice how their own sociocentric views are intensified by what they read.

The main <u>point of view</u> presented in this article is: The world news media function as profit-making enterprises that structure the news to pander to reader and society prejudices.

Questions for review:

1. How can critical thinking help you avoid the situation of "Junior Officer Ping-Pong"?
2. Why is egocentric thinking a dangerous practice as a leader?

3 *The Nature of Strengths*

⟣Learning Objectives:

- ⟣ Identify and explain your top 5 talent themes.
- ⟣ Differentiate between strength, talent, knowledge, and skills and describe their relationship.
- ⟣ Identify knowledge and skills that will help develop talents into specific strengths.
- ⟣ Apply your developed talents to perform in a given scenario.

Reprinted from Clifton, D. O., Anderson, E., & Schreiner, L. A. (2006). *StrengthsQuest: Discover and Develop Your Strengths in Academics, Career, and Beyond.* New York, NY: Gallup Press.

At the 1996 Olympic Games in Atlanta, Kerri Strug was a gymnast on the United States women's gold-medal team. Her performance on the vault, as she nursed an injured ankle, remains one of the most memorable in Olympic history.

With 32,000 people in the Georgia Dome and millions watching her on television, Kerri fell on her first attempt at her most difficult twisting vault, severely spraining her left ankle. With less than a minute between vaults, and in great pain, she again attempted the vault, further injuring her ankle — but this time successfully landing on both feet. So she stood erect on one foot, raising both hands to salute the judges, then collapsed to her knees.

The crowd went wild. Kerri's vault earned a 9.712, and the U.S. women won the gold medal.

During that same year, Kerri was a freshman at UCLA. One of her classes required a research paper similar to a mini-doctoral dissertation. Students had to formulate their own research question and develop a questionnaire that was consistent with their research question. Then, the students would administer the questionnaire, collect and analyze the data, draw conclusions, and write a report that described the process. The written report was to be 35-40 pages long.

Taking the Clifton StrengthsFinder assessment was one of the class requirements. When Kerri took it, she scored extremely high in the Focus theme. But doesn't that make sense? Who else but a person with tremendous Focus talents could concentrate on completing her most difficult vault on an injured ankle in front of 32,000 screaming fans while Olympic gold hung in the balance? Who else could block out all of those distractions and then land on one foot without falling?

While Kerri certainly had other talents that enabled her to succeed, her Focus talents played a critical role. Without them, she might never have enjoyed such stunning Olympic success.

But there's more to the story. Toward the end of the fall term, as research papers were coming due, Kerri turned her paper in three days early, before any of the other 300-plus UCLA students in the class. She did this while traveling nearly every weekend on a national tour with fellow Olympic medalists. Even more remarkable was the way that Kerri could go out on an arena floor, do a routine, and then go underneath the stands and work on the paper. She would then go back out on the floor and do another routine and return to do more homework.

You see, Kerri also applied her Focus talents to succeed in academics.

Kerri is a remarkable young woman. But the excellence she achieved wasn't due simply to the fact that she naturally possessed talents. She recognized her Focus talents and built on them by adding skills and knowledge to create strength — the ability to produce consistent, near-perfect performance. She obviously did so at the Olympics — even while in severe pain and under tremendous pressure — but she was also able to apply her Focus in academics, where she achieved despite rigorous assignments and the myriad pressures of her athletic career.

Kerri has presented each of us with more than a shared pride in her Olympic success. We can learn from her. You, too, have talents. And in those talents you have the ability to meet challenges and achieve just as surely as Kerri did.

The Basics of Strengths

Talent: The Beginning of Strength

What is a strength? That's a good question, but strength begins with talent, so let's start there. A talent is a naturally recurring pattern of thought, feeling, or behavior that can be productively applied. A great number of talents naturally exist within you, and each of them is very specific. They are among the most real and most authentic aspects of your personhood. Your specific set of talents is a major part of what makes you a unique person, and that uniqueness holds great value for you and those around you. And your talents work in various combinations each time you do something very well, in your own unique way.

There is a direct connection between your talents and your achievements. Your talents empower you. They make it possible for you to move to higher levels of excellence and fulfill your potential. This is why it is so important for you to know, understand, and value your talents.

A talent represents a capacity to *do* something. In fact, when you are able to do something very well, you can be sure that at least one of your talents is involved. Just think about all the things you do very well. You'll realize that you have many talents!

And talents help you do something well not just once; they help you do it well over and over again. Because talents are naturally recurring patterns, they are "automatic," almost like breathing, so they repeatedly help you achieve.

That's not all, either. Each of your many talents can enable you to do more than one thing very well. We're not saying that each of your talents enables you to do *everything* very well, but know that each of them can be applied to multiple areas of achievement.

The great value in your talents is not merely that they help you achieve, but that they help you achieve at levels of *excellence*. Your greatest talents are inextricably linked to your top achievements and to what you do best. Your talents make you exceptional. Therefore, coming to know, understand, and value your talents is directly linked to achieving in classes, careers, and throughout your life.

Talent Versus Other Concepts of Ability

The concept of talent is more specific in terms of the quality it describes and the things that various types of talent help a person to do very well. Traditional concepts and measures of ability (for example, I.Q. and aptitude testing) are more global and are not designed to explain what a person can specifically do.

The concept of talent also goes beyond the limits of traditional concepts of academic abilities (for example, in the areas of reading, math, and composition) in that it also addresses the qualities that help a person achieve in all aspects of life.

◙ The 34 Themes of Talent Measured by the Clifton StrengthsFinder

What is a theme? Essentially, it's is a group of similar talents.

Kerri Strug once again provides a good illustration. Kerri used a wide variety of talents in the Focus theme to achieve in athletics and academics. Among them was her talent for focusing on the precise steps required to perform complicated gymnastic maneuvers, and, during the intense pressure of the Olympics, her talent for blocking out the distraction of intense pain to produce a gold-medal performance.

Kerri used other types of talents, too. Her talents in the Adaptability theme enabled her to achieve excellence in athletics and academics at the same time. Her talent to balance two extremely high priorities, easily moving from one to the other, was crucial to her success in each area.

As a result of studying top achievers for more than three decades,

Gallup was able to identify more than 400 themes of talent. The 34 most prevalent themes are measured by StrengthsFinder.

◙ Back to Your Question: What Is a Strength?

Now, let's go to the definition of a strength: A strength is the ability to provide consistent, near-perfect performance in a given activity.

As you read earlier, the concept of strengths begins with talent. Each person naturally has a group of talents. Talents are like "diamonds in the rough," whereas strengths are like diamonds that show brilliance after they have been carefully cut and polished.

Your greatest areas of talent, your most likely sources of potential strengths, are identified by StrengthsFinder.

> Strength = Talent + Knowledge + Skill

Just as finished diamonds start as diamonds in the rough, strengths begin with talents. And just as rough diamonds are naturally found in the earth, talents are naturally found within you. But while diamonds are refined with blades and polishing wheels, strengths are produced when talents are refined with *knowledge* and *skill*.

Unlike talent, which must naturally exist within you, skills and knowledge can be acquired. Skills are the basic ability to perform the specific steps of an activity. Knowledge consists of facts and lessons learned.

Many of the skills and much of the knowledge that are combined with talent to create a strength come through experience, and sometimes a great deal of it. Skills and knowledge are also developed in a "book learning" sense, such as in the academic arenas of high school, college, technical school, and training classes.

When you have supplemented your greatest talents with knowledge and skill to the point at which you can provide consistent, near-perfect performance in a given activity, you have a strength. And in applying and even further refining your strengths, you move closer and closer to fulfilling your natural potential as an individual.

Each person has a unique and profound set and combination of talents that are developed and used to different degrees. This combination of talents makes each person like no other.

While each person defines success for himself or herself, achievement and excellence result from fully developing and applying strengths. Some roles require several strengths, all working together, to produce excellence.

You probably already have some strengths, and you certainly will have plenty of opportunity to develop more strengths throughout your lifetime.

▣ What Do Strengths Produce?

As you develop strengths by building on your greatest talents, achievements will naturally follow. But there is also a great sense of personal satisfaction that results from knowing that you are becoming more and more of whom you have the potential to be. In a sense, the development and application of strengths generate a feeling that you are fulfilling your personal destiny. This can produce enormous satisfaction and enhance the quality of your life.

While the experiences of individual people differ tremendously, most report that it is a rewarding experience to be fully living in tune with their natural talents by building and using strengths. Almost everyone says increased confidence and optimism as they become aware of, affirm, and celebrate their talents. Many describe the experience as "coming alive," or even feeling joy as they develop and apply strengths. Reports about the exact inner experiences may differ, but nearly everyone who develops and uses strengths reports a sense of positive and pleasant psychological rewards.

Our initial goal is for you to become more aware of your talents and your potential strengths. We hope you are filled with appreciation for your particular talents, for the positive differences they have already made in your life, and for the excellence strengths can produce in your future achievements, relationships, and other life experiences.

▣ Findings From Gallup's Study of the Best

Here is what Gallup knows about top achievers: *They fully recognize their talents and build on them to develop strengths.* In contrast, underachieves, the merely average, and even above-average achievers often fail to recognize their powerful talents and develop strengths. But the best achievers are certain to do so.

Top achievers apply their greatest talents in roles that best suit them. Clearly, to achieve, one must apply his or her abilities, and many do so to some level of success. But the best apply their most naturally powerful talents and do so in roles that are best suited to those talents. The ability to achieve with excellence in one area is not proof of the ability to perform equally well in another area. A proper "fit" between an individuals talents and the task at hand is essential.

Top achievers invent ways to apply their greatest talents to their achievement tasks. Every role, position, and career entails a group of tasks that must be completed, and quite often the person who performs them must consciously seek, even invent, ways to apply his or her talents to that end — even when one's role is well suited to his or her talents.

Your Strengths Quest Begins With You

As described earlier, the seeds of your personal greatness — your talents — are already in you. Therefore, your strengths quest — your quest to achieve excellence and become all you can be through your own natural talents — is really a quest to discover, develop, and apply who you truly are. Your strengths quest begins as you look within yourself as an individual to recognize your own natural talents.

Your quest will then continue as you build on your talents to develop strengths — abilities to provide consistent, near-perfect performances in specific activities. As you do this, your self-identity and personal values should become clearer, and as a result, you will likely become more confident, optimistic, and focused. As you achieve through your greatest talents, you will likely aspire to higher goals.

Your strengths quest is a lifelong adventure. Each of the three aspects — discovery, development, and application — will continue throughout your life. This exciting and fulfilling process should bring you a lifetime of great satisfaction and joy.

. . .

You have taken the Clifton StrengthsFinder, received your Signature Themes report, and discussed your Signature Themes with three people who know you very well. Now, it's time for you to affirm the Signature Themes indicated by your StrengthsFinder responses.

Affirming a Signature Theme simply means that you *agree* that it is one of your dominant areas of talent. It also means being able to see how your talent in that theme enables you to do certain things very well. Affirming your Signature Themes may seem easy, but many people experience some difficulty in doing so. Listed below are some of those difficulties and the reasons for them.

Difficulties in Affirming Our Signature Themes

1. *Many people are blind to their own greatest talents, and often to the greatest talents of others.* Some of our talents are called upon so frequently that we take them for granted. We don't consider them special, and we don't even perceive them as talents. Consequently, our Signature Themes may not seem important, valuable, or even special to us.
2. *Our talents sometimes threaten others. Rather than admit their insecurity, some people criticize us for having talents they wish they had.* As a result, we might mistakenly come to think that our Signature Themes hold weaknesses rather than talents.
3. *In some cases, we end up in positions or roles that simply don't fit our dominant talents.* Or, those talents may conflict with the roles and expectations of the positions we are in. This can make us feel like there is something wrong with us. But the problem may only be a mismatch between our dominant talents and the expectations of a role we are in.
4. *The fear of becoming proud and arrogant may interfere with seeing and affirming our Signature Themes.* In reality, pride and arrogance often stem from feelings of inadequacy. Affirming our dominant areas of talent usually results in humble gratitude for having been blessed with them.

5. *Some people have difficulty affirming their Signature Themes because they don't see how the talents in them will help them achieve their goals.* If that is the case, they will benefit from a better understanding of their talents. Talents are always valuable, and they can often be applied toward achievement in less obvious, or even surprising, ways.

Questions You Might Be Asking

▣ If a Particular Theme Is Not Among Your Signature Themes, Is It Necessarily an Area of Weakness?

No. The Clifton StrengthsFinder *does not* simultaneously measure weakness and talent. StrengthsFinder measures talent, and that's all it does. So, if a particular theme is not among your Signature Themes, it simply means that at least five other themes are more dominant in you. For example, your Responsibility theme might not be among your Signature Themes. That doesn't mean you are irresponsible. It just means that your overall talents in at least five other themes are more dominant than those in your Responsibility theme.

By focusing on your Signature Themes, you will concentrate your attention on where you have the greatest potential for achieving excellence and personal fulfillment. Focusing on any other area may serve as nothing more than a distraction.

▣ What If You Believe You Have Dominant Talent in a Theme That Was Not Identified as a Signature Theme?

Our response is simple and direct: Claim it! Affirm and celebrate your talents in that theme, then build on them to fully develop and apply strengths. Just remember that we limited your Signature Themes to five because focusing on your *most* dominant areas of talent will provide the greatest opportunities for achievement.

▣ Is Having Talent Always a Positive Experience?

Talent is always positive in the sense that it enables a person to do certain things very well. Your talents always hold potential for positive results in terms of achievements, success, personal fulfillment, and a better quality of life.

At the same time, talents place demands on the people who have them. And from that standpoint, talents can present a bit of a challenge.

Some people honestly say that they wish that their talents weren't so powerful in certain themes because they make their lives more demanding. They simply may experience more pressure because other people place higher expectations on them to achieve.

4 *Personality Types*

Learning Objectives:

- Identify and describe your MBTI.
- Interpret the four basic components of the MBTI psychological type model.
- Evaluate leader strengths and vulnerabilities by type.

Introduction to Myers-Briggs Personality Type & the MBTI[1]

Personality Type or **Psychological Type** are terms most commonly associated with the model of personality development created by Isabel Briggs Myers (aka Briggs Meyer, Meyer Briggs, Briggs & Myers) the author of the world's most widely used personality inventory, the **MBTI** or **Myers-Briggs Type Indicator.** ® Myers' and her mother, Katharine Briggs, developed their model and inventory around the ideas and theories of psychologist Carl Jung, a contemporary of Sigmund Freud and a leading exponent of Gestalt personality theory.

Beginning in the early 1940's, Myers & Briggs extended Jung's model with the initial development of the **MBTI**. They put Jung's concepts into language that could be understood and used by the average person. Isabel Myers' book *"Gifts Differing"*, published posthumously in 1980, provided a comprehensive introduction to the Jung/Myers theory. Myers' book and her philosophy of celebrating human diversity anticipated the workplace diversity movement.

The MBTI is a registered trademark of Myers-Briggs Type Indicator Trust and is published by CPP, Inc (formerly Consulting Psychologist Press) who also distributes the Inventory. The MBTI is available from CPP and its licensees in approximately 20 foreign languages. In addition, alternate versions of the inventory have been scientifically customized and validated for other languages and cultures for which a straight translation of English language terms would yield inaccurate results.

Why is understanding my personality type and others' personality types important for me as a leader?

MBTI Personality Theory

The MBTI asks the candidate to answer a series of 'forced-choice' questions, where one choice identifies you as belonging to one of four paired traits. The basic test takes twenty minutes, and at the end you are presented with a precise, multi-dimensional summary of your personality. The MBTI test classifies people into types based on four bi-polar dimensions.

Description of the Four Scales

▣ Extraversion-Introversion (E-I)

Distinguishes a preference for focusing attention on, and drawing energy from, the outer world of people and things versus the inner world of ideas and impressions.

---

[1] Reinhold, R. (n.d.). MBTI: An Introduction to the Myers-Briggs Type Indicator & Personality Types. Retrieved from http://www.personalitypathways.com/MBTI_intro.html

Sensing-Intuition (S-N)

Distinguishes a preference for gathering data directly through the senses as facts, details, and precedents (Sensing) versus indirectly as relationships, patterns, and possibilities (Intuition).

 ## Thinking-Feeling (T-F)

Distinguishes a preference for deciding via objective, impersonal logic (Thinking) versus subjective, person-centered values (Feeling).

 ## Judging-Perceiving (J-P)

Distinguishes an outward preference for having things planned and organized (Judging) versus a flexible style based more on staying open to options than deciding (Perceiving).

There are four positions in the type code, and each one indicates something important about the type. For example:

E OR I	S OR N	T OR F	J OR P
Energy Attitude	Perception Function	Judgment Function	Orientation to the outer world

The Basic Model: Two Kinds of Mental Processes, Two Kinds of Mental Orientations

 ## Two Kinds of Mental Processes

In her studies of people and extensive reading of Jung's theories, Myers concluded there were four primary ways people differed from one another. She labeled these differences "preferences"—drawing a similarity to "hand preferences" to illustrate that although we all use both of our hands, most of us have a preference for one over the other and "it" takes the lead in many of the activities in which we use our hands.

The **first** set of mental preferences relates to how people **"Perceive"** or take in information. In the Myers MBTI Type Code, this is the second letter.

S Those who prefer *Sensing* Perception favor clear, tangible data and information that fits in well with their direct here-and-now experience.

N In contrast, those who prefer *Intuition* Perception are drawn to information that is more abstract, conceptual, big-picture, and represents imaginative possibilities for the future.

The **second** set of mental preferences identifies how people form **"Judgments"** or make decisions. In the Myers MBTI Type Code, this is the third letter.

T Those who prefer *Thinking* Judgment have a natural preference for making decisions in an objective, logical, and analytical manner with an emphasis on tasks and results to be accomplished.

F Those whose preference is for *Feeling* Judgment make their decisions in a somewhat global, visceral, harmony and value-oriented way, paying particular attention to the impact of decisions and actions on other people.

What are some of the possible consequences of many senior military leaders being "ST"s in relation to creativity and adaptability?

Does gender affect whether your judgment function is "Thinking" or "Feeling"?

One of the practical applications of the MBTI and understanding these preferences is in supporting better **Teamwork**. Differences in these mental preferences lead to quite different value structures and communication styles, which can hamper mutual understanding and cooperation.

For example, people who share **Sensing and Thinking** preferences find they are naturally on the same wavelength; they easily understand one another, making good teammates and partners. Likewise, people who share **Intuition and Feeling** have a similar kinship among them. However, in the "real" world, it is more likely that you'll find a mixed bag of people, a variety of types, in the same work group. While this diversity can be a useful strength, contributing to greater depth and breadth of team competence, there will be natural communication barriers within the team due to their natural mental language differences.

Such differences can be overcome, and the communication gap bridged, with mutual respect and practice learning to "talk" and "think" in a second or third language. A MBTI workshop can be seen as an introduction to learning the language, habits and culture of other types.

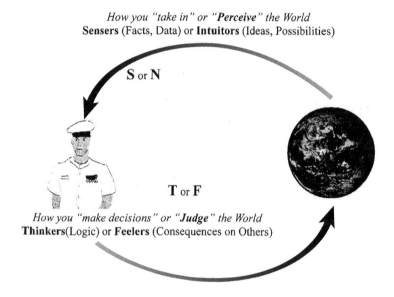

How you "take in" or "Perceive" the World
Sensers (Facts, Data) or **Intuitors** (Ideas, Possibilities)

S or **N**

T or **F**

How you "make decisions" or "Judge" the World
Thinkers(Logic) or **Feelers** (Consequences on Others)

FIGURE 4.1   People can be classified on their two mental processes – Perception and Judgment.

▣ Two Kinds of Mental Orientations

There are two other mental preferences that are part of the Myers-Briggs model: **Energy Orientation** and **Outer World Orientation**. The first one is the dimension of personality discovered by Carl Jung that became widely adopted by general psychology: Extraversion-Introversion. The second is the dimension of personality that is Myers' unique contribution to Jung's theory, an element she inferred from Jung's work but was not clearly addressed as an essential component of his theory of types. This is the style or orientation one uses in dealing with the external world: Judging or Perceiving.

Energy Orientation pertains to the two forms of **Energy Consciousness** each of us experiences on a daily basis. We occupy two mental worlds: one is inwardly turned, the other is outward. One of these worlds is our elemental source of energy; the other secondary. In the Myers MBTI Type Code, this is the first letter.

 Those who prefer *Introversion* draw their primary energy from the inner world of information, thoughts, ideas, and other reflections. When circumstances require an excessive amount of attention spent in the "outside" world, those preferring Introversion find the need to retreat to a more private setting as if to recharge their drained batteries.

 In contrast, those who prefer *Extraversion* are drawn to the outside world as their elemental source of energy. Rarely, if ever, do extraverted preference people feel their energy batteries are "drained" by excessive amounts of interaction with the outside world. They must engage the things, people, places and activities going on in the outside world for their life force.

Can you be a good leader as an introvert?

While the E-I dimension was Jung's gift to general psychology, unfortunately it has been widely distorted into a well-unwell scale with characteristics of Introversion being cast in a negative light and conversely characteristics of Extraversion cast in a positive light. This cultural bias frequently leads natural introverted types to mis-identify their primary preference as Extraversion.

Extraverted Orientation relates to which mental preference one relies upon in dealing with/relating with the **Outside World**. It is the mental function that takes the lead in the extraverted portion of a person's personality. When this leading function is one of the two Judging mental preferences, then this orientation is called **Judging**. When this leading function is one of the two Perceiving mental preferences, then this orientation is called **Perceiving**. In the Myers MBTI Type Code, this is the fourth letter.

Why are most midshipmen ESTJs or ISTJs?

 Those who prefer *Judging* rely upon either their **T** or **F** preference to manage their outer life. This typically leads to a style oriented towards closure, organization, planning, or in some fashion managing the things and or people found in the external environment. The drive is to order the outside world. While some people employ an assertive manner, others "ordering touch"—with respect to people—may be light.

 Those who prefer *Perceiving* rely upon either their **S** or **N** preference to run their outer life. This typically results in an open, adaptable, flexible style of relating to the things and people found in the outside world. The drive is to experience the outside world rather than order it; in general lack of closure is easily tolerated.

There are many personality models that have been developed from the beginning of recorded history, all of which have their strengths and shortcomings. No "true" model of human personality has yet been developed, and one can argue fairly convincingly that human personality is just too complex of an animal to ever be able to model perfectly. However, the models that have been developed do seem to approximately and reasonably model human personality to an accuracy that makes them useful and predictive. So, assuming, that we can model human personality with "reasonable accuracy", what value would such a model have? I can see two values: 1) helping an individual understand themselves and thus relate better with himself, and 2) helping an individual understand others so that they are better able to relate with them—not only for personal relationships such as friendships, but for other relationships as well.[2]

Understanding YOUR Four-Letter MBTI Code

What is your *Perception Function*? _____

What is your *Judgment Function*? _____

Do these surprise you or would you have expected these results? Why or why not?

_____

_____

_____

_____

Questions for review

1. Can understanding you and your roommates' MBTI explain why some of you get along and some of you do not?

2. As a "Youngster," how will you use your knowledge of personality types to be a more effective leader?

3. Does your personality type explain how you think and act all the time, or do you occasionally think or act in a manner inconsistent with your personality type? Why?

4. As a team leader, if you could choose your team based on personality types, would you create a team of diverse or homogenous personality types? Why?

[2] Noring, J. (1993, May 21). A Summary of Personality Typing. Retrieved from http://www.ibiblio.org/pub/academic/psychology/alt.psychology.personality/FAQ.almost

5 *Values*

Learning Objectives

- Identify sources of values.
- Classify the stages of values development.
- Differentiate between internal and external value conflicts.

> . . . David O. McKay taught, "The greatest battles of life are fought out daily in the silent chambers of the soul." If you win the battles there, if you settle the issues that inwardly conflict, you feel a sense of peace, a sense of knowing what you're about. And you'll find that the public victories—where you tend to think cooperatively, to promote the welfare and good of other people, and to be genuinely happy for other people's successes—will follow naturally.
>
> —Stephen Covey, The Seven Habits of Highly Effective People *(1989)*

> People who are self-aware, who have imagination and conscience, can see when the script they are living is not in harmony with their values— their life is not the product of their own design, but the result of a creation they have deferred to other people and circumstances. We need to approach our roles in life with values and directions clear, to rescript ourselves so the paradigms from which behavior and attitude flow are congruent with deepest values and in harmony with correct principles.
>
> —Milton Rokeach, Understanding Human Values *(1979)*

Theories of Values and Values Development

When was the last time you thought about your values—those qualities or standards that you believe are desirable, worthy, and important? Can't remember? Maybe never? You're probably not alone. Most people have a set of values, but they don't think much about them. Instead, their lives resemble a collection of habits— habits that developed when a situation arose that needed to be resolved. Some people think about values only when they are faced with a crisis that requires immediate action.[1] Yet your values are directly related to the kind of person you are, your goals and aspirations, the way you behave, and the way you relate to other people.

This chapter helps you look at values in a number of ways. It begins with a definition of values and then explores the typical sources of our values. It also discusses the stages of values development and describes some ways of clarifying values and managing values conflicts.

What Are Values?

Values have been defined in many ways, and Schwartz & Bilsky's definition is summarized as, "values are (a) concepts or beliefs, (b) about desirable end states or behaviors,

---

[1] Leatz, C. A. (1993). *Career success/personal stress: How to stay healthy in a high-stress environment.* New York: McGraw Hill.

(c) that transcend specific situations, (d) guide selection or evaluation of behavior and events, and (e) are ordered by relative importance."[2] Values coincide with personal beliefs about what is good and just, right and wrong, ethical and unethical, moral and immoral. In this way, we find that values are important to our self-concept and personal identity, help us in achieving goal-directed behavior, and giving us a sense of purpose and direction in our lives. Values are important because they influence our perceptions and preferences and motivate us to act.[3] According to Williams, "Values are core conceptions of the desirable within every individual and society. They serve as standards or criteria to guide not only action but also judgment, choice, attitude, evaluation, argument, exhortation, [and] rationalization."[4]

Frankl based his theories of logotherapy on the human striving to find meaning in life.[5] But he cautioned that values do not drive a person—they pull rather than push. Implicit in the concept of pulling is the freedom of the individual to choose to accept or reject an idea. No one is driven to good behavior; in every instance we must decide to behave morally, not to satisfy some moral drive or to ease the conscience, but for the sake of some value to which we commit ourselves. The connections among beliefs, knowledge, and values are strong—changes in beliefs affect values and changes in values affect our perceptions of reality.[6]

The goals we set for ourselves, the plans we map out for our lives, result from our value systems, but aren't necessarily the same things as our value systems. Gaus offers this suggestion to help distinguish a plan of life from a value system: "The plan concerns the organization of commitments to act that flow from one's value system. . . . Valuings imply action commitments; one who adopts a plan of action has organized his activity in light of his comparative valuings, resources, and circumstances. Understood thus, plans do not directly determine or organize what one values, but rather how one's value system translates into efficient action in particular circumstances."[7]

Can we value material things? Why or why not?

Over the past decade, research in positive psychology led by Dr. Marty Seligman has provided a connection between values and what philosophers call virtues and character. The original core virtues as discussed by Aristotle are: wisdom, courage, humanity, justice, temperance, and transcendence. Character is the combination of values that act as psychological mechanisms driving behavior that defines our personal identity. The *Values in Action (VIA) Classification of Strengths* inventory measures 24 character strengths (values) that comprise most people's value systems.[8] When considering these character strengths, we find that all are desirable to some extent, but individually, we each identify more strongly with certain values. The VIA provides a method of assessing the degree to which we identify more or less with particular values. Figure 5.1 on page 57 organizes the character strengths by the virtue each supports.

---

[2] Schwartz, S. H. & Bilsky, W. (1987). Toward a Universal Psychological Structure of Human Values. *Journal of Personality and Social Psychology, 53.* 551.

[3] Hanna, S. L. (1995). *Person to person: Positive relationships don't just happen* (2nd ed.). Englewood Cliffs, NJ: Prentice Hall.

[4] Rokeach, M. (Ed.) (1979). *Understanding human values: Individual and societal.* New York: The Free Press.

[5] Frankl, V. E. (1963). *Man's search for meaning.* New York: Washington Square Press.

[6] Rokeach, M. (Ed.) (1979). *Understanding human values: Individual and societal.* New York: The Free Press.

[7] Gaus, G. F. (1990). *Value and justification: The foundations of liberal theory.* Cambridge: Cambridge University Press, 239.

[8] Park, N. (2004). Strengths and Positive Youth Development. *Annals of the American Academy of Political and Social Science, 591,* 40–54.

▣ Sources of Values

While it is still debated as to the development of values and character, there are several researchers who continue to claim that there are biological factors that influence values and value development. The most compelling evidence is found in twin studies, which has found that behavior related to empathy and other prosocial behaviors are heritable in both adults and children.[9] Similarly, psychologists have found links between temperament/personality related to sociability and emotionality and values indicating a further biological component of values.[10] While this evidence supports biological factors, most experts agree that value development is influenced by both biology and culture.

We learn them from others—parents, families, peers, schools, religion, government, the media, etc. The primary sources of values for most of us are family and parents. The things our parents valued shaped both the way they behaved as parents and their expectations for the ways their children would behave. You can expect that your values will affect the way you raise your children, too. The strength of the influence of parental values can be seen in the parent messages that keep replaying in our minds, even well into adulthood: "A penny saved is a penny earned," "Vegetables are good for you," "Buckle up for safety." The values we learned from our parents are reflected in conscience, too. Many years after leaving home, a person can still feel guilty pangs about buying something on impulse or occasionally missing church—an indication that the individual's parents valued frugality and religion, and those values strongly influence that person's internal critic.

The value messages parents send can often be conflicting, as well. A child may hear that the parents value fairness and equality of all people, but when the child brings home a new friend of a different race, he or she may hear another message. It's no wonder that children are confused—and that confusion carries over when as adults they attempt to clarify values.[11]

Messages from television, radio, and advertisements are powerful influences on values, too. Just consider the value messages those media send about youth and body image. Is it any wonder that our society tends to devalue aging, or that so many of us are obsessed with diet, sometimes to the point that obsession becomes illness?

Our own experiences also influence the development of our values. Personally experiencing betrayal or dishonesty may clarify for us the degree to which we value loyalty and honesty. The strong support of parents and siblings or friends will reinforce for us the value of family and friendship.

Not only do we develop personal values, we also develop collective values that we share with others in the societies to which we belong—within families, on the job, in school, and within geopolitical groups like neighborhoods, towns, states, and nations. Research shows that we can find value differences related to race, ethnicity, gender, social class/occupation/education, immigrant status, age cohort, religion and nationality.[12]

[9] Matthews , K. A. Batson, C. D. Horn, & J. Rosenman , R. H. (1981). "Principles in his nature which interest him in the fortune of others…": The heritability of empathic concern for others. *Journal of Personality, 49,* 237–247.

[10] Roccas S., Sagive LSSH, Knafo A. (2002). The big five personality factors and personal values. *Personality and Social Psychology Bulletin, 28,* 789–801.

[11] Hanna, S. L. (1995). *Person to person: Positive relationships don't just happen* (2nd ed.). Englewood Cliffs, NJ: Prentice Hall.

[12] Hitlin, S. and Piliavin, J. A. (2004). Values: Reviving a dormant concept. *Annual Review of Sociology, 30,* 359–393.

These value differences are important to not only understanding our own values, but also the values of those we work with in our diverse military.

Values Development

As we mature in other ways, we also mature in building our system of values. Values take time to develop; research into values clarification has identified three stages most people move through as they develop value systems: acceptance (prizing), preference (choosing), and commitment (acting).[13]

In the early stage of values development, we accept, prize, or cherish something largely because we have been influenced (by parents, media, experience, etc.) to value it. In the parallel stage of personal development, we are still largely focused on the external and tend to behave primarily in reaction to the actions of others. For example, a child of 6 or 7 identifies with going to church and considers it important only because it is important to his or her parents.

In the preference stage of values development, we choose to believe and behave in a certain way, not merely because of external influence, but because we have considered the alternatives and the consequences and have freely chosen to place value on the belief or behavior. This stage generally emerges between the ages of 8 and 16, when personal development is shifting from an external focus to an internal one. For example, at this stage a young person may value church attendance because the person enjoys it and wants to go.

In the final stage of values development, our values are clear and ingrained and we feel a strong commitment to them. At this stage, we are willing to act in accordance with our values and beliefs, consistently and regularly, and would be ready to take a stand to protect them. Most people are ready to commit to values by the time they

Stages of Value Development

Value Development Level	Description	Personal Development Level
Acceptance (Prizing)	Ascribing worth or value to something; prizing or cherishing it; willing to identify with it or publicly affirm it	External/Reactor (ages 0–8)
Preference (Choosing)	Seeking out and pursuing a value on one's own; freely choosing from alternatives after considering consequences	Shifting (ages 8–16)
Commitment (Acting)	Willing to act and take a stand on one's values; acting with consistency and repetition	Crystallized (ages 16–23)

[13] Simon, S. B., Howe, L. W., and Kirschenbaum, H. (1972). *Values clarification: A handbook of practical strategies for teachers and students.* New York: Hart.

reach adulthood (ages 16–23), when their life focus has crystallized. For example, at this stage a person may attend church consistently because she or he values religion and finds church services spiritually fulfilling. An adult who tells you he values going to church because that's "just what you're supposed to do" probably has not developed a firm commitment to religion as a value. He has remained in the acceptance phase of the values development process.

▣ Changing Values

Have your values changed since you became a Midshipman?

As we mature, our values may change. That doesn't mean that our core values shift dramatically, but that things that once seemed to shape our lives no longer exert as strong an influence. In their place have emerged new values (or perhaps they were always there, just not as powerful as they are now) that reflect the new direction our lives are taking. For example, a mother of young children may highly value a strong public school system and will lobby for strong schools and an elementary curriculum that challenges and encourages children. When that same woman is in her forties and her children are attending college, the passionate value she placed on strong elementary schools may have waned. She still may believe in the value of a public school system, but her actions may now reflect a stronger passion for worthwhile and accessible college programs that will prepare her grown children for successful life careers. Her early values haven't evaporated altogether—the basic belief in education hasn't gone away—but the shape of her values in that regard has changed as her life circumstances have changed.

People often find themselves achieving victories that are empty, successes that have come at the expense of things they suddenly realize were far more valuable to them. People from all walks of life—doctors, academicians, performers, politicians, business professionals, athletes, and plumbers—often struggle to achieve a higher income, more recognition, or a certain degree of professional competence, only to find that their drive to achieve the goal blinded them to the things that really mattered most and now are gone.[14]

Do your top three values align with the Navy Core values of honor, courage, and commitment?

Flexibility is vital to a strong and healthy value system, but strength doesn't imply unchanging, rigid values. Instead, it means we are able and willing to continually process values and in doing so, modify them or change their priority. Lack of flexibility makes us judgmental, closes doors, and dismisses the possibility that the value systems of others may be just as legitimate as our own. Without the flexibility to adjust our thinking, we may destroy good relationships or completely reject new relationships because the other person simply doesn't believe as we do.[15]

▣ Managing Values Conflicts and Influencing the Values of Others

When our values coalesce to the point of clarity and action, we are ready to take a stand and act in accordance with them. Usually a stand emerges when our values are challenged, confronted, or attacked in some way. In the face of such a challenge

---

[14] Covey, S. R. (1989). *The seven habits of highly effective people.* New York: Simon & Schuster.

[15] Hanna, S. L. (1995). *Person to person: Positive relationships don't just happen* (2nd ed.). Englewood Cliffs, NJ: Prentice Hall.

(which may come from other people, the community, or new information we uncover about nature, people, or things), values that we might have held in the abstract suddenly are called forth in the form of concrete action. Say, for example, you value your environmental responsibility to pass the earth on relatively intact to future generations. You have only recently learned that the fluorocarbons in aerosol cans do serious damage to the ozone layer. So you take a stand to not use any products that come in aerosol cans. You act on that stand the next time you face a fierce flying insect and the only weapon available is a can of Raid. If you value your environmental responsibility strongly enough, you'll risk a sting rather than sending even a minute amount of fluorocarbons into the atmosphere.

Challenges sometimes evoke values we didn't realize we held dearly. For example, a young family has always spent time together on a regular summer vacation. This year, the oldest child is 10 years old and playing for the first time on a summer league softball team. It turns out that the scheduled games overlap the time the family had set aside for vacation. The family discusses the things it values that are relevant to this situation: sports play as a source of good health, teamwork as a means of learning to cooperate with and be responsible to others, as well as family togetherness and the mental and emotional benefits of a relaxing vacation. Ultimately, they take this stand: When they are in town, softball games get highest priority; but family trips are more important than attending every game.

We usually order our values hierarchically and use them to guide our behavior at certain moments. Because we view some values as more important than others, we often make trade-offs in our lives based on the relative importance we attach to certain values. For example, if you value intellectual development more than you value physical development, given a limited amount of time, you may spend it in the library studying rather than in the gym working out.[16] Values are so fundamental to human behavior that when our personal values are not congruent with our other value sets or the values of others, we may experience serious conflict and the stresses that result can be difficult to manage.

Ethics or values conflicts are not always framed in the context of right versus wrong. More often we are confronted with value dilemmas that present something that is right on both sides—and we can't do both right things at the same time. The rightness on each side reflects two of our core values in conflict with each other. People who have no core values can experience no ethical dilemmas—they don't value any rightness and so are unaware of the ethical universe in which value-driven people live.[17]

Interpersonal conflicts driven by values are the most difficult to resolve. Because values are so closely tied to beliefs, and because beliefs are largely subjective, when we find ourselves in conflict that stems from a fundamental difference in values, the result is likely to be a standoff. Neither party to a conflict is likely to relinquish his or her hold on values (especially those that have crystallized for us and to which we are firmly committed), so argument or moralizing will have little effect on the conflict and will most probably make it more intense. So how can you manage a values conflict? How can you influence the values of another?

Internal Values Conflict- Internal conflict involves two of our core values in conflict with each other, right vs. right.

External Values Conflict- External conflict involves the value systems of two separate entities, your personal values vs. those of another person, group, or community.

What internal conflicts are Midshipmen most likely to experience?

[16] Verderber, R. F., and Verderber, K. S. (2003). *Inter-act: Using interpersonal communication skills* (10th ed.). Belmont, CA: Wadsworth.

[17] Kidder, R. M. (1994). *Shared values; troubled times: Global ethics for the twenty-first century.* E. N. Thompson Forum on World Issues, University of Nebraska–Lincoln. Lincoln, NE: Cooper Foundation and University of Nebraska–Lincoln.

As leaders, how can we overcome external conflicts between our peers, subordinates or superiors?

Confrontation is not the answer. But more subtle approaches may work. Simply modeling the values you want to see others adopt can be a powerful strategy. If you truly value human dignity, for example, you'll walk away from conversations that turn to demeaning women or people of other races. Reinforcing the values you hold dear can also influence the values of others. If you and a co-worker are at odds because you strongly value cooperation in the workplace and your colleague seems to value only her own well-being, you may be able to gradually influence that person to value cooperation if you compliment her each time she demonstrates even the slightest willingness to be part of the team.

Sometimes you simply have to acknowledge that the other person's value system is different from yours. In some cases, the only resolution to a values-based conflict may be to agree to disagree and move beyond it.

▣ Conclusion

We often form friendships by aligning ourselves with those who share our values; it is more difficult to develop an intense relationship with those whose fundamental values are different from our own. But just as we try to understand cultural differences that may initially seem to be barriers to interpersonal interactions, so too should we be open-minded enough to at least attempt to learn why someone else values things that we do not. Most likely we can find many common values in spite of differences on one or two value issues.

Values are fundamental to the way we interact with others. They are the foundation of the life goals we set for ourselves, the building blocks of self-concept and self-esteem, the guiding forces in our exertion of power and influence over others, the bases for many of the conflicts we experience (as well as the roots of conflict resolution). It is no wonder, then, that developing a value system is fundamental to interpersonal communication and interpersonal leadership.

◉ Large Group Exercise: Cave Rescue

Adapted from Francis and Young, 1979.[18]

▣ Purpose

To help you identify some of the things you value and to help you correlate actions to values.

▣ You Will Need

Cave Rescue Briefing Sheet
Cave Rescue Biographical Sheet
Cave Rescue Ranking Sheet

---

[18] Francis, D., and Young, D. (1979). *Improving work groups: A practical manual for team-building.* San Diego: University Associates.

☑ Activity

Read the briefing sheet and become familiar with the situation you have been asked to help with. The biographical sheet is explained in the briefing. Use the ranking sheet as instructed.

When you have completed your ranking sheet individually, work with others in a small group to reach consensus about your rankings. Once your group has reached consensus, select someone to announce your decision and your rationale to the rest of the class.

Cave Rescue Briefing Sheet

You are a member of a research management committee responsible for administering research projects in the behavioral sciences at State University. You have been called to an emergency meeting because of a catastrophe in one of the projects for which the committee is responsible.

The project, which is a study of human behavior in confined spaces, is conducting an experiment in a remote part of the country. The experiment involves seven people who have been living underground in a cave system for several days. The group's only outside contact is via a radio link to a research station at the cave entrance. The volunteers in the cave have issued a call for help: They have been trapped by falling rocks, and water is slowly rising; they expect it will eventually fill the cave.

The only available rescue team reports that rescue will be extremely difficult and, with the equipment available, only one person can be brought out each hour. It is quite likely the rising water will drown some of the trapped volunteers before they can all be removed from the cave.

Through the radio link, the volunteers have been informed about the impossibility of rescuing everyone. They are unwilling to decide the sequence by which they will be rescued. Your research management committee must decide the order of rescue. Lifesaving equipment will arrive at the cave in about 50 minutes. By that time, you must provide the rescue team with the rescue sequence.

The only available information about the trapped volunteers has been drawn from the project files. You'll find that information on the Cave Rescue Biographical Information Sheet. You can use any criteria you wish to help you make a decision.

Complete a Cave Rescue Ranking Sheet individually, then work with members of your group to reach a consensus about the best order of rescue. Once your group has made its decision, complete another Cave Rescue Ranking Sheet for the group and select a spokesperson to announce your decision and your rationale.

Cave Rescue Biographical Sheet

Helen: White, female, American, age 34. Married, homemaker, four children, aged 7 months to 8 years. Husband is city council member. Was a promising psychology student when she left university to marry. Lives in suburb near university. Hobbies are ice skating and cooking. Became involved in the volunteer project through association with Owen, another volunteer. Project coordinator suspects Helen and Owen have developed a covert sexual relationship.

Tozo: Female, Japanese, age 19. Single, sociology student at State University. Parents live in Tokyo, father is wealthy industrialist and national authority on traditional Japanese mime theater. Outstandingly attractive, has dated several men from the upper crust. Recently featured in TV documentary on Japanese women.

John: Black, male, American, age 37. Married, five children, aged 6 years to 19 years. Campus coordinator of Catholic Social Services at State University. Worked full time while attending school; earned master's degree in social work. Heavily involved with Black militant group for several years. Hobbies are camping with his family and photography.

Owen: White, male, American, age 47. Unmarried, physical education instructor at University High School. Served in Army right after high school, was infantry platoon leader in the first Iraq war, earned several distinguished decorations. Medical discharge due to serious leg wound (recovery complete except for occasional pains). Earned master's degree in physical education, using GI Bill benefits. Life is a bit unsettled, drinking problem. Hobbies: modifying and driving stock cars.

Paul: White, male, English, age 47. Divorced (six years), no children. Medical research scientist at University Hospital. Recognized world authority on treatment of rabies. Currently testing a new experimental, low-cost rabies treatment, but much of his research data are still in working notebooks. Hobbies are classical music and sailing. Some emotional difficulty related to divorce and ex-wife's recent remarriage. Twice convicted of indecent exposure (last occasion was 11 months ago).

Edward: White, male, American, age 59. Married, two grown children, seven grandchildren. General manager of small factory (71 employees) that produces rubber belts for machines. Recently negotiated a large contract for his company that, if signed, would create 85 new jobs for the company; will complete details when he returns to work. Socially and politically active; senior freemason and city council member. Hobbies: spelunking (cave exploration). Plans to write a book on the subject when he retires.

Jean: Black, female, Jamaican, age 72. Unmarried, no relatives. Living in U.S. since 1979, but has not sought American citizenship. Ph.D. in biological sciences; working with a government grant to explore biological organisms that live in caves. Most recent work with tree organisms has led to development of experimental vaccine that could be the forerunner to an AIDS vaccine. Recent Peabody Award winner from Stanford University. Assignment in current project: Study the behavior of people in confined spaces and gather microbes for future medical research.

Does your personality type affect how you read / interpret these biographical descriptions?

mother →

media →

children → lots of jobs

Cave Rescue Values Sheet (Individual)

Instructions: Answer the 3 questions about each person. Then rank the seven people trapped in the cave in terms of the value of rescuing them. List numbers in the left-hand column. (Number 1 gets out first, etc.) Complete this sheet on your own.

#	Name	What I value about this person	What about this person has a neutral affect on me	What about this person might lower my ranking of them
2	Helen	mother of many young children	Volunteer	covert sexual relations
1	Tozo	young, smart	Parents live in Tokyo, TV documentary	Gold digger
6	John	children camps, coordinator	camping	Black Militant group
5	Owen	Army, distinguished decorations	leg wound	drinking problem
3	Paul	Medical Research Robots	Divorced	Emotional difficulty
4	Edward	General Manager, new jobs	⇒ Spelunking Book	old
7	Jean	forerunner to AIDS vaccine	no relatives	not a US citizen

Curiosity →
Zest →
Bravery →
leadership →
love of learning →
Fairness →
Service to others →

Cave Rescue Ranking Sheet (Group)

As a group, you must arrive at consensus about your rankings. This doesn't mean you have to agree unanimously, but the majority of your group should be able to live with the final order you come up with. When you determine the order, select someone to present your decision to the class

	NAME	PRIMARY REASON FOR RANKING
1		
2		
3		
4		
5		
6		
7		

What procedures did you use to determine consensus?

What were the principal criteria you used to rank the trapped volunteers?

Foundations of Character

Courage   "Courage is rightly esteemed the first of human qualities... because it is the quality which guarantees all others." — Winston Churchill Emotional strengths that involve the exercise of will to accomplish goals in the face of opposition, external or internal.

Integrity Speaking the truth but more broadly presenting oneself in a genuine way and acting in a sincere way; being without pretense; taking responsibility for one's feelings and actions

Bravery [Valor] Not shrinking from threat, challenge, difficulty, or pain; speaking up for what is right even if there is opposition; acting on convictions even if unpopular; includes physical bravery but is not limited to it.

Perseverance [Persistence] Finishing what one starts; persisting in a course of action in spite of obstacles; "getting it out the door"; taking pleasure in completing tasks.

Vitality [Zest, Enthusiasm, Vigor, Energy] Approaching life with excitement and energy; *not* doing things halfway or halfheartedly; living life as an adventure; feeling alive and activated.

Wisdom   "The nation that will insist upon drawing a broad line of demarcation between the fighting man and the thinking man will find its fighting done by fools and its thinking done by cowards." — LtCol Sir William Butler Cognitive strengths that entail the acquisition and use of knowledge.

Love of Learning Mastering new skills, topics, and bodies of knowledge, whether on one's own or formally; obviously related to the strength of curiosity but goes beyond it to describe the tendency to add systematically to what one knows.

Ingenuity [Creativity] Thinking of novel and productive ways to conceptualize and do things; includes artistic achievement but is not limited to it.

Perspective Being able to provide wise counsel to others; having ways of looking at the world that make sense to oneself and to other people.

Curiosity [Interest, Novelty-seeking, openness to experience] Taking an interest in ongoing experience for its own sake; finding subjects and topics fascinating; exploring and discovering.

Open-mindedness [Judgment, Critical thinking] Thinking things through and examining them from all sides; not jumping to conclusions; being able to change one's mind in light of evidence; weighing all evidence fairly.

Justice   "Justice is the first virtue of social institutions as truth is of systems of thought." — John Rawls Civic strengths that underlie healthy community life.

Fairness Treating all people the same according to notions of fairness and justice; *not* letting personal feelings bias decisions about others; giving everyone a fair chance.

Loyalty [Social responsibility, Citizenship, Teamwork] Working well as a member of a group or team; being loyal to the group; doing one's share.

Leadership: Encouraging a group of which one is a member to get things done and at the same time maintain good relations within the group; organizing group activities and seeing that they happen.

FIGURE 5.1   **Foundations of Character**[1]

[1] Modified from VIA Institute on Character. (2004). The VIA Classification of Character Strengths. retrieved from http://www.viacharacter.org/VIAINSTITUTE/Classification.aspx

Humanity   "An individual has not started living until he can rise above the narrow confines of his individualistic concerns to the broader concerns of all humanity." — Martin Luther King, Jr. Interpersonal strengths that involve tending and befriending others.

   Compassion [Kindness] Doing favors and good deeds for others; helping them; taking care of them.

   Emotional Intelligence [Social Intelligence] Being aware of the motives and feelings of other people and oneself; knowing what to do to fit into different social situations; knowing what makes other people tick.

   Gratitude Being aware of and thankful for the good things that happen; taking time to express thanks.

   Love Valuing close relations with others, in particular those in which sharing and caring are reciprocated; being close to people.

Temperance   "No [one] is fit to command another that cannot command him[or her]self." —William Penn Strengths that protect against excess.

   Self-control [Self regulation] Regulating what one feels and does; being disciplined; controlling one's appetites and emotions.

   Humility/Modesty Letting one's accomplishments speak for themselves; *not* seeking the spotlight; not regarding oneself as more special than one is.

   Forgiveness and mercy Forgiving those who have done wrong; accepting the shortcomings of others; giving people a second chance; *not* being vengeful.

   Prudence Being careful about one's choices; not taking undue risks; not saying or doing things that might later be regretted.

Transcendence   "I have one life and one chance to make it count for something . . . I'm free to choose what that something is, and the something I've chosen is my faith. Now, my faith goes beyond theology and religion and requires considerable work and effort. My faith demands — this is not optional — my faith demands that I do whatever I can, wherever I am, whenever I can, for as long as I can with whatever I have to try to make a difference." — President Jimmy Carter Strengths that forge connections to the larger universe and provide meaning.

   Spirituality [Religiousness, Faith, Purpose]: Having coherent beliefs about the higher purpose and meaning of the universe; knowing where one fits within the larger scheme; having beliefs about the meaning of life that shape conduct and provide comfort.

   Optimism [Hope, Future-mindedness, Future orientation] Expecting the best in the future and working to achieve it; believing that a good future is something that can be brought about.

FIGURE 5.1   Foundations of Character[1] *(Continued)*

[1] Modified from VIA Institute on Character. (2004). The VIA Classification of Character Strengths. retrieved from http://www.viacharacter.org/VIAINSTITUTE/Classification.aspx

Appreciation of beauty and excellencee [Awe, Wonder, Elevation] Noticing and appreciating beauty, excellence, and/or skilled performance in various domains of life, from nature to art to mathematics to science to everyday experience.

Humor [playfulness] Liking to laugh and tease; bringing smiles to other people; seeing the light side; making not necessarily telling jokes.

Questions for review

1. How can we use critical thinking to express our opinions regarding values and resolve value conflicts?

2. As a leader, why is it important to understand how to handle internal and external value conflicts?

6 *Reflection*

Learning Objectives:

- Analyze the statement: "*In the military, we often become addicted to action.*"
- Distinguish between reflection and reflective action.
- Identify four ways to reflect that are listed in your text.
- Describe the importance of reflection as military officer. Identify examples.

Reprinted from Quinn, R. E. (2004). *Building the bridge as you walk on it: A guide for leading change.* San Francisco, CA: John Wiley & Sons, Inc.

> *When we take the time to integrate action and reflection, we begin to behave differently. . . . As we become more purpose-centered, internally driven, other-focused, and externally open, we more fully integrate who we are with what we are doing. At this point, what we are doing enlarges our best self, and our best self enlarges what we are doing.*

Here we will examine reflective action. It was Plato who once argued that the unexamined life is not worth living. To this someone once responded, "Yes, and the unlived life is not worth examining." Reflective action is a concept that combines both arguments. It is not easy to integrate both reflection and action. In the military for example, there is a tremendous imperative toward action. If we err between action and taking the time to reflect, we err on the side of action.

Given the bias toward action in modern life, let us begin our examination of the practice of reflective action from the other direction—from the viewpoint of a man who had chosen a life of reflection and contemplation.

Most of us in the organizational world are engulfed in action, at the expense of contemplation and reflection. This extreme is just as isolating as the extreme of contemplation divorced from action.

In the military, we often become addicted to action. We develop organizational cultures that carry the expectations that people will come in early and leave late. We reinforce the compulsive patterns of type A personalities. We complain endlessly about the loss of balance in our lives and the pain of burnout. We assume that there is no place for reflection. We dare not speak of the need for spiritual awareness and personal integration. In this distorted world where we have institutionalized the split of action and reflection, we are trapped in the vortex of slow death. People often recognize the problem but lack the courage to do anything about it. They choose slow death over deep change.

Why do you think service members might struggle with the idea of practicing reflection?

Reflective Action

The positive tension of the state of reflective action can be seen in Table 6.1. We can be so mindful and reflective that we become stagnant and inactive. On the other hand, and much more commonly in organizational life, we can be so active and energetic that we become mindless and unreflective.

The challenge is to be both reflective and active. We can do this by making a practice of regularly reflecting on what is happening in our lives. At first, we make time for contemplation when we are away from our usual tasks so as to increase our capacity for mindfulness during the tasks. Eventually we act and learn simultaneously. We are both mindful and energized while creating the life we want to live.

Table 6.1. Reflective Action.

NEGATIVE	POSITIVE	INTEGRATIVE	POSITIVE	NEGATIVE
This person is so mindful and reflective as to be stagnant or inactive.	This person is mindful and reflective.	This person practices reflective action.	This person is active and energetic.	This person is so active and energetic as to be mindless or unreflective.
Stagnant; inactive	Mindful; reflective	Reflective and active	Active; energetic	Mindless; unreflective

Reflective action: This person is active and energetic while also being mindful and reflective. While deeply engaged in the world, the person also spends time in reflective contemplation. Contemplation when away from a task increases the capacity for mindfulness during the task. The person acts and learns simultaneously and is both mindful and energized while actively creating.

Personal orientation: I continually renew my understanding of who I am and why and how I am doing the things I do by learning from action and acting from an ever-expanding consciousness. I live in a reciprocal relationship between action and reflection. I practice reflective action.

Practicing Reflective Action

Some Navy and Marine Corps officers have attributed "not making the same mistake twice" to their systematic method of maintaining a journal. Perhaps the most common way to integrate action and reflection is through the habit of journal writing. Some people record the events of each day in a process akin to diary writing by simply recording what happened during the day. *Reflective action requires more than just recording events.* It requires examination of who we are and how that matches with what we are doing. It often requires an exploration of the link between our present and our past.

While maintaining a journal serves many people as their method of reflection, there are several means of reflection one can use. *Systematically reflecting* refers to the manner or process of reflection that works best for you. Examples include meeting with teammates each week to discuss how practices have gone, using your daily Physical Training (PT) as time to think about the day's activities, or conversing with a friend to discuss your thoughts. An example from Plebe Summer is the daily Thoughts of the Day you completed each night. A good system of reflection might be to maintain a journal of all the leadership traits, both positive and negative, you have observed among the upper class. Periodically reflecting on these entries may help to avoid the traits you dislike and remind you of the traits you wish to exemplify.

Often times we reflect when it is natural or during times when it is most important to reflect. This type of reflection is an example of *natural reflection.* Generally after one has made a poor decision or made a mistake, time is spent trying to figure out why or how it could have been done better. While we have no way of knowing when these events will happen, the circumstances can compel us to think about the situation in a deep and meaningful way. This form of reflection can be very productive if we are objective in our assessment of the situation and we learn something positive from the experience.

Inserting some form of regularity or routine into one's reflection is an example of *recurrent reflection.* Recurrent reflection refers to *when* you reflect and not necessarily *how* you do so. Examples of this form of reflection are doing so every night before bed, during church, or during the ten minutes between third and fourth period. Some people find it important to maintain a formal schedule and like having

Reflection is a careful and deep consideration about our own experiences, observations, values, priorities and goals. During reflection we assess, analyze, synthesize, evaluate, discern and make new discoveries about ourselves and others.

Reflective action applies this internalized process (introspection) to the outside world where we act in ways that are congruous with our values, priorities and goals.

a very specific time to spend in reflection. Putting aside time to think through the happenings of each day might serve useful in maintaining yourself as a reflective person that can act using lessons learned.

Being mindful of the past so that you can actively and energetically tackle future tasks embodies the idea of reflective action. Although many consider reflection to be a very personal and private process, reflection can be done *either alone or with others*. By asking for the help of a shipmate, friend or family member to think through why something happened, you will often find a different and potentially richer, point of view. In the fleet, junior officers are encouraged to seek the advice of the senior enlisted that have "been there and done that." By engaging others in reflecting on your daily life, you might find that you can avoid mistakes that have already been made by someone else.

Questions for review:

1. What do you think was meant when the Greek philosopher wrote, "The unexamined life is not worth living?"

2. Do you think it is important as a midshipmen and future officer to include regular reflection into your schedule? And if so, why?

Part
Two

Self-Leadership

7 *Personal Mission Development*

⊙ Learning Objectives:

- ⊙ Distinguish between Gardner's "truer version of happiness" and the "storybook version."
- ⊙ Classify the three questions that a Life Mission Statement should address.
- ⊙ Formulate a one sentence Life Mission Statement.

Commitment and Meaning

The quest for meaning is as old as history and a central theme in all great literature. For John W. Gardner the meaning of life is largely found in the commitments one makes to something beyond the self. This discussion of meaning and commitment is taken from his book Self-Renewal.[1]

In maturity one undertakes commitments to something larger than the service of one's "convulsive little ego," to use William James's memorable phrase—religious commitments, commitments to loved ones, to the social enterprise and to the moral order. In a free society we shall never specify too closely what those commitments should be.

Young people today would have a far easier time understanding the role of commitment in their lives if they were not misled by the juvenile interpretation of the "pursuit of happiness" that is widely held today. It is not unduly harsh to say that the contemporary idea of happiness cannot possibly be taken seriously by anyone whose intellectual or moral development has progressed beyond that of a three-week-old puppy. From Aristotle to Jefferson, philosophers who have thought seriously about happiness would be startled to discover how that word is now interpreted.

What makes you happy? What do you foresee making you happy in 10 years? 20 years?

The truth is that few humans are capable of achieving the vegetative state implied in the current conception of happiness. Despite almost universal belief to the contrary, gratification, ease, comfort, diversion and a state of having achieved all one's goals do not constitute happiness for humans. The reason Americans have not trapped the bluebird of happiness, despite the most frantic efforts the world has ever seen, is that happiness as total gratification is not a state to which we can aspire. The irony is that we should have brought such unprecedented dynamism to the search for such a static condition.

> The American commitment is not to affluence, nor to all the cushioned comforts of a well-fed nation, but to the liberation of the human spirit, the release of human potential, the enhancement of individual dignity. Those are the great themes of our life as a people. Everything else is a means to those ends.
>
> Some of our fellow citizens do not honor those ends. But many live by the American commitment and live to further that commitment. They come from all walks of life. They constitute the brotherhood and sisterhood of those who care enough about the American commitment to do something about it. It is an army without banners, and its campaigns are not reported on the front page—but it is marching.
>
> Every time a teacher strives to give honest individual attention to a child, she is advancing the cause. Every time an employer seeks to create

[1] Gardner, J. W. (1964). *Self-Renewal: The Individual and the Innovative Society.* New York: Harper & Row.

the working environment in which individual employees can flourish and grow, he is helping. So is every mother who provides the special combination of love and instruction that makes for early emergence of a sense of responsibility.

Anyone can contribute and I count the contribution as a measure of those I meet. I don't want to know what their religion is or their political party, or the size of their bankroll. I want to know what they have done lately about the American commitment.

—*Speech at Education Symposium, University of Texas, Austin, 1972*

It might be possible for an impoverished nation to harbor the delusion that happiness is simply comfort and pleasure and having enough of everything. But we have tried it, and we know better.

One can accept this fact without at the same time underrating the pleasant things in life. One is rightly suspicious of those who tell poor people that they should be content with poverty, or hungry people that hunger is ennobling. Every human being should have the chance to enjoy the comforts and pleasures of good living. All we are saying here is that they are not enough. If they were, the large number of Americans who have been able to indulge their whims on a scale unprecedented in history would be deliriously happy. They would be telling one another of their unparalleled serenity and bliss instead of trading tranquilizer prescriptions.

So we are coming to a conception of happiness that differs fundamentally from the storybook version. The storybook conception tells of desires fulfilled; the truer version involves striving toward meaningful goals—goals that relate the individual to a larger context of purposes. Storybook happiness involves a bland idleness; the truer conception involves seeking and purposeful effort. Storybook happiness involves every form of pleasant thumb-twiddling; true happiness involves the full use of one's powers and talents. Both conceptions of happiness involve love, but the storybook version puts great emphasis on being loved, the truer version more emphasis on the capacity to give love.

This more mature and meaningful view opens up the possibility that one might even achieve happiness in striving to meet one's moral responsibilities, an outcome that is most unlikely under the present view unless one's moral responsibilities happen to be uncommonly diverting.

Note that we speak of happiness as involving a "striving toward" significant goals, not necessarily the attaining of those goals. It is characteristic of some kinds of human striving that the goals may be unattainable. Those who dedicate their lives to the achieving of good government or to the combating of human misery may enjoy small victories but they can never win the longer battle. The goal recedes before them. Such striving, says Allport, "confers unity upon personality, but it is never the unity of fulfillment, of repose, or of reduced tension."

For this reason, self-renewing people never feel that they have "arrived." They know that the really important tasks are never finished—interrupted, perhaps, but never finished and all the significant goals recede before one. Those who think that they have arrived have simply lost sight of those goals (or perhaps never saw them in the first place).

Don't pray for the day when we finally solve our problems. Pray for freedom to continue working on the problems the future will never cease to throw at us.

—*Journals*

What is meant by "meaningful goals"? What are some examples of meaningful goals that you have?

It is widely believed that humans in their natural state will do only what is required to achieve strictly physical satisfactions, but as every anthropologist can testify, this is not true. Primitives are intensely committed to their social group and to the moral order as they conceive it. One has to be fairly well steeped in the artificialities of civilization before one can imagine that indulgence of physical satisfactions might be a complete way of life.

Anyone can see that most men and women are quite prepared to (and do) undergo hardship and suffering in behalf of a significant goal. Indeed, they often actually court hardship in behalf of something they believe in. "Virtue will have naught to do with ease," wrote Montaigne. "It seeks a rough and thorny path."

This is not to say that the aims that humans conceive beyond the needs of the self are necessarily ones that would win our admiration. They may be expressions of the highest idealism or they may be crude, even vicious. That is a salient feature of the problem. If we make the mistake of imagining that only the material wants of people need be satisfied and offer them no significant meanings, they are likely to seize upon the first "meanings" that present themselves, however shallow and foolish, committing themselves to false gods, to irrational political movements, to cults and to fads. It is essential that the human hunger for dedication find worthy objects.

It would be wrong to leave the implication that we are selfless creatures who only wish to place ourselves at the service of some higher ideal. Having rejected the oversimplified view of our nature as wholly materialistic and selfish, we must not fall into the opposite error. Humans are complex and contradictory beings, egocentric but inescapably involved with their fellow beings, selfish but capable of superb selflessness. We are preoccupied with our own needs, yet we find no meaning in life unless we relate ourselves to something more comprehensive than those needs. It is the tension between our egocentrism and our social and moral leanings that has produced much of the drama in human history.

Of course one always thinks one's neighbor should be more dedicated. Our own passion for dedication is contaminated by selfishness, laziness, and inconstancy, but our ardor for the other fellow's dedication is pure and undefiled. The employer believes that employees should be more dedicated to their work (meaning usually that they should work harder for less pay). Older people think young people should be more dedicated. We are all familiar with the moral zeal that rises in our breast when we think of the standards the other fellow ought to live up to. Artemus Ward said, "I have already given two cousins to the war, and I stand ready to sacrifice my wife's brother. . . ."

Nothing that is said here should be taken as an encouragement of such vicarious morality. Nor is anything that we say here to be taken as a defense of other misguided forms of commitment. There will never be a way of preventing fools from dedicating themselves to silly causes. There is no way to save some intense and unstable minds from a style of dedication that is in fact fanaticism.

Aside from these obvious dangers, there are other more subtle hazards in dedication. Anyone who thinks, for example, that a determination to "do good to others" is not accompanied by certain hazards should remember Thoreau's comment: "If I knew . . . that a man was coming to my house with the conscious design of doing me good, I should run for my life." Doing good to others may be an expression of the purest altruism or it may simply be a means of demonstrating one's superiority or of living vicariously.

Hunger for Meaning

Humans are in their nature seekers of meaning. They cannot help being so any more than they can help breathing or maintaining a certain body temperature. It is the way their central nervous systems work.

In most societies and most ages, however primitive they may have been technologically, the hunger for meaning was amply served. Though some of the religions, mythologies, and tribal superstitions with which the hunger for meaning was fed were crude and impoverished, they did purport to describe a larger framework in terms of which one's life gained significance.

With the arrival of the modern age a good many misguided souls conceived the notion that we could do without such nourishment. And for a breath-taking moment it did seem possible, in view of the glittering promises that modern life offered. Under the banner of a beneficial modernity, the individual was to have security, money, power, sensual gratification and status as high as anyone. He would be a solvent and eupeptic Walter Mitty in a rich and meaningless world.

But even (or especially) those who came close to achieving the dream never got over the nagging hunger for meaning.

At one level, our search for meanings is objectively intellectual. We strive to organize what we know into coherent patterns. Studies of perception have demonstrated that this tendency to organize experience is not an afterthought or the result of conscious impulse but an integral feature of the perceptual process. At the level of ideas, our inclination to organize meaningful wholes out of our experience is equally demonstrable. We try to reduce the stream of experience to orderly sequences and patterns. We produce legends, theories, philosophies.

To an impressive degree, the theories of nature and the universe that we have developed are impersonal in the sense that they take no special account of our own aspirations and status (though they are strictly dependent on our conceptualizing power and rarely wholly divorced from our values). Out of this impersonal search for meaning has come modern science.

But we have never been satisfied to let it go at that. We have throughout history shown a compelling need to arrive at conceptions of the universe in *terms of which we could regard our own lives as meaningful*. We want to know where *we* fit into the scheme of things. We want to understand how the great facts of the objective world relate to us and what they imply for our behavior. We want to know what significance may be found in our own existence, the succeeding generations of our kind and the vivid events of our inner life. We seek some kind of meaningful framework in which to understand (or at least to reconcile ourselves to) the indignities of chance and circumstance and the fact of death. A number of philosophers and scientists have told us sternly that we must not expect answers to that sort of question, but we pay little heed. We want, in the words of Kierkegaard, "a truth that is true for me." We seek conceptions of the universe that give dignity, purpose and sense to our own existence.

When we fail in this effort we exhibit what Tillich describes as the anxiety of meaninglessness—"anxiety about the loss of an ultimate concern, of a meaning which gives meaning to all meanings." As Erikson has pointed out, the young person's search for identity is in some respects this sort of search for meaning. It is a search for a framework in terms of which young persons may understand their own aims, their relation to their fellow beings and their relation to larger purposes. In our society every individual is free to conduct this search on his own terms and to find, if he is lucky, the answer that is right for him.

Meaning, Purpose, and Commitment

There are those who think of the meaning of life as resembling the answer to a riddle. One searches for years, and then some bright day one finds it, like the prize at the end of a treasure hunt. This is a profoundly misleading notion. The meanings in any life are multiple and varied. Some are grasped very early, some late; some have a heavy emotional component, some are strictly intellectual; some merit the label religious, some are better described as social. But each kind of meaning implies a relationship between the person and some larger system of ideas or values, a relationship involving obligations as well as rewards. In the individual life, meaning, purpose and commitment are inseparable. When one succeeds in the search for identity one has found the answer not only to the question "Who am I" but to a lot of other questions too: "What must I live up to? What are my obligations? To what must I commit myself?"

A free society will not specify too closely the kinds of meaning different individuals will find or the things about which they should generate conviction. People differ in their goals and convictions and in the whole style of their commitment. We must ask that their goals fall within the moral framework to which we all pay allegiance, but we cannot prescribe the things that will unlock their deepest motivations. Those earnest spirits who believe that one cannot be counted worthy unless one burns with zeal for civic affairs could not be more misguided. And we are wrong when we follow the current fashion of identifying moral strength too exclusively with fighting for a cause. Nothing could be more admirable nor more appealing to us as a performance-minded people. But such an emphasis hardly does justice to the rich variety of moral excellences that humans have sought and occasionally achieved in the course of history.

> For men and women who have accepted the reality of change, the need for endless learning and trying is a way of living, a way of thinking, a way of being awake and ready. Life isn't a train ride where you choose your destination, pay your fare and settle back for a nap. It's a cycle ride over uncertain terrain, with you in the cyclist's seat, constantly correcting your balance and determining the direction of progress. It's difficult, sometimes profoundly painful. But it's better than napping through life.
>
> —*Self-Renewal (Rev. ed.), 1981, p. xii*

A good many of the most valuable people in any society will never burn with zeal for anything except the integrity and health and well-being of their own families—and if they achieve those goals, we need ask little more of them. There are other valuable members of a society who will never generate conviction about anything beyond the productive output of their hands or minds—and a sensible society will be grateful for their contributions. Nor will it be too quick to define some callings as noble and some as ordinary. One may not quite accept Oliver Wendell Holmes's dictum—"Every calling is great when greatly pursued"—but the grain of truth is there.

Questions for review:

1. What are the differences between the "storybook version of happiness" and Gardner's "truer version"?
2. What is the importance of setting meaningful goals that may never be achieved? Isn't this counter to good goal setting practice?

Personal Mission Worksheet

For most of us, it started as children:

"What do you want to do when you grow up?"

It's still a pretty good question. It's also the idea behind having a <u>Life Mission</u> — intentional reflection regarding the person you are committed to becoming.

In other words: **When all is said and done…will you be proud and satisfied with what you've said and what you've done?**

For military members, our pledge to uphold the Constitution gives us a unified mission. Each of us has taken an oath to "support and defend the Constitution of the United States" against anyone or anything that threatens it. A well-developed life mission statement can have the same meaning on a personal level—a creed that guides our lives and inspires us to protect it from all competing interests.

As we begin this chapter, reflect on the following words from Vice Admiral James Bond Stockdale:

> " . . .every good leader is a good teacher. He is able to give those around him a sense of perspective and to set the moral, social, and particularly the motivational climate among his followers. This is not an easy task. It takes wisdom and self-discipline; it requires the sensitivity to perceive philosophic disarray in one's charges and the knowledge of how to put things in order. I believe that a good starting point is that old injunction 'know thyself.' A leader must aspire to strength, compassion, and conviction several orders greater than required by society in general."

Up to this point in an effort to "know thyself," you have explored, among other things, your value system, your personality type, and your natural talents. All this knowledge will be of little use if you do not have a purpose or a direction in which to apply yourself. This chapter will help you take all that you have learned thus far, and purposefully apply it to your life so that you may live a life with a purpose. In other words:

"Make your life a mission – not an intermission."

—*Arnold Glasgow*

Part One

As a child, what did you dream of becoming?

_____

_____

What motivates you?   What angers you?

_____   _____

_____   _____

_____   _____

What things do you do that you consider being of the most value?

_____

_____

Name three people whom you admire and the characteristics they demonstrate that cause you to admire them.

1. _____

_____

_____

2. _____

_____

_____

3. _____

_____

_____

Describe yourself in one word. _____

You are now 70 and you have your family and closest friends gathered around you. They have asked you to tell them what is really important in life. What would you tell them?

_____

_____

_____

_____

Before I die, I want to:

Be _____

Go _____

Have _____

Do _____

Help _____

What is your personality type (MBTI)? _____

What does your personality type typically value?

_____

What types of things does your personality type typically enjoy doing the most?

_____

Previously, we discussed our values. List some of your most important values.

_____   _____

_____   _____

_____   _____

_____   _____

Considering all of the information above, what are the three MOST IMPORTANT values of your life?

The most important value of my life is: _____

Why?

_____

_____

_____

The 2nd most important value of my life is: _____

Why?

_____

_____

_____

The 3rd most important value of my life is: _____

Why?

_____

_____

_____

Part Two

What did you do for fun as a child?

_____

_____

What came easy to you as a child?

_____

_____

What were your favorite subjects in school?

_____

Think about the last time you were really excited about life, when you lost all track of time? What were you doing? Where were you? Who was with you? What were the results?

_____

_____

_____

_____

What do you do better and easier than anyone you know?

_____

_____

What are the activities that you cannot, not do? To be true to yourself, you must do these:

_____

_____

If money, education, and experience were no object, describe the work activity you would be involved in ten years from now?

_____

_____

What do you do that causes other people to say, "You are really good at < >, it seems so natural for you"?

_____

_____

From the Strengths Finder assessment (Strengths Quest Book) what are your top 5 talent themes – what do they mean as far as how you get things done?

_____ – _____

_____ – _____

_____ – _____

_____ – _____

_____ – _____

What activities can these 5 themes **work together** to do?

_____

_____

_____

_____

Considering all of the information in Part Two, what three activities bring you the most fulfillment when doing them?

_____, _____, and _____

Part Three

You have been given $1 million to pass along to a charity, cause, or organization that you believe in. Who would you give the money to and how would you want the money spent?

_____

_____

You are now 90 years old and all of the people whose lives you have ever improved during your life are gathered around you. The largest group of people is made up of:

_____

What type of people do you most enjoy working with?

_____

Complete the following statement: "At the end of my life I want people to say I

Believed in: _____

Fought for: _____

Was dedicated to: _____

Symbolized: _____

What types of people need your abilities the most?

_____

What in your life is more important than your life?

_____

Putting It All Together

An effective mission statement answers three questions. Those are:

1. What am I going to do?
2. To or for whom am I going to do it?
3. How, or in what way, will I do it?

What you are going to do in life should be based upon what you value most and how you are made. Go back to Part One of this chapter. Look at the three most important values of your life and why you chose them as your top three. Also, look at your MBTI type and consider what types of things give you the most satisfaction in life.

Write down 2 or 3 things that you can do for the rest of your life that are based upon your top three values. These should be activities that are ongoing and not things that stop once you have accomplished them (i.e. serving others vs. becoming a Naval Aviator).

A. _____

B. _____

C. _____

To or for whom you are going to live your mission should also be based upon your core values. It should be some group or something that you are not only willing to die for, but also willing to dedicate your daily life to.

You have already reviewed your three most important values. Now review your answers in Part Three of this chapter.

What one or two things (group, cause, idea, belief system, etc.) are you willing to spend your life adding value to?

D. _____

E. _____

How, or in what way, you are going to live out your missions depends on what your strengths are (remember a Strength = Talent + Skills + Knowledge). When we act from our strengths we are more likely to find satisfaction in our lives. Therefore, it makes sense that to live a life of satisfaction and purpose we should use our strengths to live out our mission in life.

Review Part Two of this chapter and then fill in the spaces below.

The activities that bring me the most fulfillment when doing them are:

F. _____ G. _____ H. _____

Now use your answers in the worksheet as the building blocks for your Life Mission Statement. Personalize it, put it in your own words, and make it make sense to you. It should be easy to remember, and inspire you to keep going when life gets hard.

8 Motivation and Goals

Learning Objectives:

- Distinguish between a need and a motive.
- Describe Maslow's Hierarchy of Needs.
- Distinguish between performance goals and learning goals.
- Outline the SMART criteria for goal setting.
- Create SMART goals to be applied to your life as a midshipman.

How Do Needs and Motives Influence Motivation?[1]

According to a widely accepted explanation of human behavior, people have needs and motives that propel them toward achieving certain goals. Needs and motives are closely related. A **need** is an internal striving or urge to do something, such as a need to drink when thirsty. It can be regarded as a biological or psychological requirement. Because the person is deprived in some way (such as not having enough fluid in the body), the person is motivated to take action toward a goal. In this case the goal might be simply getting something to drink.

A **motive** is an inner drive that moves a person to do something. The motive is usually based on a need or desire and results in the intention to attain an appropriate goal. Because needs and motives are so closely related, the two terms are often used interchangeably. For example, "recognition need" and "recognition motive" refer to the same thing.

Maslow's Need Hierarchy

The best-known categorization of needs is **Maslow's need hierarchy.** At the same time, it is the most widely used explanation of human motivation. According to psychologist Abraham H. Maslow, people strive to satisfy the following groups of needs in step-by-step order:

1. *Physiological needs* refer to bodily needs, such as the requirements for food, water, and sleep.
2. *Safety needs* refer to actual physical safety and to a feeling of being safe from both physical and emotional injury.
3. *Social needs* are essentially love or belonging needs. Unlike the two previous levels of needs, they center around a person's interaction with other people.
4. *Esteem needs* represent an individual's demand to be seen as a person of worth by others—and to him- or herself.
5. *Self-actualizing needs* are the highest level of needs, including the needs for self-fulfillment and personal development.

A diagram of the need hierarchy is presented in Figure 8-1. Notice the distinction between higher-level and lower-level needs. With few exceptions, higher-level needs are more difficult to satisfy. A person's needs for affiliation might be satisfied by being a member of a friendly work group. Yet to satisfy self-actualization needs, such as self-fulfillment, a person might have to develop an outstanding reputation in his or her company.

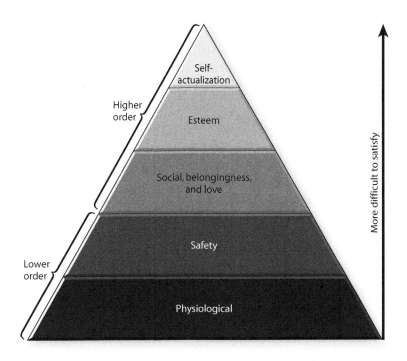

FIGURE **8.1** **Maslow's Need Hierarchy**

The need hierarchy implies that most people think of finding a job as a way of obtaining the necessities of life. Once these are obtained, a person may think of achieving friendship, self-esteem, and self-fulfillment on the job. When a person is generally satisfied at one level, he or she looks for satisfaction at a higher level. As Maslow describes it, a person is a "perpetually wanting animal." Very few people are totally satisfied with their lot in life, even the rich and famous.

The extent of need satisfaction is influenced by a person's job. Some construction jobs, for example, involve dangerous work in severe climates, thus frustrating both physiological and safety needs. Ordinarily there is much more opportunity for approaching self-actualization when a person occupies a prominent position, such as a top executive or famous performer. However, a person with low potential could approach self-actualization by occupying a lesser position. In the current era, workers at all levels are threatened with the frustration of security needs because so many companies reduce the number of employees to save money.

How do Maslow's needs and the other needs described in this chapter relate to self-motivation? First you have to ask yourself, "Which needs do I really want to satisfy?" After answering the question honestly, concentrate your efforts on an activity that will most likely satisfy that need. For instance, if you are hungry for power, strive to become a high-level manager or a business owner. If you crave self-esteem, focus your efforts on work and social activities that are well regarded by others. The point is that you will put forth substantial effort if you think the goal you attain will satisfy an important need.

How Does Goal Setting Work?[2]

Despite abundant goal-setting research and practice, goal-setting theories are surprisingly scarce. An instructive model was formulated by Locke and his associates. According to Locke's model, goal setting has four motivational mechanisms.

▣ Goals Direct Attention

Goals direct one's attention and effort toward goal-relevant activities and away from goal-irrelevant activities. If, for example, you have a term project due in a few days, your thoughts and actions tend to revolve around completing that project. Scooter Store, which was included among the list of the 100 best companies to work for in America in 2004 by *Fortune,* uses this motivational function of goal setting on a daily basis. Every morning the company's managers assemble their workers in a 14-minute huddle to discuss the day's goals.

▣ Goals Regulate Effort

Not only do goals make us selectively perceptive, they also motivate us to act. The instructor's deadline for turning in your term project would prompt you to complete it, as opposed to going out with friends, watching television, or studying for another course. Generally, the level of effort expended is proportionate to the difficulty of the goal.

▣ Goals Increase Persistence

Within the context of goal setting, persistence represents the effort expended on a task over an extended period of time: It takes effort to run 100 meters; it takes persistence to run a 26-mile marathon. Persistent people tend to see obstacles as challenges to be overcome rather than as reasons to fail. A difficult goal that is important to an individual is a constant reminder to keep exerting effort in the appropriate direction. Annika Sorenstam is a great example of someone who persisted at her goal of being the best female golfer in the world. She has won 62 tournaments since starting on the LPGA tour in 1994.

She already has qualified for the LPGA and World Golf Halls of Fame, has won a career Grand Slam, shot the only round of 59 in women's pro golf and has won six Player of the Year titles.

[In 2003] her new challenge was playing in a PGA Tour event, where she made a lasting impression but failed to make the cut. When it was over, she said she didn't care to compete in more men's tournaments but needed to move on.

Moving on meant winning two more LPGA majors. Just like Tiger Woods, major titles and a single-season Grand Slam have become her new focus.

"Nobody else has done it, so I think that says it all," she said. "But I like to set high goals, I like to motivate myself. If you believe it in your mind, I think you can do it."

▣ Goals Foster the Development and Application of Task Strategies and Action Plans

If you are here and your goal is out there somewhere, you face the problem of getting from here to there. For example, the person who has resolved to lose 20 pounds

---

[2] Kreitner, R. & Kinicki, A. (2007). *Organizational Behavior* (7th ed.). New York: McGraw-Hill.

must develop a plan for getting from "here" (his or her present weight) to "there" (20 pounds lighter). Goals can help because they encourage people to develop strategies and action plans that enable them to achieve their goals. By virtue of setting a weight-reduction goal, the dieter may choose a strategy of exercising more, eating less, or some combination of the two.

Performance vs Learning Goals[3]

How does a learning goal differ from a performance-outcome goal? What explains the superiority of a learning goal over a performance goal on a task that is complex for an individual? How can specific challenging learning goals be applied in business settings?

The primary distinction between a performance and a learning goal is the framing of the instructions given to employees. *Hence, the difference between these two types of goals is first and foremost a "mindset."* The respective instructions focus attention on two different domains—motivation versus ability. A performance goal, as the name implies, frames the instructions so that an employee's focus is on task performance (e.g., attain 20 percent market share by the end of the next fiscal year). The search for information to attain the goal is neither mentioned nor implied because knowledge and skills are considered a given on tasks that require primarily choice, effort, or persistence on the part of the people who have been assigned the goal. Similarly, a learning goal as the name implies, frames the instructions in terms of knowledge or skill acquisition (e.g., discover three effective strategies to increase market share). A learning goal draws attention away from the end result. The focus is on the discovery of effective task processes. Once an employee has the knowledge and skills necessary to effectively perform the task, a specific challenging performance goal should be set to direct attention to the exertion of effort and persistence required to achieve it. The performance goal cues individuals to use strategies or performance routines that the person has learned previously are effective. Setting a learning goal on a task that is relatively straightforward for an individual wastes time, and is ineffective in that the person has already mastered the requisite performance routines and is aware of the requisite job behaviors. In short, learning goals help people progress to the point where performance outcome goals become beneficial for increasing one's effectiveness. The focus of a learning goal is to increase one's knowledge (ability); the focus of a performance goal is to increase one's motivation to implement that knowledge. Therefore, both learning and performance goals are needed to be successful. But, as noted earlier, our research shows that a performance goal should not be set until an employee has the knowledge to attain it.

Performance Goal
Based on performance measures and outcomes

Learning Goal
Based on knowledge or skill acquisition

Setting Smart Goals

In accordance with available research evidence, goals should be "SMART." SMART is an acronym that stands for specific, measurable, attainable, results oriented, and time bound. Table 8-1 contains a set of guidelines for writing SMART goals. There are two additional recommendations to consider when setting goals. First, for complex tasks, [leaders] should train [subordinates] in problem-solving techniques and encourage them to develop a performance action plan. Action plans specify the strategies or tactics to be used in order to accomplish a goal.

---

[3] Latham, G. & Seijts, G. (2005). Learning versus performance goals: When should each be used. *Academy of Management Executive, 19*(1), 124–131.

Table 8-1 Guidelines for Writing SMART Goals

Specific	Goals should be stated in precise rather than vague terms. For example, a goal that provides for 20 hours of technical training for each [sailor and marine] is more specific than stating that a manager should send as many people as possible to training classes. Goals should be quantified when possible.
Measurable	A measurement device is needed to assess the extent to which a goal is accomplished. Goals thus need to be measurable. It also is critical to consider the quality aspect of the goal when establishing measurement criteria. For example, if the goal is to complete a managerial study of methods to increase productivity one must consider how to measure the quality of this effort. Goals should not be set without considering the interplay between quantity and quality of output.
Attainable	Goals should be realistic, challenging, and attainable. Impossible goals reduce motivation because people do not like to fail. Remember, people have different levels of ability and skill.
Results oriented	[Command] goals should focus on desired end-results that support the [Navy's] vision. In turn, an individual's goals should directly support the accomplishment of [command] goals. Activities support the achievement of goals and are outlined in action plans. To focus goals on desired end-results, goals should start with the word *to* followed by verbs such as *complete, acquire, produce, increase,* and *decrease.* Verbs such as *develop, conduct, implement,* or *monitor* imply activities and should not be used in a goal statement.
Time bound	Goals specify target dates for completion.

SOURCE: Kinicki, A.J. (2005). *Performance Management Systems.* Superstition Mt., AZ: Kinicki and Associates Inc.

Questions for review:

1. Think about what motivates you. How can understanding what motivates yourself and others be useful as a leader?

2. What do we observe more at USNA: performance goals or learning goals? List some examples of each in midshipman life.

3. Why are SMART goals more likely to facilitate goal commitment?

9 *Staying On Track*

Learning Objectives:

- List and describe the five ways to "stay on track."

- Apply the five ways to "stay on track" to various situations.

- Differentiate between what can and cannot be controlled in given situations and explain how this differentiation will produce a greater probability of success.

- Analyze the statement: "What most people do not see is the price of doing wrong that is guaranteed, but not tangible."

Previously in this text we have discovered our purpose and how we can make sure we live a life congruent with that purpose. However, having knowledge of the life we want to live as well as the motivation and discipline to do so is not enough. Too many people with great determination to live a life of purpose have been derailed due to unforeseen circumstances.

As you read through this chapter it is important to keep in mind that getting sidetracked from the life you want to live almost never happens all at once. Few people are ever perfectly on track one day, and wake up the next day completely off track. Instead people tend to give their life away slowly; one small decision at a time. The following are some ways that leaders can remain focused and keep their life on the path they choose for it.

1. Know What You Can and Cannot Control

What things couldn't you control during plebe summer? What could you control?

Sometime in your life you have probably heard someone say that we live in a society where people refuse to take responsibility for their own actions. While that does happen, it is more often the case that people *do not realize they have control over their actions in the first place.* For example, have you ever heard statements similar to the following?

> "He made me hit him. I told him not to call me a name."
> "I can't help but be cynical in a place like this."
> "Don't MAKE me come over there!"

All of these statements represent someone giving control of their actions over to someone or something else. No one "makes" us hit anyone else; it is a choice we make. Circumstances cannot *make* us be cynical. What kind of attitude we have is our choice. No child can *make* his mother or father "come over there," yet still children all over America hear that on a regular basis.

According to psychologist Michael Bader people become negative and give up when they no longer believe in their ability to affect positive change in their own life. This happens when the culture they are a part of defines "both reality (the way things are) and morality (the way they're supposed to be)."[1] He goes on to say that, "…at the heart of the matter is a belief that the world is fixed, and that ultimately, there's not a lot that one can do, despite one's suffering and wishes for relief."[2] This belief creates a feeling of helplessness, and that helplessness results in a person giving up on trying to make life better as well as hostility towards the culture they live in.

To live a life of purpose it is important to realize that we *always* have the ability to "affect positive change" in our own life in some way. In order to do that we must

---

[1] Bader, M. (2006). Cynicism. *Tikkun, 21*(5), 42–43.
[2] Ibid.

understand what parts of our life we can and cannot control, and then align the parts we can control with our mission. We cannot always control our circumstances, but we can control our actions and reactions to those circumstances. We cannot always control what emotions we feel, but we can control our actions and attitudes no matter what emotions we have. We can control our opinions and our own joy! We have the ability to choose whether or not we will optimistically pursue our life's mission or let external factors determine what sort of life we live.

2. Learn from Disappointment

I recently saw a commercial for a major fast-food restaurant that had a bunch of people standing around kicking trees. Suddenly one person boldly proclaims, "I deserve a hot, juicy burger!" His reason for deserving it, "...because I have a mouth, and it wants one." While this commercial may be amusing, it is also indicative of a dangerous cultural belief. That belief is if you want something then you must deserve it, and if you deserve it then you should expect to get it. It conveys the message that it is normal to expect to get whatever you want and to never be disappointed.

The simple fact is this message is wrong. Getting everything we want is *not* normal. Have you gotten everything you ever wanted? Do you know anyone that has? If we unrealistically expect to never be disappointed we set ourselves up to not only fail, but to be unreasonably angry about that failure.

Dean, Brandes, & Dharwadkar summarize the causal factors concept of one reason people end up being angry and bitter towards the society they are a part of by stating that it requires three major components. First, a person must form; "...unrealistically high expectations of oneself or others that generalize to expectations of society, institutions, authorities, and the future."[3] Second, the person must have an; "...experience of disappointment in oneself and others."[4] Finally the person must have; "...feelings of disillusion and betrayal by one's self or others."[5]

We all have unrealistically high expectations at times, and we will all be disappointed at some point in our life. However if instead of putting our energy into finding a way to learn from that disappointment we become angry and bitter towards those around us we may very well give up on ourselves, those around us, and the organizations we are a part of.

Having a set of values and principles that guide your life is essential for leaders. Expecting yourself and others to live according to those values and principles is also essential. However it is important to realize that while the values and principles may be perfect, people are not. When you are disappointed because a leader did things that went against values they professed what do you do? Do you let anger turn to bitterness or do you choose to learn from the situation? What do you do when a leader makes a decision that negatively affects you? Do you assume they don't know what they're doing? Do you assume they are just out to get you, or do you try to see things from their point of view so you can learn, even if after doing so you still don't agree with them?

Disappointment is not something we should be shocked by, something to be feared, or something to be hated. It is a natural part of growth and improvement. It is something that we should expect, deal with when it comes, and look for the opportunity to learn from it. Disappointment is not necessarily bad; it is only hard.

Why is experiencing failure such an important aspect of plebe year? How will these experiences help you as a junior officer?

[3] Dean, J. W., Brandes, P., & Dharwadkar, R. (1998). Organizational cynicism. *Academy of Management Review 23* (2), 341–352.
[4] Ibid.
[5] Ibid.

If you plan on being a world-changing leader, if you plan on living a life of purpose, then you must be prepared to be disappointed at times. This is not to say that you should go through life being constantly worried about what may happen next. It is simply to say that when disappointment happens, leaders do not let it control their life because they realize that it is what you do after being disappointed that counts.

3. When Frustrated, Look for Multiple Points of View and Implications

Has shortsightedness ever led you to underestimate your impact on a particular person or situation?

As stated previously, leaders change the world! However it is often not very obvious to the leader that they are changing the world, or making any difference at all. Many people get sidetracked from their life of purpose because they believe they lack the ability to make a positive change within their environment (Abraham, 2000). The thought process usually follows a path similar to the following:

> "I have tried several times to have a significant impact on my environment, but cannot see a difference. Therefore I am wasting my time and energy and should just give up."

An example of this is a police officer that takes criminals off of the street every day only to see ten others replace the one he or she removed, or to have the ones removed returned to the street by the court system. According to Rebecca Abraham this sort of, "constant reminder that one's best efforts are in vain deprives their work of meaning...[and] Over time, the burden of taking every insult, failure, and rejection personally yields burnout."[6]

There are two fundamental flaws in this thought process. The first flaw is that people often only look at one point of view to determine if they are having an impact or not. In the example above, the police officer may not have had a major statistical impact on the number of criminals he removed from the street. However he may very well have saved the lives of many people by successfully removing only one or two murderers. From his point of view he made little impact on his environment, but ask the people that would have been killed what kind of an impact the police officer had. Ask their family and friends, or the children they would have never had. From their point of view the impact of the police officer is world changing.

The second fundamental flaw in the thought process is determining the present impact only. It is almost impossible to fully know the impact one's work will or will not have in the future. In other words it is impossible to know all of the implications of one's actions. *The Grapes of Wrath* is largely considered to be the best American novel ever written. However John Steinbeck, after he had just finished writing it, wrote in his journal, "I am sure of one thing—it isn't the great book I had hoped it would be. It's just a run-of-the-mill book. And the awful thing is that it is absolutely the best I can do."[7] He went on to win the Pulitzer Prize in 1939 for *The Grapes of Wrath*, and won the Nobel Prize for Literature in 1962.

In many professions, often times the most noble ones, the full results of one's work are not known until well after the work has been done. This is the case with police, the clergy, teachers, parents, and also leaders. We must not give up living a life of purpose

[6] Abraham, R. (2000). Organizational Cynicism: Bases and consequences. *Genetic, Social, and General Psychology Monographs, 126*(3), 269–292.

[7] Steinbeck, J. (1989). *Working Days: The Journals of the Grapes of Wrath*. Penguin Books.

because we do not think we are having the impact we want to. When we get frustrated it is vital that we view the situation from many points of view. It is also vital that we consider not just the immediate impact, but also the possible future impact of our actions. By giving up we destroy our chances of having any impact at all.

4. Remember that Fairness is Subjective

Recently I overheard some midshipmen talking about the current liberty policy. One of them emphatically exclaimed, "It's not fair!" As I kept walking down the hallway I wondered, "Is he right? Is the policy actually not fair?" When I went to the Academy I had less liberty than they do now so it seemed perfectly fair to me. Most of the Plebes would give almost anything to get as much liberty as the upper-classmen had. It would seem fair to them. So why would it not seem fair to the midshipmen I passed in the hall?

We tend to base our concept of fairness on perceived equity. Equity Theory states that a person will feel the situation is equitable or fair when the amount of effort he or she put in, compared to the rewards received for that effort, is equal to the amount of effort someone else put in compared to the rewards they received for that effort.[8] For example, if I studied for a test for 4 hours and received a B on a test, and my roommate studied for the same test for 4 hours but received an A, I would think the situation was not equitable or fair.

The concept is simple enough, but putting the concept into practice is anything but simple. One problem is that we tend to determine what is equitable or fair by comparing ourselves to others around us or that are similar to us.[9] The midshipmen that claimed their amount of liberty is unfair were very likely comparing themselves to other midshipmen that once had more liberty. If they had compared themselves to some classes before them that had less liberty they would have been excited at the amount they received.

How does perceiving that something is unfair take us "off track"?

Another problem is that people tend to overestimate their own effort while underestimating the effort of others. In the example above it is possible that my roommate got an A because he studied more effectively or took fewer breaks. All of this means that what is fair and what is not fair is determined by the person, and can greatly differ depending on the person's point of view as well as the amount of information he or she has.

How can the subjective nature of fairness derail our life mission? In any organization there is a psychological contract that is created between the organization and those that are a part of it. The psychological contract assumes that the leaders of the organization will act in a manner that is fair, impartial, and equitable. When a member of the organization perceives inequity (unfairness), they become bitter towards whomever or whatever they perceive to be the cause of the inequity.[10] This bitterness can cause people to focus on perceived unfairness and stop focusing on their life's mission.

The next obvious question is what can be done about it? First, think critically about the situation as discussed in the previous two chapters. Under critical analysis many things do not seem as bad as they once may have. Second, solicit the opinion of respected others, that were not involved in the situation. Honest and direct advice

[8] Kreitner, R. & Kinicki, A. (2008). *Organizational Behavior* (8th ed.). New York: McGraw-Hill.
[9] Ibid.
[10] Andersson, L., & Bateman, T. S. (1997). Cynicism in the workplace: Some causes and effects. *Journal of Organizational Behavior, 18,* 449–470.

from a respected friend will help reveal different points of view. Third, when bitterness starts to happen because of perceived unfairness, focus on your life mission. Hold onto your core values, remember what your life's purpose is, and refuse to let bitterness keep you from doing it.

5. Accept the Price of Doing Right and Know the Full Price of Wrong

Recently the news has been flooded with the story of a prominent politician that hired a prostitute. While this is the most current story of this type, it is by no means the only one. It seems like almost every other month that a similar story is in the news. The reaction of whoever is involved is usually the same as well. They apologize to the public and to their family, and then express deep regret that they have done such a thing. Many emphatically express how their behavior went against all of the values they hold dear.

Doing things that go against our values and mission in life is not limited to politicians or to acts as egregious as cheating on your spouse. Recent surveys estimate that more than 75 percent of college students have cheated on an exam.[11] Yet most Americans claim to value honesty. The percentage of marriages that end in divorce is more than 40 percent,[12] but we still claim to value the institution of marriage. Many leaders claim to value setting a good example, but then choose to drink so much it becomes impossible to do so.

While it may be easy to think that the people mentioned above are somehow fundamentally different than we are, the fact is they are not. We may promise ourselves that we will not get divorced or fail to set a good example for those we lead. However, very few go into marriage with the intention of getting divorced and very few leaders intentionally fail to set the example, yet both of these things still happen on a regular basis. To think that we are somehow fundamentally better people than all of those that have come before us and failed is the height of arrogance, and sets us up to fail as well.

One reason many people fail is that they do not accept the price of doing right, and they do not fully understand the price of doing wrong. Friedrich Nietzsche stated, "The individual has always had to struggle to keep from being overwhelmed by the tribe. If you try it, you will be lonely often, and sometimes frightened. But no price is too high to pay for the privilege of owning yourself." If you choose to live your life mission, and that mission is a noble one, you must understand and accept that it will require you to go against what others want you to do. At times it will require you to feel lonely, rejected, and even hurt by those around you. However what you get for that price is a life with a purpose. One that is fulfilling, has integrity, and can change the world!

The price of doing right is not immediately obvious when in any given situation. Conversely, most people believe that the price of doing wrong is not only obvious, but also not guaranteed. They measure the price of wrong in possible, tangible consequences. For example, a midshipman decides that it is okay to get drunk because he doesn't believe they are going to have a breathalyzer test that night so it is not likely he

What are some examples of tangible outcomes of breaking the rules at USNA? What are the more underlying intangible consequences?

[11] Education Portal. (2007, August 4). 75 to 98 Percent of College Students Have Cheated. Retrieved from http://education-portal.com/articles/75_to_98_Percent_of_College_Students_ Have_Cheated.

[12] National Center of Health Statistics (2007, July 6). New Marriage and Divorce Data. Retrieved from http://nchspressroom.wordpress.com/category/divorce-rate/.

will get caught, and therefore get put on restriction. The only consequence he considers is whether or not he will get put on restriction. It is tangible, and not guaranteed.

What most people do not see is the price of doing wrong that is guaranteed, but not tangible. In the example above the midshipman does not think about the fact that he will lose some of his integrity. He will stop living a purposeful life, at least for a period of time. He will lose some of the respect, whether they say so or not, of those around him. He will lose some self-respect, and find guilt, for going against his values.

Living our life mission requires that we accept the price of doing so. However it also requires that we examine the full price, both tangible and intangible, of doing wrong in any given situation.

"Staying on Track" in the Most Difficult of Times[13]

Admiral Stockdale's time as a prisoner of war serves as a great example of someone that lived a life of purpose under extremely hard circumstances. Read the following excerpt from a speech he delivered at King's College in London, and consider how he stayed on track in living a life of purpose in his situation.

On September 9, 1965, I flew at 500 knots right into a flak trap, at tree-top level, in a little A-4 airplane—the cockpit walls not even three feet apart—which I couldn't steer after it was on fire, its control system shot out. After ejection I had about thirty seconds to make my last statement in freedom before I landed in the main street of a little village right ahead. And so help me, I whispered to myself: "Five years down there, at least. I'm leaving the world of technology and entering the world of Epictetus."

"Ready at hand" from the *Enchiridion* as I ejected from that airplane was the understanding that a Stoic always kept *separate* files in his mind for (A) those things that are "up to him" and (B) those things that are "not up to him." Another way of saying it is (A) those things that are "within his power" and (B) those things that are "beyond his power." Still another way of saying it is (A) those things that are within the grasp of "his Will, his Free Will" and (B) those things that are beyond it. All in category B are "external," beyond my control, ultimately dooming me to fear and anxiety if I covet them. All in category A are up to me, within my power, within my will, and properly subjects for my total concern and involvement. They include my opinions, my aims, my aversions, my own grief, my own joy, my judgments, my attitude about what is going on, my own good, and my own evil.

To explain why "your own good and your own evil" is on that list, I want to quote Aleksandr Solzhenitsyn from his gulag book. He writes about that point in prison when he realizes the strength of his residual powers, and starts what I called to myself "gaining moral leverage," riding the updrafts of occasional euphoria as you realize you are getting to know yourself and the world for the first time. He calls it "ascending" and names the chapter in which this appears "The Ascent":

> It was only when I lay there on the rotting prison straw that I sensed within myself the first stirrings of *good*. Gradually it was disclosed to me that the line separating good and evil passes not between states nor between classes nor between political parties, but right through every human heart, through all human hearts. And that is why I turn back to the years of my imprisonment and say, sometimes to the astonishment of those about me, "Bless you, prison, for having been a part of my life."

[13] Stockdale, J. B. (1995). *Thoughts of a Philosophical Fighter Pilot.* Stanford, CA: Hoover Institution Press.

I came to understand that long before I read it. Solzhenitsyn learned, as I and others have learned, that good and evil are not just abstractions you kick around and give lectures about and attribute to this person and that. The only good and evil that means anything is right in your own heart, within your will, within your power, where it's up to you. *Enchiridion 32*: "Things that are not within our own power, not without our Will, can by no means be either good or evil." *Discourses*: "Evil lies in the evil use of moral purpose, and good the opposite. The course of the Will determines good or bad fortune, and one's balance of misery and happiness." In short, what the Stoics say is "Work with what you have control of and you'll have your hands full."

What is not up to you? beyond your power? not subject to your will in the last analysis? For starters, let's take "your station in life." As I glide down toward that little town on my short parachute ride, I'm just about to learn how negligible is my control over my station in life. It's not at all up to me. I'm going right now from being the leader of a hundred-plus pilots and a thousand men and, goodness knows, all sorts of symbolic status and goodwill, to being *an object of contempt*. I'll be known as a "criminal." But that's not *half* the revelation that is the realization of your own *fragility*—that you can be reduced by wind and rain and ice and seawater or *men* to a helpless, sobbing wreck—unable to control even your own bowels—in a matter of *minutes*. And, more than even that, you're going to face fragilities you never before let yourself believe you could have—like after mere minutes, in a flurry of action while being bound with tourniquet-tight ropes, with care, by a professional, hands behind, jackknifed forward and down toward your ankles held secure in lugs attached to an iron bar, that, with the onrush of anxiety, knowing your upper body's circulation has been stopped and feeling the ever-growing induced pain and the ever-closing in of claustrophobia, you can be made to blurt out answers, sometimes correct answers, to questions about anything they know you know. (Hereafter, I'll just call that situation "taking the ropes.")

"Station in life," then, can be changed from that of a dignified and competent gentleman of culture to that of a panic-stricken, sobbing, self-loathing wreck in a matter of minutes. So what? To live under the false pretense that you will forever have control of your station in life is to ride for a fall; you're asking for disappointment. So make sure in your heart of hearts, in your inner self, that you treat your station in life with *indifference,* not with contempt, only with *indifference.*

And so also with a long long list of things that some unreflective people assume they're assured of controlling to the last instance: your body, property, wealth, health, life, death, pleasure, pain, reputation. Consider "reputation," for example. Do what you will, reputation is at least as fickle as your station in life. *Others* decide what your reputation is. Try to make it as good as possible, but don't get hooked on it. Don't be ravenous for it and start chasing it in tighter and tighter circles. As Epictetus says, "For what are tragedies but the portrayal in tragic verse of the sufferings of men who have admired things external?" In your heart of hearts, when you get out the key and open up that old rolltop desk where you really keep your stuff, don't let "reputation" get mixed up with your *moral purpose* or your *will power*; they *are* important. Make sure "reputation" is in that box in the bottom drawer marked "matters of indifference." As Epictetus says, "He who craves or shuns things not under his control can neither be faithful nor free, but must himself be changed and tossed to and fro and must end by subordinating himself to others."

I know the difficulties of gulping this down right away. You keep thinking of practical problems. Everybody has to play the game of life. You can't just walk around saying, "I don't give a damn about health or wealth or whether I'm sent to prison or not." Epictetus took time to explain better what he meant. He says everybody should play the game of life—that the best play it with "skill, form, speed, and grace." But, like most games, you play it with a ball. Your team devotes all its energies to getting the ball across the line. But after the game, what do you do with the ball? Nobody much cares. It's not worth anything. The competition, the game, was the thing. The ball was "used" to make the game possible, but it in itself is not of any value that would justify falling on your sword for it.

Once the game is over, the ball is properly a matter of indifference. Epictetus on another occasion used the example of shooting dice—the dice being matters of indifference, once their numbers had turned up. To exercise *judgment* about whether to accept the numbers or roll again is a *willful* act, and thus *not* a matter of indifference. Epictetus's point is that our *use* of externals is not a matter of indifference because our actions are products of our will and we totally control that, but that the dice themselves, like the ball, are material over which we have no control. They are externals that we cannot afford to covet or be earnest about, else we might set our hearts on them and become slaves of such others as control them.

These explanations of this concept seem so modern, yet I have just given you practically verbatim quotes of Epictetus's remarks to his students in Nicopolis, colonial Greece, two thousand years ago.

So I took those core thoughts into prison; I also remembered a lot of attitude-shaping remarks. Here's Epictetus on how to stay off the hook: "A man's master is he who is able to confer or remove whatever that man seeks or shuns. Whoever then would be free, let him wish nothing, let him decline nothing, which depends on others; else he must necessarily be a slave." And here's why never to beg: "For it is better to die of hunger, exempt from fear and guilt, than to live in affluence with perturbation." Begging sets up a demand for quid pro quos, deals, agreements, reprisals, the pits.

If you want to protect yourself from "fear and guilt," and those are the crucial pincers, the real long-term destroyers of will, you have to get rid of all your instincts to compromise, to meet people halfway. You have to learn to stand aloof, never give openings for deals, never level with your adversaries. You have to become what Ivan Denisovich called a "slow movin' cagey prisoner."

All that, over the previous three years, I had *unknowingly* put away for the future. So, to return to my bailing out of my A-4, I can hear the noontime shouting and pistol shots and whining bullets ripping my parachute canopy and see the fists waving in the street below as my chute hooks a tree but deposits me on the ground in good shape. With two quick-release fastener flips, I'm free of the parachute, and immediately gang tackled by the ten or fifteen town roughnecks I had seen in my peripheral vision, pounding up the road from my right.

I don't want to exaggerate this or indicate that I was surprised at my reception. It was just that when the gang tackling and pummeling was all over, and it lasted for two or three minutes before a man with a pith helmet got there to blow his police whistle, I had a very badly broken leg that I felt sure would be with me for life. My hunch turned out to be right. Later, I felt some relief—but only minor—from another Epictetus admonition I remembered: "Lameness is an impediment to the leg, but not to the Will; and say this to yourself with regard to everything that happens. For you will find such things to be an impediment to something else, but not truly to yourself."

. . .

Epictetus turned out to be right. After a very crude operation, I was on crutches within a couple of months, and the crooked leg, healing itself, was strong enough to hold me up without the crutches in about a year. All told, it was only a temporary setback from things that were important to me, and being cast in the role as the sovereign head of an American expatriate colony that was destined to remain autonomous, out of communication with Washington, for years on end was very important to me. I was forty-two years old—still on crutches, dragging a leg, at considerably less than my normal weight, with hair down near my shoulders, my body unbathed since I had been catapulated from the *Oriskany*, a beard that had not seen a razor since I arrived—when I took command (clandestinely, of course, the North Vietnamese would never acknowledge our rank) of about fifty Americans. That expatriate colony would grow to over four hundred—all officers, all college graduates, all pilots or backseat electronic wizards. I was determined to "play well the given part."

The key word for all of us at first was "fragility." Each of us, before we were ever in shouting distance of another American, was made to "take the ropes." That was a real shock to our systems—and, as with all shocks, its impact on our inner selves was a lot more impressive and lasting and important than to our limbs and torsos. These were the sessions where we were taken down to submission, and made to blurt out distasteful confessions of guilt and American complicity into antique tape recorders, and then to be put in what I call "cold soak," a month or so of total isolation to "contemplate our crimes." What we actually contemplated was what even the most laid-back American saw as his betrayal of himself and everything he stood for. It was there that I learned what "Stoic Harm" meant. A shoulder broken, a bone in my back broken, a leg broken twice were *peanuts* by comparison. Epictetus: "Look not for any greater harm than this: destroying the trustworthy, self-respecting well-behaved man within you."

When put into a regular cell block, hardly an American came out of that experience without responding something like this when first whispered to by a fellow prisoner next door: "You don't want to talk to me; I am a traitor." And because we were equally fragile, it seemed to catch on that we all replied something like this: "Listen, pal, there are no virgins in here. You should have heard the kind of statement I made. Snap out of it. We're all in this together. What's your name? Tell me about yourself." To hear that last was, for most new prisoners just out of initial shakedown and cold soak, a turning point in their lives.

But the new prisoner's learning process was just beginning. Soon enough he would realize that things were not at all like some had told him in survival training— that if you made a good stiff showing of resistance in the opening chapters, the interrogators would lose interest in you and you would find yourself merely relegated to boredom, to "sitting out the war," to "languishing in your cell," as the uninitiated novelists love to describe the predicament. No, the war went on behind bars—there was no such thing as the jailers giving up on you as a hopeless case. Their political beliefs *made* them believe you could be made to see things their way; it was just a matter of time. And so you were marched to the interrogation room endlessly, particularly on the occasions of your being apprehended breaking one of the myriad rules that were posted on your cell wall—"trip wire" rules, which paid dividends for the commissar if his interrogator could get you to fall prey to his wedge of *shame*. The currency at the game table, where you and the interrogator faced one another in a duel of wits, was *shame*, and I learned that unless he could impose shame on me, or unless I imposed it on myself, he had nothing going for him. (Force was available, but that required the commissar's okay.)

For Epictetus, emotions were acts of will. Fear was not something that came out of the shadows of the night and enveloped you; he charged *you* with the total responsibility of starting it, stopping it, controlling it. This was one of Stoicism's biggest demands on a person. Stoics can be made to sound like lazy brutes when they are described merely as people indifferent to most everything but good and evil, people who make stingy use of emotions like pity and sympathy. But add this requirement of total personal responsibility for each and every one of your emotions, and you're talking about a person with his hands full. I whispered a "chant" to myself as I was marched at gunpoint to my daily interrogation: "control fear, control guilt, control fear, control guilt." And I devised methods of deflecting my gaze to obscure such fear or guilt as doubtless emerged in my eyes when I temporarily lost control under questioning. You could be bashed for failure to look at the face of your interrogator; I concentrated on his left earlobe, and he seemed to get used to it—thought I was a little cockeyed, probably. Controlling your emotions is difficult but can be *empowering*. Epictetus: "For it is *within you*, that both your destruction and deliverance lie." Epictetus: "The judgment seat and a prison is each a place, the one high, the other low; but the *attitude of your will* can be kept the same, if you *want* to keep it the same, in either place."

We organized a clandestine society via our wall tap code—a society with our own laws, traditions, customs, even heroes. To explain how it could be that we would order each other into more torture, order each other to refuse to comply with specific demands, intentionally call the bluff of our jailers and in a real sense force them to repeat the full ropes process to another submission, I'll quote a statement that could have come from at least half of those wonderful competitive flyboys I found myself locked up with: "We are in a spot like we've never been in before. But we deserve to maintain our self-respect, to have the feeling we are fighting back. We can't refuse to do every degrading thing they demand of us, but it's up to you, boss, to pick out things we must all refuse to do unless and until they put us through the ropes again. We deserve to sleep at night. We at least deserve to have the satisfaction that we are hewing to our leader's orders. Give us the list; what are we to take torture for?"

I know this sounds like strange logic, but in a sense it was a first step in claiming what was rightfully *ours*. Epictetus said, "The judge will do some things to you which are thought to be terrifying; but how can he *stop you* from taking the punishment *he threatened*?" That's *my* kind of Stoicism. You have a right to make them hurt you, and they don't like to do that. When my fellow prisoner Ev Alvarez, the very first pilot they captured, was released with the rest of us, the prison commissar told him: "You Americans were nothing like the French; we could count on them to be reasonable." Ha!

I put a lot of thought into what those first orders should be. They would be orders that *could be obeyed*, not a "cover your ass" move of reiterating some U.S. government policy like "name, rank, serial number, and date of birth," which had no chance of standing up in the torture room. My mind-set was "we here under the gun are the experts, we are the masters of our fate, ignore guilt-inducing echoes of hollow edicts, throw out the book and write your own." My orders came out as easy-to-remember acronyms. The principal one was BACK US: Don't Bow in public; stay off the Air; admit no Crimes, never Kiss them goodbye. "US" could be interpreted as United States, but it *really* meant "Unity over Self." Loners make out in an enemy's prison, so my first rule of togetherness in there was that each of us had to work at the lowest common denominator, never negotiating for himself but only for *all*.

Prison life became a crazy mixture of an old regime and a new one. The old was the political prison routine, mainly for dissenters and domestic enemies of the state. It was designed and run by old-fashioned Third World Communists of the Ho Chi Minh cut. It revolved around the idea of "repentance" for your "crimes" of antisocial behavior. American prisoners, street criminals, and domestic political enemies of the state were all in the same prison. We never saw a "POW camp" like the movies show. The communist jail was part psychiatric clinic and part reform school. North Vietnam protocol called for making *all* their inmates demonstrate shame—bowing to all guards, heads low, never looking at the sky, frequent sessions with your interrogator if, for no other reason, to check your *attitude* and, if judged "wrong," then maybe down the torture chute of confession of guilt, of apology, and then the inevitable payoff of atonement.

The new regime, superimposed on the above, was for Americans only. It was a propaganda factory, supervised by English-speaking young bureaucratic army officers with quotas to fill, quotas set by the political arm of the government: press interviews with visiting left-wing Americans, propaganda films to shoot (starring intimidated "American air pirates"), and so on.

An encapsulated history of how this bifurcated prison philosophy fared is that the propaganda footage and interviews started to backfire. Smart American college men were salting their acts with sentences with double meanings, gestures read as funny-obscene by Western audiences, and practical jokes. One of my best friends, tortured to give names of pilots he knew who had turned in their wings in opposition to the war, said there were only two: Lieutenants Clark Kent and Ben Casey (then-popular fictional characters in America). That joke was headlined on the front page of the *San Diego Union*, and somebody sent a copy back to the government in Hanoi. As a result of that friendly gesture from a fellow American, Nels Tanner went into three successive days of rope torture, followed by 123 days in leg stocks, all while isolated of course.

So after several of these stunts, which cost the Vietnamese much loss of face, North Vietnam resorted to getting their propaganda only from the relatively *few* (less than 5 percent) of the Americans they could trust *not* to act up: real loners who, for different reasons, never joined the prisoner organization, never wanted to get into the tap code network, well-known sleazeballs we came to call *finks*. The vast majority of my constituents were enraged by their actions and took it upon themselves to diligently memorize data that would convict them in an American court-martial. But when we got home our government essentially dropped the charges I had preferred.

The great mass of all other Americans in Hanoi were by all standards "honorable prisoners," but that is not to say there was anything like a homogeneous prison regime we all shared. People like to think that because we were all in the Hanoi prison system, we had all these common experiences. It's not so. These *differing* regimes became marked when our prison organization stultified the propaganda efforts of this two-headed monster they called the "Prison Authority." They turned to vengeance against the leadership of my organization and to an effort to break down the morale of the others by baiting them with an amnesty program in which they would compete for early release by being compliant with North Vietnam's wishes.

In May 1967, the public address system blared out: "Those of you who repent, truly repent, will be able to go home before the war is over. Those few diehards who insist on inciting the other criminals to oppose the camp authority will be sent to a special dark place." I immediately put out an order forbidding any American to accept early release, but that is not to say I was a lone man on a white horse. I didn't have to sell that one; it was accepted with obvious relief and spontaneous jubilation by the overwhelming majority.

Guess who went to the "dark place." They isolated my leadership team—me and my cohort of ten top men—and sent us into exile. The Vietnamese worked very hard to learn our habits, and they knew who were the troublemakers and who were "not making any waves." They isolated those I trusted most; everybody had a long record of solitary and rope-mark pedigrees. Not all were seniors; we had seniors in prison who would not even communicate with the man next door. One of my ten was only twenty-four years old—born after I was in the navy. He was a product of my recent shipboard tendencies: "When instincts and rank are out of phase, take the guy with the instincts." All of us stayed in solitary throughout, starting with two years in leg irons in a little high-security prison right beside North Vietnam's "Pentagon"—their Ministry of Defense, a typical old French building. There are chapters upon chapters after that, but what they came down to in my case was a strung-out vengeance fight between the "Prison Authority" and those of us who refused to quit trying to be our brother's keepers. The stakes grew to *nervous breakdown* proportions. One of the eleven of us died in that little prison we called Alcatraz, but even including him, there was not a man who wound up with less than three and a half years of solitary, and four of us had more than four years. To give you a sense of proportion on how the total four hundred fared on solo, one hundred had none, more than half of the other three hundred had less than a year, and half of those with less than a year had less than a month. So the average for the four hundred was considerably less than six months.

Howie Rutledge, one of the four of us with more than four years, went back to school and got a master's degree after we got home, and his thesis concentrated on the question of whether long-term erosion of human purpose was more effectively achieved by torture or isolation. He mailed out questionnaires to us (who had also all taken the ropes at least ten times) and others with records of extreme prison abuse. He found that those who had less than two years' isolation and plenty of torture said torture was the trump card; those with more than two years' isolation and plenty of torture said that for long-term modification of behavior, isolation was the way to go. From my viewpoint, you can get used to repeated rope torture—there are some tricks for minimizing your losses in that game. But keep a man, even a very strong-willed man, in isolation for three or more years, and he starts looking for a friend—*any* friend, regardless of nationality or ideology.

Epictetus once gave a lecture to his faculty complaining about the common tendency of new teachers to slight the stark realism of Stoicism's challenges in favor of giving the students an uplifting, rosy picture of how they could meet the harsh requirements of the good life painlessly. Epictetus said: "Men, the lecture-room of the philosopher is a hospital; students ought not to walk out of it in pleasure, but in pain." If Epictetus's lecture room was a hospital, my prison was a laboratory—a laboratory of human behavior. I chose to test his postulates against the demanding real-life challenges of my laboratory. And as you can tell, I think he passed with flying colors.

It's hard to discuss in public the real-life challenges of that laboratory because people ask all the wrong questions: How was the food? That's always the first one, and in a place like I've been, that's so far down the scale you want to cry. Did they harm you physically? What was the nature of the *device* they used to harm you? Always the device or the truth serum or the electric shock treatment—all of which would totally defeat the purpose of a person seriously trying to break down your will. All those things would give *you* a feeling of moral superiority, which is the last thing he would want to have happen. I'm not talking about brainwashing; there is no such thing. I'm talking about having looked over the brink and seen the bottom of the pit and realized the truth of that linchpin of Stoic thought: that the thing that brings down a man is not *pain* but *shame*!

Why did those men in "cold soak" after their first rope trip eat their hearts out and feel so unworthy when the first American contacted them? Epictetus knew human nature well. In that prison laboratory, I do not know of a single case where a man was able to erase his conscience pangs with some laid-back pop psychology theory of cause and effect. Epictetus emphasizes time and again that a man who lays off the causes of his actions to third parties or forces is not leveling with himself. He must live with his own judgments if he is to be honest with himself. (And the "cold soak" tends to make you honest.) "But if a person subjects me to fear of death, he compels me," says a student. "No," says Epictetus, "It is neither death, nor exile, nor toil, nor any such things that is the cause of your doing, or not doing, *anything*, but only your opinions and the decisions of your Will." "What is the fruit of your doctrines?" someone asked Epictetus. "Tranquility, fearlessness, and freedom," he answered. You can have these only if you are honest and take responsibility for your own actions. You've got to get it *straight*! *You* are in charge of *you*.

Did I preach these things in prison? Certainly not. You soon learned that if the guy next door was doing okay, that meant that he had all his philosophical ducks lined up in his own way. You soon realized that when you dared to spout high-minded philosophical suggestions through the wall, you always got a very reluctant response.

No, I never tapped or mentioned Stoicism once. But some sharp guys read the signs in my actions. After one of my long isolations outside the cell blocks of the prison, I was brought back into signaling range of the fold, and my point of contact was a man named Dave Hatcher. As was standard operating procedure on a first contact after a long separation, we started off not with gushes of news but with first, an agreed-upon danger signal, second, a cover story for each of us if we were caught, and third, a backup communications system if this link was compromised—"slow movin' cagey prisoner" precautions. Hatcher's backup communication for me was a note drop by an old sink near a place we called the Mint, the isolation cell block of Hatcher's "Las Vegas" wing of the prison—a place he rightly guessed I would soon enough be in. Every day we would signal for fifteen minutes over a wall between his cell block and my "no man's land."

Then I got back into trouble. At that time the commissar of prisons had had me isolated and under almost constant surveillance for the year since I had staged a riot in Alcatraz to get us out of leg irons. I was barred from all prisoner cell blocks. I had special handlers, and they caught me with an outbound note that gave leads I knew the interrogators could develop through torture. The result would be to implicate my friends in "black activities" (as the North Vietnamese called them). I had been through those ropes more than a dozen times, and I knew I could *contain* material—*so long as they didn't know I knew it*. But this note would open doors that could lead to more people getting killed in there. We had lost a few in big purges—I think in torture overshoots—and I was getting tired of it. It was the fall of 1969, and I had been in this role for four years and saw nothing left for me to do but check out. I was solo in the main torture room in an isolated part of the prison, the night before what they told me would be my day to spill my guts. There was an eerie mood in the prison. Ho Chi Minh had just died, and his special dirge music was in the air. I was to sit up all night in traveling irons. My chair was near the only paned glass window in the prison. I was able to waddle over and break the window stealthily. I went after my wrist arteries with the big shards. I had knocked the light out, but the patrol guard happened to find me passed out in a pool of blood but still breathing. The Vietnamese sounded the alert, got their doctor, and saved me.

Why? It was not until after I was released years later that I learned that that very week, Sybil had been in Paris demanding humane treatment for prisoners. She was on world news, a public figure, and the last thing the North Vietnamese needed was me dead. There had been a very solemn crowd of senior North Vietnamese officers in that room as I was revived.

Prison torture, *as we had known it in Hanoi*, ended for everybody that night.

Of course it was months before we could be sure that was so. All I knew at the time was that in the morning, after my arms had been dressed and bandaged, the commissar himself brought in a hot cup of sweet tea, told my surveillance guard to take off my leg irons, and asked me to sit at the table with him. "Why did you do this, Sto-dale? You know I sit with the army's General Staff; they've asked for a full report this morning." (It was not unusual for us to talk like that by that time.) But he never once mentioned the note, nor did anybody else thereafter. *That* was unprecedented. After a couple of months in a tiny isolated cell we called Calcutta to let my arms heal, they blindfolded me and walked me right into the Las Vegas cell block. The isolation and special surveillance were over. I was put solo, of course, in the Mint.

Dave Hatcher knew I was back because I was walked under his window, and though he could not peek out, he could listen and over the years had attuned his ear to my walking "signature," my limping gait. Soon enough, the rusty wire over the sink in the washroom was bent to the north—Dave Hatcher's signal for "note in the bottle under the sink for Stockdale." Like an old fighter pilot, I checked my six o'clock, scooped the note up fast, and concealed it in my prison pajama pants, carefully. Back in my cell, after the guard locked the door, I sat on my toilet bucket—where I could stealthily jettison the note if the peephole cover moved—and unfolded Hatcher's sheet of low-grade paper toweling on which, with a rat dropping, he had printed, without comment or signature, the last verse of Ernest Henley's poem *Invictus*:

> It matters not how strait the gate,
> How charged with punishment the scroll,
> I am the master of my fate:
> I am the captain of my soul.

Questions for review:

1. What is meant by the phrase *"what most people do not see is the price of doing wrong that is guaranteed, but not tangible"*?

2. How did Admiral Stockdale experience each of the "five ways to stay on track" while incarcerated in a North Vietnamese prison camp?

3. How have you experienced each of "five ways to stay on track" while at USNA?

Part
Three

Leading Others

10 *Civility*

Learning Objectives:

- Identify and describe Carter's Five Tenets of civility.
- Apply the five tenets of civility to a given scenario.
- Describe why leaders have a responsibility to ensure a climate of civility within their organization (division, platoon, team, etc).

Civility: A Key Factor for Leadership

CAPT James A. Campbell, USN (RET)
Class of 1972 Distinguished Military Professor for Character Education

Plebe Summer is over! Today you move to your new company area, from 6th wing to 1st wing ... bummer. And WOW, all that stuff! You never realized how much you were issued since you didn't use most of it over the summer. And on top of that, you have to move a computer too! You need to get some things at the Mid Store for cleaning and maybe some deodorant ... you'll definitely need some after this move. You decide to go after breakfast.

Your shoes are looking good; they should, since you spent about an hour on them last night! But just as you're heading out the door, your roommate blows by you and wipes out the toe of your left shoe. "Sorry, man," he shouts over his shoulder as he beats you out the door. There's no time to change shoes so you'll have to risk it at formation. "No chance," you mumble as you chop into the P-way. "I'm screwed." Sure enough, you get flamed on by your 2/C and put on "All Calls." Nice. He didn't have to beat you out the door. Did you see a smirk on his face?

Having been ordered to change shoes by your Squad Leader, you arrive to your squad table late to find no seats ... thanks again, roommate! You finally find a seat at another company's table and request permission to come aboard. As the Firstie stares at you, she grudgingly grants permission. She wants to know why you're late, and you try the obligatory "No excuse, Ma'am." It doesn't work. She wants the real reason. You retell the story, and she asks to see the shoes you are wearing, which aren't your best. Of course, that draws another flame session while standing at attention, and as you take your seat, you note that most of the food is gone. "I guess it doesn't matter anyway," you think to yourself as breakfast ends and you're all dismissed. You can pick up some snacks in the Mid Store, along with the deodorant, in your brief few minutes of free time before the big move.

You're unable to find your favorite deodorant so you ask one of the attendants (a high schooler just working for the summer) if there might be some in the back. He responds, "What you see is what you get." Fair enough—what's the big deal anyway? Deodorant is deodorant, right? This guy isn't interested in helping you anyway; he turns away and continues flirting with one of the other female workers. You grab some deodorant and a snack and go to checkout. You give the clerk your Mid Store card. He gives you an icy stare and the words: "Don't you have cash? I'm new here and not sure how to charge your card." The hits just keep on coming!

After the cashier finally figures out how to charge your account (while you endure the heated stares from the mids waiting in line behind you),

you head back to your room, already dreading the task of schlepping your stuff from one side of the world to the other.

As you chop back to your room, each greeting of "Good morning, Sir" or "Good morning, Ma'am" is returned with either a wordless stare or something mumbled unintelligibly. It's then that you think about your lessons over the summer, the preaching about "brothers and sisters in arms," "one team, one fight," and being "professional." Did you miss something? Was that all a bunch of fluff? So much for brothers and sisters in arms, you think. I'm treated like crap around here. What a fine Navy day so far, and it is not even 0830!

Any or all of the above story sound familiar? If so, then you have experienced a lack of *civility*. In the next few pages, let's try to identify this concept called civility, its connection to leadership, specifically military leadership, and how you can work to establish a habit of civility while at the Naval Academy.

Stephen Carter, the author of the book, *Civility: Manners, Morals, and the Etiquette of Democracy,* defines civility as the "**. . . sum of the many sacrifices we are called to make for the sake of living together. When we pretend that we travel alone, we can also pretend that these sacrifices are unnecessary.**" Carter considers integrity and civility absolutely necessary for us to function in our roles as human beings, and I would add, in our roles as commissioned officers. Integrity, as you have learned, helps align our moral compass. Civility, then, provides us the tools to interact with others on this journey called life. Civility is not just manners, but an attitude of dignity and respect for our fellow citizens and for ourselves. What does civility look like in the routine of day-to-day business? Consider the following story.

In one of my far-too-few shore tours, I had the pleasure of traveling to England and Scotland in 1998 to work with members of the Royal Navy's submarine force as they prepared to launch their final Vanguard-class ballistic missile submarine. The missile, missile launch, and fire control systems were ours, so the United States had oversight for the operational testing and acceptance of that submarine's missile-related systems. My primary point of contact was a captain in the Royal Navy named Marcus. Marcus was the poster child for the English gentleman, as suave and refined as 007. Most of my travel in the United Kingdom was by rail, which would have been unusual in the United States. As I rode the train, I was struck by a sign located by each seat, requesting that passengers respect their fellow passengers and not use cell phones. Interestingly enough, I did not see anyone using a cell phone until one day when Marcus and I boarded the train in Bath to travel to London. Marcus' cell phone rang. To my amazement, he answered it! I was dumbfounded; I could also sense the stares from several passengers. Marcus, the ultimate gentleman, had breached the code of civility on this particular journey! Before I could collect my thoughts, a gentleman a few seats away rose and approached Marcus as he was talking. The gentleman leaned in, saying nothing, and pointed to the sign about cell phone use. Then he left. It was now Marcus' turn to be dumbfounded. He immediately terminated the call and was immensely embarrassed, not believing he had been so inconsiderate. He apologized profusely to those near him for his rudeness.

I was struck by several things during that short event, including the concept itself: respect your fellow passengers on this ride. The issue was resolved with no one raising their voice (or a finger); in fact, there was no conversation at all, and the "perpetrator" apologized to those around him. The civility of that event remains with me to this day. I suspect that

What is your definition or understanding of civility and how does it differ or align with Steven Carter's definition?

it might not have been so memorable had it occurred in the United States—or maybe memorable for other reasons. How have your cell phone experiences compared to this one?

Now let's consider the concept of civility in connection with leadership. The following two stories are about military leaders with whom you should be familiar. But these stories are not about combat. These stories both occur in the post-Civil War period of 1865 and had far-reaching consequences.

The first involves the Confederate surrender at Appomattox:

On the morning of April 9, 1865, [MGEN Joshua] Chamberlain learned of the desire by Lee to surrender the Army of Northern Virginia when a Confederate staff officer approached him under a flag of truce. "Sir," he reported to Chamberlain, "I am from General John Gordon. General Lee desires a cessation of hostilities until he can hear from General Grant as to the proposed surrender." The next day, Chamberlain was summoned to Union headquarters where Major General Charles Griffin informed him that of all the officers in the Federal Army, General Grant had selected Chamberlain to preside over the ceremony of the surrender and parole of the Confederate infantry at Appomattox Court House on April 12.

Thus Chamberlain was responsible for one of the most poignant scenes of the Civil War. As the Confederate soldiers marched down the road to surrender their arms and colors, Chamberlain, on his own initiative, ordered his men to come to attention and "carry arms" as a show of respect. Chamberlain described what happened next:

"The gallant John B. Gordon, at the head of the marching column, outdoes us in courtesy. He was riding with downcast eyes and more than pensive look; but at this clatter of arms he raises his eyes and instantly catching the significance, wheels his horse with that superb grace of which he is master, drops the point of his sword to his stirrup, gives a command, at which the great Confederate ensign following him is dipped and his decimated brigades, as they reach our right, respond to the 'carry.' All the while on our part not a sound of trumpet or drum, not a cheer, nor a word nor motion of man, but awful stillness as if it were the passing of the dead."

Chamberlain's salute to the Confederate soldiers was unpopular with many in the North, but he defended his action in his memoirs, *The Passing of the Armies*. Many years later, Gordon, in his own memoirs, called Chamberlain "one of the knightliest soldiers of the Federal Army."[1]

The second story is about Robert E. Lee in Richmond:

The scene is St. Paul's Episcopal Church in Richmond, Virginia—April 1865. The nation had been recently and nearly completely destroyed by the cataclysm of civil war. The social fabric, particularly of the South, had been torn. People resented change and the agents of change. A recently-freed African American man observed the service from the rear of the church. When it was time for communion, he walked to the rail to receive alongside the church's white parishioners. The congregation was aghast.

This seemingly small matter ran completely counter to anything almost anyone in that church had experienced—or would even tolerate. The minister and other communicants were stunned and didn't move.

---

[1] Joshva Chamberlain. (n.d.). Retrieved from http://en.wikipedia.org/wiki/Joshua_Chamberlain# Appomattox

Just then, a grandfatherly yet ramrod straight gentleman rose from a pew near the front. Robert E. Lee, the man called "the greatest soldier in the history of the English-speaking peoples" by Winston Churchill, understood the situation immediately. He knelt beside the man and both received communion. In an instant a situation was diffused, and more importantly, a message was sent to the congregation, the community, and entire region that change, positive change, was inevitable.

While Lee's actions on that Sunday morning did not themselves end the struggle for the civil rights of African Americans, for that struggle continues today, but that message and the message of rapprochement with the laws and ideals of former enemies became the starting point for healing a nation. Lee would continue to urge his former soldiers to put away their arms and ill will toward the United States. He was, in many regards, singularly responsible for thousands of former Confederate soldiers' (and the generations that followed) willingness to reintegrate fully into American life.[2]

Is there a common thread that runs through each of the stories of Chamberlain, Lee, and my friend Marcus? I would offer that, when you look at their actions and consider Carter's definition of civility, that thread would be "sacrifice." Each man placed the needs and feelings of others ahead of his own in the choices he made. They sacrificed their own desires and egos in deference to others. For Chamberlain and Lee, after a bloody, protracted civil war with families divided and many destroyed, their acts of civility were profound and far-reaching. These were men of high visibility and impeccable reputation, and the ripple-effect of their singular acts did much to restore a divided country. For Marcus, he sacrificed his desire to save face and admitted his error to those around him. His act also had a ripple effect, just not of the same magnitude. Each, by the power of their position and example, were able to influence others, which is the ultimate end state of leadership—the art of influencing others.

At this point, you may be thinking, "But we are training to be combat leaders. Do I extend acts of civility to the enemy?" The short answer to the question is yes. History is replete with examples of civility on the battlefield, among combatants on the same side and those who were considered enemies. A developed habit of civility, based on respect, is not weakness, but rather an attitude that can keep one's soul intact in spite of the horrors of combat. The following is from the book (and movie by the same name) *A Bridge Too Far*. As the Allies were driving to cross the Rhine into Germany, the British had unknowingly run headlong into a crack Panzer force at the bridge in the Dutch city of Arnhem and were in the process of being annihilated. The German commander, General Model, at the request of the British, allowed a cease fire to extract the British wounded into German field hospitals and bury their dead before recommencing the battle. In today's environment, this action would seem to be unachievable and maybe it is; however, this topic of honorable conduct on the battlefield will be addressed in more depth in your ethics course next year.

Great stories, but how can we put this concept of civility into practice on a daily basis here at the Naval Academy? Considering that we are servants of the nation, it is appropriate to look at Carter's "etiquette of democracy."[3] I have not listed all of the tenets (Carter has fifteen), but putting these five to work each day will have a significant impact on those with whom you share this journey at the Naval Academy.

How can civility be seen as a weakness and why also would this line of thinking be problematic? How can civility make America great?

[2] Horn, S.F. (1949). *The Robert E. Lee Reader*. New York, NY: Konecky & Konecky, 462.
[3] Carter, S.L (1999). *Civility*. New York, NY: Basic Books, 277–285.

1) **Our duty to be civil toward others does not depend on whether we like them or not.**

Remember the words of Coach Boone in *Remember the Titans* as he exhorts his players to come together, become a team, and overcome the social pressures of integration: "I don't care if you like each other, but you will respect each other." He knew, like we all do, that we will never like all of our coworkers, teammates, company mates, or shipmates, but if any organization, command, or team is to succeed, its people must work together. The ability to do that is built on a foundation of respect for each other and the trust that develops from that respect.

2) **Civility requires that we sacrifice for strangers, not just for people we happen to know.**

Consider the terms military *service* or community *service*. Each of these concepts represents, at its heart, doing something for a person or group of people that you do not personally know and for which you receive nothing. Start small. You will never know all of your classmates, but consider what you might sacrifice for the betterment of the class. Then expand your sacrifice for the betterment of the Brigade, then the Navy, then your fellow citizens. Civility, sacrifice, and service all presuppose an obligation to a larger and mostly anonymous group of fellow citizens.

3) **Civility has two parts: generosity, even when it is costly, and trust, even when there is risk.**

This tenet of civility is a little more difficult. Consider the first part: generosity. Since you have little money right now, one thing you can be generous with is your time. Some would consider that time is a more valuable resource than money. I am one of those people. We can always write a larger check because we can get more money. But you cannot give more time, because once expended it is gone, never to be recouped. We all are only issued 24 hours per day—both the rich and the poor. To determine your values, check where you spend your time. The second part is even more difficult. It is very hard at this point in time to do what is implied here: to trust that the judgment of others is as good as your own. As you acquire more seniority and responsibility, you will find more and more people have their hands on the control stick of your life. Never more obvious was this to me than in command of a submarine. You learn to trust your people—at great risk to yourself. No one said that being civil was easy.

4) **Civility requires that we listen to others with knowledge of the possibility that they are right and we are wrong.**

This is the intellectual virtue of humility and one of the foundations of critical thinking. Intellectual humility depends on recognizing that you should not claim to know more than you do and that someone else may know more. Knowing and admitting when one is wrong is not weakness nor does it weaken your authority. Quite the converse—it will enhance the trust that your Sailors and Marines have in your leadership. You should endeavor, however, through study and experience to develop your competence so that the times you are wrong are few. When you are in error, admit it.

5) **Civility requires that we express ourselves in ways that demonstrate our respect for others.**

Carter's summary is most appropriate: "We show respect for ourselves and others when we trouble ourselves to think carefully about what we say, rather than grabbing for the first expletive that comes to mind." Demeaning someone in an effort to raise your acceptance in a group is neither civil nor an indication of a good leader. Those around you will wonder what you think and say about them when they are not around. The foundation of trust will erode, eventually undermining your leadership and team-building efforts.

In summary, civility, sacrifice, and leadership are inextricably linked. Civility and effective leadership can only be achieved if we are willing and able to sacrifice *our* wants and needs to the wants and needs of *others*, whether they are your peers, fellow citizens, or your Sailors and Marines. Civility as an attitude of selflessness and sacrifice is not a sign of weakness. On the contrary, acts of civility strengthen bonds and build trust between people, teams, organizations, and cultures. Being civil, when circumstances and human nature dictate otherwise, takes more self-control and inner strength than giving in to the temptation of the moment. Lord Moran, in his landmark book, *The Anatomy of Courage,* observes ". . . namely that a man of character in peace becomes a man of courage in war. He cannot be selfish in peace and yet be unselfish in war. Character, as Aristotle taught, is a habit, the daily choice of right instead of wrong; it is a moral quality which grows to maturity in peace and is not suddenly developed on the outbreak of war. If you know a man in peace, you know him in war."

Alexis deTocqueville once noted "America is great because America is good ... when America ceases to be good, it will cease to be great." In order to remain good, we must start with learning how to be good to each other—to be civil.

Questions for review:

1. Why do you think that civility is an important topic for midshipmen and future officers of the armed forces?

2. What are the differences between mere etiquette, being polite and civility as presented by Steven Carter?

3. Can you think of a reason why this leadership quality might apply more to the current overseas posture for our nation's military than in previous wars?

11 *Active Listening*

Learning Objectives:

- Explain the concept of active listening and describe the crucial role it plays in the communication process.
- Identify and describe the three different types of barriers to communication.
- Apply active listening in leadership roles that are available as a 3/C.

Active Listening

Know how to listen and you will profit even from those who talk badly.

— *Plutarch*

Reprinted from Fritz, S. (1999). *Interpersonal Skills for Leadership*. Englewood Cliffs, NJ: Prentice Hall, Inc.

Introduction to Theories of Active Listening

Why should a textbook on Self Leadership include a lesson on listening? People who study the way humans communicate have found that most people spend 70 percent of their waking day engaged in some form of communication; college students may spend as much as three-fifths of that time listening. That means if you are awake for 16 hours, you're communicating in some way during 11 of those hours, and you spend between six and seven hours listening. Studies of student listening habits have shown that good listeners earn better grades. Still, many college students are remarkably inefficient listeners. At any given time, only 20 percent of the students present at a college lecture are paying attention, and only 12 percent are actively listening.

Listening is a crucial element of the communication process that also includes speaking, writing, and reading. Yet very little time (if any) is devoted to teaching people the skills they need to become better listeners. We learn in elementary school how to write, read, and speak, but virtually no class time is spent teaching techniques to make listening more effective. While the other three modes of communication are important, listening deserves at least as much attention in the skill-building process.

Barriers to Active Listening and How to Overcome Them

To become more active listeners, we need to acknowledge listening problems that could become barriers to good communication. Most problems are one of three types: environmental, physiological, or psychological. You will soon see, however, that most listening problems are psychological in nature.

Environmental Barriers Many distractions that keep us from listening actively are physical, coming from outside us or from within. External noises (traffic, a radio playing in another room, other conversations) compete with the speaker for our attention. Not only do we have to listen over other sounds, we often have to repress other sensory stimuli that may interfere with our ability to listen attentively. It's harder to give your full attention to the act of listening if you're too hot or too cold, sitting in an uncomfortable chair, or wearing tight-fitting shoes.

To overcome environmental barriers, you need to do everything you can to minimize physical distractions when it is important for you to listen carefully. Turn off the TV or radio. Consciously screen out other noises you can't so easily control, or move to a quiet place. Get comfortable. Turn your back to visual distractions. Prepare to listen by directing your attention to the speaker. Adjust your physical posture to enable you to listen. Make eye contact.

Physiological Barriers   Another barrier to active listening is caused by the different rates at which we think and speak. A person is capable of thinking at a rate about five times faster than he or she can speak. While the average rate of speech is 125 to 150 words per minute, the brain can think at a rate between 500 and 1000 words per minute. That difference can cause a listener's mind to wander, leading to daydreaming and unconscious self-talk. The speaker's message may have to compete with random, unrelated snippets of thought: "I like her shoes," "I need to remember to turn in that history paper before four o'clock," etc.

It's not easy to eliminate this physiological hurdle altogether, but you can try to reduce it. As you listen, try to keep pace with the speaker. Use your mental energy to think about what the speaker is saying and to analyze and interpret his or her words. Paraphrase silently if you don't have an immediate opportunity to paraphrase aloud. Try to be aware of intrusive mental noise and block it out. If you find your mind shifting to an unrelated subject, deliberately bring it back to the message.

Mishearing also accounts for some errors in listening. One obvious physiological barrier to active listening arises whenever a physical condition affects the organs of hearing. A cold, an ear infection, or other conditions that prevent the eardrum, ossicles, and cochlea from functioning normally will certainly interfere with your ability to simply hear sounds. At other times we may hear incorrectly because the speaker has used a word that is hard to interpret: homonyms (plain/plane, tied/tide) can cause confusion, as can words that mean more than one thing (bill, check, let). Another source of erroneous interpretation is the speaker's use of slang expressions or incorrect pronunciation (youse/use; grammar/grandma).

If you hear something that seems to make no sense or leads you to an apparently incongruous interpretation of the speaker's message, try to correct what may be a mishearing. (Could Eliza Doolittle possibly have meant the rain in Spain stays mainly in the *plane*? Probably not—she must have meant *plain*.)

Psychological Barriers   Almost everyone comes equipped with a set of psychological filters through which any spoken message must pass. Psychological factors that influence listening include "preconceived ideas, moods, assumptions, labels, stereotypes, past experiences, emotions, hopes, memories, and even degree of self-esteem". We form fast impressions of both speaker and message, and our filters strongly influence those impressions. As a result, we may erect these psychological barriers to active listening: selective listening, negative listening attitudes, personal reactions to words, and poor motivation to listen well.

Selective listening. Selective listening is the process of choosing to hear only what we consider important and disregarding the rest. For example, if you go into your annual review with your supervisor, and, among other things, she tells you that some clients say they think your telephone manner is somewhat stiff and formal, your self-esteem filter may catch only that criticism and you won't hear your supervisor praise your record-keeping skills, your diligence, and your dependability. The only thing

Environmental Barrier- External barrier that affects everyone simultaneously

Physiological Barrier- Internal barrier that cannot be controlled

Psychological Barrier- Internal barrier that can be controlled

Psychological Barriers to Active Listening

@ Selective Listening
@ Negative Listening Attitudes
@ Personal Reactions
@ Poor Motivations

that sticks with you is the critical remark—psychological noise has made it impossible for you to hear the positive things that were said.

Be on your guard for selective listening. Practice listening for the whole message, not just those parts that get caught in your psychological filters.

Negative listening attitudes. Attitudes, too, shape our ability to listen. Negative listening attitudes interfere with reception of the entire message and lead to selective listening. In addition, those attitudes go hand in hand with behaviors that are counterproductive to good communication. Your attitude sends both verbal and nonverbal signals to the speaker; negative attitudes may make the speaker feel nervous, uncomfortable, and unappreciated. Your feedback clearly tells the speaker, "I'm bored," "I don't care about what you're saying," "I'm anxious to get out of here," "I don't respect your views," or "My ideas are more valuable than yours." The speaker may decide to stop talking and the communication fails.

Hold your reactions and attitudes in check. If you begin to feel a negative listening attitude creep up on you, force yourself to practice behaviors of the positive opposite. For example, if you feel yourself growing bored, sit up straight, look at the speaker, and analyze what she is saying in terms of its relevance to you. Some people say that "attitude follows behavior"—if you *act* interested, you may soon find that you *are* interested.

Personal reactions to words. We respond to words at two levels of meaning: the denotative and the connotative. Denotative meanings are those literal meanings assigned to words to which we all subscribe. But connotative meanings develop when certain words are used in certain contexts and come to be associated with words beyond the denotative level. Everyone has a red flag filter that catches words that may cause strong reactions—like *liberal, feminist, income tax,* or *communist.* For example, if you hear a speaker use *girls* in reference to adult females, the rest of the message may get lost in your reaction to the connotation you associate with the term *girls* and the related assumptions you make about persons who would refer to women as *girls.*

When a speaker uses a word that waves a red flag at you, look past it. Instead of giving in to the emotional deafness such a word is likely to inspire, focus on the entire message and try to see where the word fits in the overall context.

In other cases, connotative meanings may smudge the message with inadvertent humor or ambiguity. Consider this situation: When Marge visited California for the first time several years ago, she rolled up the legs of her jeans and waded into the Pacific Ocean. Unfortunately, she didn't roll them up far enough, and one of the waves she hadn't anticipated doused her to mid-thigh. She called her children that evening to describe her experience and told them, "I wet my pants in the Pacific Ocean." They laughed because the connotation of the phrase "wet my pants" was stronger than the literal meaning Marge had intended.

We also need to beware of chance associations a speaker's words may trigger in us as we listen. The speaker may be telling you about a problem she is trying to resolve with the instructor of her art history class, but the word *art* makes you think of painting and painting makes you think about the garage you are building but haven't been able to finish because it has been too rainy to paint it, and suddenly you are focusing not on your friend's problem, but your own. The message has fallen by the wayside along the path of your free association.

It's important to focus on the denotative meanings of words. Use nonverbal cues to help you determine what the speaker meant. If the connotation was unintended, let it go. If other cues tell you the connotative mix-up was intended, enjoy the resultant humor. If a speaker's word triggers an unrelated association, you may need to make a conscious effort to suppress it. Just attend to the speaker's words extra carefully and intently for a couple of minutes to force the intrusive association away.

Poor motivation. Another psychological impediment to active listening is lack of preparation. You can listen most actively if you know your listening goals. Without goals, you have no point on which to focus, and, consequently, no motivation to stay attuned to the speaker's message. So, while the other person is speaking, you may be thinking your own thoughts or preparing your rebuttal, without giving the speaker's ideas the attention they deserve.

To deal with motivational problems, you must clearly define your reasons for listening. The ladder shown in the box suggests the increasing level of complexity of listening goals. The higher the goal on the ladder, the more intense your listening needs to be. When you know what your goal is, you can identify and practice listening behaviors that will help you achieve your objective.

> **Listening Goals Ladder**
> Response/Action
> Analysis
> Retention
> Understanding
> Enjoyment

▣ To Be a Good Listener

Good listening behaviors can be learned, but like any skill, they require practice to be perfected. Here are ten guidelines for good listening that you can practice right away. They work in any listening situation and can lead to more sophisticated and refined listening habits.

1. Stop talking. Listen quietly until the speaker's message is complete.
2. Avoid, reduce, or eliminate distractions.
3. Expend the energy needed to give the speaker the benefit of your attention.
4. Use pauses to reflect on what the speaker is saying.
5. Identify the speaker's main ideas and central themes.
6. Judge the content of the message, not the speaker's delivery style.
7. Use paraphrasing, note-taking, and questions when appropriate to ensure understanding.
8. Interpret loaded emotional words appropriately; don't overreact.
9. Give useful feedback.
10. Listen between the lines and beyond the words: Listen for the speaker's feelings as well as facts.

Questions for review:

1. How can you use the concepts of active listening in your role as a 3/C Midshipman?
2. Think about the three types of barriers to communication. As a Naval Officer, in what situations is it imperative to be aware of these barriers?

12 *Social Influence*

Learning Objectives:

Part 1:

- Define social influence and distinguish between the three types of social influence.
- Analyze the negative consequences that could result from each type of social influence.
- Analyze Solomon Asch and Stanley Milgram's experiments and explain what the outcomes of their research teach us about social influence.
- Apply the six principles of influence (*listed in your text*) to a leadership situation.

Part 2:

- Describe the phenomenon of *captainitis* and be able to provide military specific examples.
- Describe what role uncertainty plays in yielding to social influence.
- Another reason we yield to social influence is to gain social approval. Describe the three factors that affect the impact of social approval.

PART 1

Categories of Social Influence: Conformity, Compliance, and Obedience[1]

Social Influence

Social influence is defined as a change in behavior caused by real or imagined pressure from others. It is different from persuasion in that it refers to shifts in overt actions rather than in private attitudes and beliefs.

3 Types of Social Influence

conformity

Behavior change designed to match the actions of others.

compliance

Behavior change that occurs as a result of a direct request.

obedience

Compliance that occurs in response to a directive from an authority figure.

Social psychologists have considered three major categories of social influence: conformity, compliance, and obedience. The amount of overt social pressure associated with these categories escalates as one moves from conformity to compliance and, finally, to obedience. **Conformity** involves changing one's behavior to match the responses or actions of others, to fit in with those around us. Before a party or concert, you might ask, "What will people be wearing?" Imagine showing up in shorts and a T-shirt when everyone else is wearing formal clothing, or imagine appearing in formal wear when everyone else is dressed casually. The discomfort most of us would feel in such situations gives you some sense of the strength of the desire to fit in. Conformity can occur without overt social pressure; no one may ever have to take you aside to say, "You're dressed inappropriately," but you may still voluntarily leave to change into an outfit that looks less out of place.

Compliance refers to the act of changing one's behavior in response to a direct request. The request may come from sources as distinct as friends ("C'mon, have a beer and forget your studying!"), salespeople ("You should sign now because we can't guarantee this model will be here tomorrow"), charities ("St. Mary's Food Bank needs your contributions to feed the poor this Thanksgiving. Please give"), or panhandlers on the street ("Hey buddy, can you spare $3.75 for a cup of cappucino?"). As in the case of a restroom sign asking you to wash your hands before leaving, the requester need not be physically present to exert pressure to comply.

Obedience is a special type of compliance that involves changing one's behavior in response to a directive from an authority figure. A boss may require employees to work overtime, a military officer may command soldiers to attack the enemy, or a police officer may order drivers to take a detour. In directing others to obey, authority figures typically exert the most overt attempts at influence.

[1] Kenrick, D.T., Neuberg, S.L. & Cialdini, R.B.(2005). *Social psychology: Unraveling the mystery* (3rd ed.). Boston, MA: Pearson Education, Inc.

Before considering the factors that motivate us to yield to social influence pressures, let's explore conformity, compliance, and obedience in greater depth by examining a classic piece of research into each process. These pieces of research are noteworthy in that each revealed more impact of social influence than nearly anyone expected and each stimulated a tradition of investigation that continues today (Blass, 2000; Cialdini, 2001; Levine, 1999).

Conformity: Asch's Research on Group Influence

Group pressure can lead people to conform even when contradictory evidence is right before their eyes. This phenomenon was investigated in a series of experiments conducted by Solomon Asch (1956). Asch was interested not only in the submission of individuals to group forces but also in the capacity of people to act independent of conformity pressures.

To investigate these processes of conformity and independence, Asch asked college students in groups of eight to match the lengths of different lines. A typical line-matching problem is shown in Figure 12.1. The task was not difficult. In the control condition, in which there was no group pressure pushing toward wrong choices, 95% of the participants got all of 12 line matches right. For those in the experimental condition, however, the situation changed. They were faced with a social consensus that contradicted their own eyes. Before making their own judgments, they heard five other students (who were actually confederates of the experimenter) unanimously agree on an answer that was clearly wrong. Did they stick to their guns and give the right answers or did they go along with the crowd? As shown in Figure 12.2, only 25% of these participants ignored the group's obvious errors and gave only correct answers. The other 75% went against the evidence of their senses and conformed to some extent. Although no one went along every single time, one individual conformed on 11 of the 12 choices.

What was going on in the minds of the participants when they heard the whole group make judgments that seemed plainly wrong? One participant, who stayed independent of group pressure, became embarrassed, whispering to a neighbor at one point, "I always disagree, darn it." When the experiment was over and he was asked whether he thought the entire group was wrong, he turned to them and said, "You're *probably* right, but you *may* be wrong!" He was "exultant and relieved" when the true nature of the experiment was disclosed to him. Although he hadn't buckled under group pressure, even he had been led to doubt his own judgment. The participant who conformed 11 out of 12 times (more than any other participant) claimed later that he was swayed by the seeming confidence of the other group members. He said he actually came to believe that they were right, thinking that he alone had fallen victim to some sort of "illusion." Asch's research demonstrated that people faced with strong group consensus sometimes go along even though they think the others may be wrong. In addition, they sometimes believe that the others are right, doubting the evidence of their own senses if the members of their group seem confident enough.

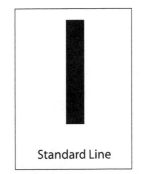

Standard Line   Comparison Lines

FIGURE 12.1 Asch's line-judging task In Asch's conformity studies, subjects were shown a standard line like that on the left and three comparison lines like those on the right. Their task was to choose the comparison line that matched the length of the standard line. It was an easy task—until the other group members began choosing incorrectly.

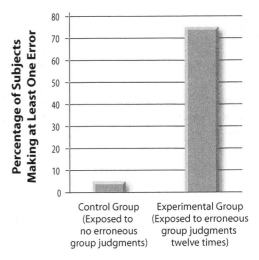

FIGURE 12.2 Effects of incorrect group judgments on conformity Subjects estimated the length of lines either after the other group members had made no errors in their own estimates (control group) or after the other group members had all judged the line lengths incorrectly (experimental group). Only 5% of control group subjects made any errors. But 75% of experimental group subjects made at least one mistake.

Source: Adapted from Asch, 1956.

Say what? The only true subject (#6) assesses for himself the length of lines (top photo) and reacts with puzzlement and dismay when other group members answer incorrectly (bottom photo).

Asch obtained his results among students who were strangers convened for a short experiment. Think how much more potent the social pressure might be when those confident others are members of one's own circle, whose goodwill is treasured. And imagine how much more potent the pressure might become within groups like religious cults, in which the members are often taught to suppress their individuality and are counseled daily on the importance of blind faith in the group's beliefs. Two months before the Heaven's Gate commune members committed suicide in 1997, they spent several thousand dollars for a high-powered telescope because they had heard rumors about a small object (which they suspected was a spaceship) that appeared to be trailing Comet Hale-Bopp. When they complained to the salesman that the telescope showed them no trace of the mysterious object, he explained that there never was a trailing object, only a rumor based on a blip of static in one very early and poor-quality image of the comet. How did they respond to this direct evidence against their group's unanimous and firmly held beliefs about a spaceship carrying their extraterrestrial contacts? They decided to continue believing in the spaceship's existence but to stop looking at the evidence: They turned in the telescope for a refund (Ferris, 1997).

▣ Compliance: The "Foot-in-the-Door" Technique

The term *foot-in-the-door* refers to door-to-door salespeople getting one foot in the door as a way to gain full entry. The psychological underpinnings of this technique were investigated in a clever series of experiments by Jonathan Freedman and Scott Fraser (1966). To address their question, "How can a person be induced to do something he would rather not do?" Freedman and Fraser left the laboratory to conduct field experiments.

In one experiment, 156 housewives in Palo Alto, California, were called on the phone and asked to do something the researchers guessed that most people would rather not do: allow a team of six men from a consumer group to come into their home for two hours "to enumerate and classify all the household products you have." The women were told that the men would need full freedom to go through the house exploring cupboards and storage spaces. Few women (only 22%) complied if this was all they were asked. However, another group of women was contacted twice, once with a small request designed simply to get a "foot in the door"—they were asked to answer a series of eight questions about household soaps (such as "What brand of soap do you use in your kitchen sink?"). It was such a minor favor that nearly everyone agreed. Three days later, these women

PARTICIPANT OBSERVATION

Robert Cialdini was facing a dilemma. He was interested in the reasons people comply with requests of all sorts. Furthermore, he thought that studying the tactics of a wide variety of *successful* "compliance pros" would be especially instructive because these individuals have learned what makes people say yes to requests—otherwise, they wouldn't be successful. But he recognized that few influence practitioners would want him tagging along to record their secrets and perhaps interfere with their effectiveness. To resolve his dilemma, Cialdini engaged in a distinct type of systematic natural observation: **participant observation.** Rather than simply watching from the side, the participant observer becomes an internal spy of sorts. Often with disguised identity and intent, the researcher infiltrates the setting of interest to examine it from within.

To study the compliance professions from the inside, Cialdini (2001) enrolled in the training programs of a broad range of these professions—sales, advertising, fund raising, public relations, recruitment, and so on—learning the same lessons that successful influence practitioners regularly pass on to trainees. Through it all, he looked for parallels, common principles of influence that rose to the surface and persisted in each of the professions. Six widely used and successful principles of influence, to which we'll refer throughout this chapter, emerged from this program of participant observation:

@ *Reciprocation.* People are more willing to comply with requests (for favors, services, information, and concessions) from those who have provided such things first. Because people feel an obligation to reciprocate, Cialdini found that free samples in supermarkets, free home inspections by exterminating companies, and free gifts through the mail from marketers or fund raisers were all highly effective ways to increase compliance with a follow-up request. For example, according to the Disabled American Veterans organization, mailing out a simple appeal for donations produces an 18% success rate, but enclosing a small gift—personalized address labels—boosts the success rate to 35% (Smolowe, 1990).

@ *Commitment/consistency.* People are more willing to be moved in a particular direction if they see it as consistent with an existing or recently made commitment. For instance, high-pressure door-to-door sales companies are plagued by some buyers' tendency to cancel the deal after the salesperson has left and the pressure to buy is no longer present. In training sessions Cialdini attended, several of the door-to-door sales companies claimed that they had significantly reduced this problem with a trick that heightens the customer's sense of personal commitment to the sale: Rather than having the sales representative write in the details of the contract, they have the customer do it.

@ *Authority.* People are more willing to follow the directions or recommendations of someone they view as an authority. So automatic is the tendency to follow an authority, Cialdini noted, that many times advertisers try to—and do—succeed merely by employing actors dressed to look like experts (scientists, physicians, police officers, and so on).

@ *Social validation.* People are more willing to take a recommended step if they see evidence that many others, especially similar others, are taking it. Manufacturers make use of this principle by claiming that their products are the fastest growing or largest selling in the market. Cialdini found that the strategy of increasing compliance by providing evidence of others who had already complied was the most widely used of the six principles he encountered.

@ *Scarcity.* People find objects and opportunities more attractive to the degree that they are scarce, rare, or dwindling in availability. Hence, newspaper ads are filled with warnings to potential customers regarding the folly of delay: "Last three days." "Limited time offer." "One week only sale." One particularly single-minded movie theater owner managed to load three separate appeals to the scarcity principle into just five words of advertising copy that read, "Exclusive, limited engagement, ends soon."

@ *Liking/friendship.* People prefer to say yes to those they know and like. If you doubt that this is the case, consider the remarkable success of the Tupperware Home Party Corporation, which arranges for customers to buy its products not from a stranger across a counter, but from the neighbor, friend, or relative who has sponsored a Tupperware party and gets a percentage of its profits. According to interviews done

Continued

Participant observation

A research approach in which the researcher infiltrates the setting to be studied and observes its working from within.

Six Principles of Influence:

@ Reciprocation

@ Commitment/Consistency

@ Authority

@ Social Validation

@ Scarcity

@ Liking/Frienship

Continued from previous page

by Cialdini, many people attend the parties and purchase the products, not out of a need for more containers that go *pffft* when you press on them but out of a sense of liking or friendship for the party sponsor.

Before we can feel secure in the conclusions of participant observation studies, we usually need to find support for their conclusions elsewhere—for example, in experimental research or in additional natural observations by other scientists. Fortunately, as we'll see in this chapter, experimental evidence and additional observations have validated the role of each of these principles in compliance decisions. For instance, in one study, each of the principles, when applied in the sales presentations of department store clerks, produced a significant increase in retail clothing purchases (Cody, Seiter, & Montagne-Miller, 1995).

were contacted by the same consumer group, but now with the larger, home-visit request. Under these circumstances, 52% of the women agreed to allow the team of men to rummage through their cupboards and closets for two hours.

Can people be influenced like this in everyday life? And how can social psychologists find out? Most of social psychology's knowledge of human behavior comes from controlled laboratory experiments, which offer an excellent way to understand the *causes* of that behavior. But these experiments have their drawbacks. For instance, laboratories are artificial settings where responding might not occur as it would in daily life. Therefore, social scientists sometimes employ other methods that are better able to capture behavior as it normally takes place. One such method is the field experiment, in which researchers perform controlled experimentation in naturally occurring settings, as Freedman and Fraser did to study the foot-in-the-door tactic. A second method doesn't require controlled experimentation at all. Instead it involves the careful observation of people as they act and interact in natural situations.

Obedience: Milgram's Shock(ing) Procedure

Political leaders, military commanders, police officers, high school principals, store managers, and parents issue commands that produce obedience on a daily basis. Social psychologist Stanley Milgram wanted to see how far the obedience-inducing power of authority could be extended. Would you obey orders from a researcher you had never before met if he or she asked you to deliver painful, potentially deadly electric shocks to an innocent victim? And if so, what would the victim have to say to get you to stop obeying such orders?

In a well-known series of studies done decades ago, Milgram (1974) placed advertisements in local newspapers to solicit participants for a "memory experiment" at Yale University. Suppose that one of those studies was being conducted today and that you signed up to participate. Here's what you'd encounter: Upon your arrival at the laboratory, you'd be introduced to another participant (actually a confederate of the experimenter). After hearing that the research would examine the effects of punishment on memory, you'd be assigned to the Teacher role and the other participant to the Learner role in the study. You'd be informed that, as part of your duties, you'd have to deliver a series of electric shocks to the Learner. At this point, the Learner would mention that he had been treated for a heart condition and express concern about the dangers of receiving electric shocks. To this, the experimenter would reply that, although painful, the shocks would produce "no permanent tissue damage."

The experimenter would then take you both to the next room, where the nervous Learner would be strapped into an apparatus looking eerily like an electric chair. That accomplished, you'd be ushered into an experimental room and shown a menacing shock-delivery machine with shock levers ascending from 15 to 450 volts. Each group of four shock levers would be assigned a progressively more frightening label, ranging from "Slight shock" through "Moderate," "Strong," "Very strong," "Intense," "Extreme intensity," to "Danger: Severe shock." A final pair of levers (for the 435- and 450-volt shocks) would apparently deliver shocks so intense that the English language had no words to describe them adequately, as they carried only the stark label "XXX."

Mean machine. *Milgram's subjects delivered shocks by operating the levers of this intimidating piece of equipment.*

Before beginning, you would receive an unpleasant sample shock of 45 volts to give you an idea of what the Learner would be experiencing. You'd then be instructed to deliver a shock to the Learner every time he erred on a memory task, advancing to the next higher shock lever with every new mistake. With each error and each more punishing shock, the confederate would voice increasingly desperate cries of pain. At first, he'd simply cry out, "Ugh." At 120 volts, he would shout out, "Hey, this really hurts!" At 150 volts, he'd plead to be released:

> That's all! Get me out of here. I told you I had heart trouble. My heart's starting to bother me now. Get me out of here, please. My heart's starting to bother me. I refuse to go on. Let me out.

Would you continue or stop? If you tried to stop, the experimenter would prod you by saying, "Please continue." If you failed to obey, the experimenter would insist, "The experiment requires that you continue." If you persisted in your disobedience, he'd state, "It is absolutely essential that you continue." Finally, he would demand, "You have no choice; you must go on."

If you continued to follow orders and deliver the shocks, the Learner's appeals would become more agonized and desperate. Finally, he'd burst into a litany of pleas, demands, and shrieks:

> Let me out of here. Let me out of here. My heart's bothering me. Let me out, I tell you. Let me out of here. Let me out of here. You have no right to hold me here. Let me out! Let me out! Let me out! Let me out of here! Let me out! Let me out!

Should that not be enough to convince you to resist the experimenter's orders, things would suddenly change. When you delivered the next shock, you'd hear nothing from the Learner's chamber. If you asked the experimenter to see if the Learner was all right, he'd refuse, saying instead, "Treat no response as a wrong response, and deliver the next higher level of shock." For the final eight shocks—into the "Danger" category and the region marked "XXX"—the Learner, once so vocal in his pain would be deadly silent.

How likely would you and other participants like you be to follow orders to go all the way to 450 volts? Before publishing his study, Milgram described the procedures to 40 psychiatrists at a leading medical school and asked them to predict the results. They expected that fewer than 4% of Milgram's subjects would continue once the Learner stopped answering and that only 0.01% would go all the way to the end. Sadly, the psychiatrists greatly underestimated the power of obedience to authority. More than 80% of the participants continued past the Learner's refusal to answer. Even more remarkably, 65% persisted to the end—defying an innocent victim's repeated screams and enduring his subsequent ominous silence—simply because the "boss" of the study commanded it (see Figure 12.3). What's more, these high levels of obedience have remained steady when researchers have repeated Milgram's procedures in more recent years (Blass, 1999).

In the years following Milgram's studies, some critics faulted him on ethical grounds, saying that he should not have subjected his participants to the stress of thinking they were harming the Learner. Others have defended Milgram, arguing that the importance of his findings outweighed this discomfort. What's your position on this controversy?

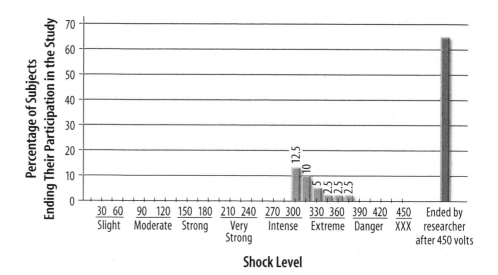

FIGURE 12.3 Obedience in the Milgram study Despite predictions to the contrary from psychiatrists at Yale Medical School, the majority (65%) of subjects obeyed a researcher's commands to deliver every available shock, up to 450 volts, to an innocent fellow subject.

Source: Adapted from Milgram, 1963.

Milgram conducted an elaborate series of follow-up studies. In one, he explored the extent to which his results were due to the scientific credibility of Yale University, where the study took place. He rented office space in a rundown section of Bridgeport, Connecticut, and ran the same procedures again. Surprisingly, a large proportion of participants (48%) obeyed the researcher's orders even under these questionable circumstances, indicating that his findings were not limited to university-based authorities. But how do we know that it was authority influence rather than some other factor—the desire to release pent-up aggression, for instance—that caused Milgram's subjects to behave so cruelly?

The evidence supporting the obedience to authority explanation is strong. First, it's clear that, without the researcher's directive to continue, the participants would have ended the experiment quickly. They hated what they were doing and agonized over their victim's agony. They implored the researcher to let them stop. When he refused, they went on, but in the process they trembled, perspired, shook, and stammered protests and additional pleas for the victim's release. In addition to these observations, Milgram provided even more convincing evidence for the interpretation of his results in light of obedience to authority. In a later experiment, for instance, he had the researcher and the victim switch scripts so that the researcher told the Teacher to stop delivering shocks to the victim, while the victim insisted bravely that the Teacher continue. The result couldn't have been clearer: 100% of the participants refused to give one additional shock when it was merely the fellow participant who demanded it. These results would hardly be expected if participants' principal motive was to release aggressive energy rather than to follow an authority.

If, as Milgram's research indicates, a majority of people will deliver painful shocks to a heart patient on the orders of a research scientist who has no real authority over them, it becomes less surprising that soldiers have killed innocent civilians and that cult members will kill themselves at the direction of more personally relevant authority figures. More recent work has examined disturbing levels of unethical obedience in organizations (Darley, 2001). For example, personnel managers may discriminate against certain racial groups when instructed to do so by an authority figure (Brief, Buttram, & Dukerich, 2001). But *why* do people obey? What goals are served by this and the other forms of social influence?

PART 2:

▣ The Goals of Social Influence

Notice that conformity, compliance, and obedience all refer not to the act of wielding influence but to the act of yielding to it. When it comes to understanding human motivation, yielding questions are more interesting—and more instructive—than wielding questions. In this chapter we emphasize the goals of those who choose to conform, comply, and obey. As we will see, people yield to social influence to achieve one or more of three basic goals: choosing correctly, gaining social approval and managing self-image.

Choosing Correctly

According to Robert W. White (1959), we all have a motive for *competence,* a motive to master our environments so that we consistently gain desired rewards and resources. Of course, consistently succeeding in any environment doesn't occur by accident. To do well, we must choose well. From a profusion of possibilities, we must make the choices most likely to bring us the rewards and resources we seek. It's for this reason that influence professionals are forever trying to convince us that if we select their products or services—from hair care to health care—we will have chosen well and gotten a "good deal." The problem when encountering influence attempts of this sort lies in recognizing when the offered deal is in fact a good one.

How can we know beforehand whether a choice for a particular toothpaste or restaurant or political candidate will prove wise and effective? Frequently, we rely on two powerful principles to steer us correctly in our influence decisions—authority and social validation.

▣ Authority

The most striking research evidence for the influence of legitimate authority comes from the Milgram obedience study. But the tendency to defer to an authority arises in many more situations than the laboratory setting that Milgram constructed (Blass, 1991; Miller, Collins, & Brief, 1995). What's more, the behaviors influenced in these situations range from the ordinary to the dramatic (Sabini & Silver, 1982). In the realm of ordinary behaviors, we can find deference to authority in something as commonplace as the tone of voice one uses in a conversation. Communication researchers who study what happens in conversations have learned that people shift their voice and speech styles toward the styles of individuals in positions of power and authority (Giles & Coupland, 1991; Pittam, 1994). One study explored this phenomenon by analyzing interviews on the *Larry King Live* television show. When King interviewed guests having great social standing and prestige (for instance, George Bush, Bill Clinton, and Barbra Streisand), his voice style changed to match theirs. But when he interviewed guests of lower status and prestige (for instance, Dan Quayle, Spike Lee, and Julie Andrews), he remained unmoved, and their voice styles shifted to match his (Gregory & Webster, 1996).

As Milgram's findings demonstrated, people also follow an authority's lead in situations involving much more dramatic consequences than changes in voice. Consider, for example, the catastrophic consequences of a phenomenon that airline industry officials have labeled "captainitis" (Foushee, 1984). Accident investigators from the Federal Aviation Administration have recognized that an obvious error by a flight captain often goes uncorrected by other crewmembers and results in a crash.

Three Reasons People Yield to Social Influence:

◉ Choosing Correctly
◉ Gaining Social Approval
◉ Personal Commitments

"Captainitis"

A phenomenon coined by the airline industry when an obvious error by a flight captain goes uncorrected by a crewmember because of the captain's position of authority, ultimately resulting in a crash

The catastrophic consequences of captainitis. Minutes before this airliner crashed into the Potomac River near National Airport in Washington, D.C., an alarming exchange occurred between pilot and copilot concerning the wisdom of taking off with ice on the wings. Their conversation was recorded on the plane's "black box."

Co-pilot: *Let's check those tops [wings] again since we've been sitting awhile.*

Captain: *No, I think we get to go in a minute.*

Co-pilot: *[Referring to an instrument reading] That doesn't seem right, does it? Uh, that's not right.*

Captain: *Yes, it is. . .*

Co-pilot: *Oh, maybe it is.*

[Sound of plane straining unsuccessfully to gain altitude]

Co-pilot: *Larry, we're going down!*

Captain: *I know it!*

[Sound of impact that killed the captain, co-pilot, and 67 passengers]

expert power
The capacity to influence that flows from one's presumed wisdom or knowledge.

It seems that, because of the captain's authority position, crewmembers either fail to notice or fail to challenge the mistake. They appear to assume that if the captain said it, it must be right.

Think back throughout your schooling, when your English teachers corrected your writing style, you probably took their criticisms into account in your next paper. That was no doubt the case for multiple reasons. First, like many authorities, teachers have power over you. They can affect your grade in the class, your standing in school, your chances for a good position after graduation, and so on. For such reasons alone, it makes good sense to follow their directions. Bur there's a second reason. Like many authorities, teachers are experts on the subject at hand. If they say that a sentence you've written is awkward, you're likely to *believe* it and to change in order to improve your writing in general. In short, following the advice of authorities helps us choose rapidly and correctly. Although some authorities are in a position to force us into obedience, it's more interesting to consider how effective they can be without the power to reward or punish—when what they have instead is **expert power**, the power that comes from acknowledged competence in the matter at hand (French & Raven, 1959; Kozlowski & Schwartzwald, 2001).

Authorities as Experts An authority's expert power can have a strong effect on compliance because it serves our strong motivation to choose correctly. Milgram (1965, p. 74) claimed that his subjects' obedience occurred not simply through overt pressure but, as well, "by the uncritical acceptance of the experimenter's definition of the situation." When authorities are presumed to know best, following their lead becomes a sensible thing. This helps explain why less educated individuals are more obedient to authority figures (Hamilton, Sanders, & McKearney, 1995; Milgram, 1974): They tend to presume that authorities know more than they do.

Because following an expert's direction is normally wise, and because authorities are frequently experts, we often use authority as a decision-making heuristic (shortcut). Assuming that an authority knows best can be an efficient way of deciding, because we don't have to think hard about the issues ourselves; all we have to do to be right is accept the authority's advice. But unthinking reliance on authority can be dangerous, too. This shortcut approach can lead us to respond to the symbols rather than the substance of genuine authority (Bushman, 1984).

The results of a study conducted by a team of physicians and nurses revealed the force that one such symbol—the mere title Dr.—has in the medical arena. Hospital nurses received a phone call from a man they'd never met but who identified himself as the doctor of a patient on their floor. He then ordered them to give twice the maximum acceptable dosage of a drug to that patient. Ninety-five percent obeyed and had to be stopped on their way to the patient's room with the unsafe drug dosage in their hands (Hofling, Brotzman, Dalrymple, Graves, & Pierce, 1966). A follow-up study asked nurses to recall a time when they'd obeyed a doctor's order that they considered inappropriate and potentially harmful to a patient. Those who admitted such incidents (46%) attributed their actions to their beliefs that the doctor was a legitimate and expert authority in the matter—the same two features of authority that appear to account for obedience in the Milgram procedure (Blass, 1999; Krackow & Blass, 1995). Incidents of this deference to the symbols of authority continue to occur. A 17-year-old convinced nurses at a Virginia hospital to carry out twelve treatments on six patients by misrepresenting himself as a doctor on the phone.

Authorities as Agents of Influence   It should come as no surprise that influence professionals frequently try to harness the power of authority by touting their experience, expertise, or scientific recognition: "Fashionable clothiers since 1841," "Babies are our business, our only business," "Four out of five doctors recommend the ingredients in . . . ," and so on. There's nothing wrong with such claims when they're real, because we usually want to know who is an authority on a topic and who isn't, it helps us choose correctly. The problem comes when we are subjected to phony claims of this sort. When we aren't thinking hard, as is often the case when confronted by authority symbols, we can be easily steered in the wrong direction by false authorities—those who aren't authorities at all but who merely present the aura of authority. For instance, people are more willing to perform a variety of unusual actions (to pick up a paper bag on the street, stand on the other side of a Bus Stop sign, put money in someone else's parking meter) if directed to do so by someone wearing a security guard's or firefighter's uniform; moreover, they are more likely to do so unquestioningly (Bickman, 1974; Bushman, 1984).

In sum, authorities are formidable sources of social influence. One reason is that they are often expert. Consequently, following their directions offers us a shortcut route to choosing correctly. However, when we defer to authority orders or advice too readily, we risk performing actions that may be unethical or unwise. Let's turn now to a second major principle that people use to help them achieve the goal of choosing correctly, social validation.

▣ Social Validation

Just as following the advice of an authority is normally a shortcut to good decisions, so is following the lead of most of one's peers. If all your friends are raving about a new restaurant, you'll probably like it, too. Therefore, we frequently decide what we should do in a situation by examining what others, especially similar others, are doing there (Baron et al., 1996). We use the actions of these others as a means of **social validation,** as an interpersonal way to locate and validate the correct choice (Festinger, 1954).

social validation
An interpersonal way to locate and validate the correct choice.

Because the desire to choose correctly is powerful, the tendency to follow the crowd is both strong and widespread. Studies have shown that, based on evidence of what their peers are doing, bystanders decide whether to help an emergency victim (Latané & Darley, 1970), citizens decide whether to pay their taxes fully (Steenbergen, McGraw, & Scholz, 1992), juveniles decide whether to commit a wide range of crimes (Kahan, 1997), spouses decide whether to "cheat" sexually (Buunk & Baker, 1995), and homeowners decide whether to recycle their trash (Schultz, 1999). In this last study, residents of a Los Angeles suburb received information describing the regular curbside recycling behavior of many of their neighbors. This information produced an immediate increase in the amount of material the residents recycled. In addition, when observed up to a month later, they were recycling more trash than ever. These improvements did not occur, however, for residents who received only a plea to recycle.

Whenever influence practitioners identify a psychological principle that people use to reach their goals, the practitioners are sure to use it to advance their own goals. We saw that this was the case for the authority principle, and it is no less the case for the principle of social validation. Sales and marketing professionals make a special point of informing us when a product is the "largest selling" or "fastest growing" in its market. Bartenders are known to "salt" their tip jars with dollar bills at the start of their shifts to give the impression that previous customers tipped with folding money. Television commercials depict crowds rushing into stores and hands depleting shelves of the advertised item. Consider the advice offered more than 350 years ago by the Spaniard Balthazar Gracian (1649/1945) to anyone wishing to sell goods and services: "Their intrinsic worth is not enough, for not all turn the goods over or look deep. Most run where the crowd is—because the others run" (p. 142). This tendency to run because others are running affects more than product sales. Indeed, it accounts for some of the most bizarre forms of human conduct on record. In the Focus on Social Dysfunction feature, we examine one such form, mass hysteria.

Although the tendency to follow the lead of our peers can lead to misguided behavior, most of the time it doesn't. Most of the time it sends us in right directions, toward correct choices. Which are the factors that spur people to use the actions of others in the process of trying to choose correctly? Social psychologists have uncovered several. We begin with one that resides in the person.

▣ Uncertainty

When people don't trust their own judgments, they look to others for evidence of how to choose correctly (Wooten & Reed, 1998). This self-doubt may come about because the situation is ambiguous, as it was in a classic series of experiments conducted by the Turkish social psychologist Muzafer Sherif (1936). Sherif projected a dot of light on the wall of a darkened room and asked subjects to indicate how much the light moved while they watched it. Actually, the light never moved at all; but, because of an optical illusion termed the *autokinetic effect,* it seemed to shift constantly about, although to a different extent for each subject. When participants announced their movement estimates in groups, these estimates were strongly influenced by what the other group members estimated; nearly everyone changed toward the group average. Sherif concluded that when there's no objectively correct response, people are likely to doubt themselves and, thus, are especially likely to assume that "the group must be right" (p. 111). Many studies have supported his conclusion (Bond & Smith, 1996; Tesser, Campbell, & Mickler, 1983).

Despite initial uncertainty, once a group has agreed on a response, members can hold onto it fiercely (Jacobs & Campbell, 1961). In one study, group members who had undergone Sherif's autokinetic effect procedure returned many months later to be tested again, but this time with no other group members present. When placed in the darkened room once more, these individuals saw the light move a distance that fit with the group answer formed a year earlier (Rohrer, Baron, Hoffman, & Swander, 1954).

People also feel unsure of themselves when the task they face is difficult. Richard Crutchfield (1955) gave college students the opportunity to conform to the majority position on a variety of tasks, ranging from perceptual problems to opinion items. The one that generated the most conformity (79%) was a numerical problem that was the most difficult of all the tasks—because it was actually impossible to solve.

MASS HYSTERIA

Throughout history, people have been subject to extraordinary collective delusions—irrational sprees, manias, and panics of various sorts. In his classic text on "the madness of crowds," Charles MacKay listed hundreds that occurred before the book's first publication in 1841. It is noteworthy that many shared an instructive characteristic—contagiousness. Often, they began with a single person or group and then swept rapidly through whole populations. Action spread to observers, who then acted and thereby validated the correctness of the action for still other observers, who acted in turn.

For instance, in 1761, London experienced two moderate-sized earthquakes exactly a month apart. Convinced by this coincidence that a third, much larger quake would occur in another month, a soldier named Bell began spreading his prediction that the city would be destroyed on April 5. At first, few paid him any heed. But those who did took the precaution of moving their families and possessions to surrounding areas. The sight of this small exodus stirred others to follow, which, in cascading waves over the next week, led to near panic and a large-scale evacuation. Great numbers of Londoners streamed into nearby villages, paying outrageous prices for any accommodations. Included in the terrified throngs were "hundreds who had laughed at the prediction a week before, [but who] packed up their goods, when they saw others doing so, and hastened away" (MacKay, 1841/ 1932, p. 260).

After the designated day dawned and died without a tremor, the fugitives returned to the city furious at Bell for leading them astray. As MacKay's description makes clear, however, their anger was misdirected. It wasn't the crackpot Bell who was most convincing. It was the Londoners themselves, each to the other.

A similar, though less historic incident took place in modern Singapore when, for no good reason, the customers of a local bank began drawing out their money in a frenzy. The run on this respected bank remained a mystery until much later, when researchers interviewing participants discovered its peculiar cause: An unexpected bus strike had created an abnormally large crowd waiting at the bus stop in front of the bank that day. Mistaking the gathering for a crush of customers poised to withdraw their funds from a failing bank, passersby panicked and got in line to withdraw their deposits, which led more passersby to do the same. Soon illusion had become reality and, shortly after opening its doors, the bank was forced to close to avoid ruin ("News," 1988).

In all, most people feel that behaviors become more valid when many others are performing them. In instances of mass delusion, this social validation extends to wildly irrational acts that seem to reflect correct choices not because of any hard evidence in their favor but merely because multiple others have chosen them.

When people feel unsure of their grasp on reality, they're more likely to defer to authority figures, too. In field tests of combat artillery units, teams that are fully rested often refuse to fire on hospitals and other civilian targets, but after 36 sleepless hours, they obey orders to fire at anything without question (Schulte, 1998).

Consensus and Similarity

Consensus   Remember Asch's (1956) conformity research? It showed that people would make obvious errors on a line-judging task merely because everybody in their group had already chosen to make that error. Imagine the pressure you would feel in such a situation if *everyone* else chose an answer that looked wrong to you. With perfect agreement among the others, you'd probably trust the group more and yourself less. In your desire to choose correctly, you might well conform because you believed that the group was right. In addition, the more group

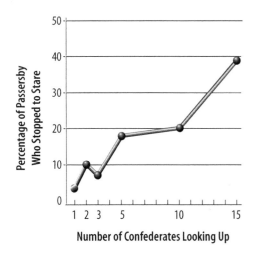

FIGURE 12.4 Looking up What could motivate pedestrians on a wintry day in New York City to stop, stand, and stare at little of obvious interest or importance? Researchers had sent confederates to stare upward for 60 seconds. The more confederates staring upward at nothing in particular, the more passersby joined the group.

Source: Adapted from Milgram, Bickman, & Berkowits, 1969.

Suppose two charity volunteers came to your door and, before asking you to contribute to their cause, they showed you a long list of your neighbors who had already donated. How would they have used consensus and similarity to influence your decision?

members who were in agreement, the stronger would be your tendency to conform (Bond & Smith, 1996; Insko, Smith, Alicke, Wade, & Taylor, 1985) (see Figure 12.4).

In contrast, imagine a slightly different situation: Before you have to give your answer, the consensus of the group is broken by one individual who chooses the line that looks right to you. Now, when it's your turn to speak, what would you do—go along with the majority or join the rebel? Most likely, you'd become much less likely to agree with the majority. Even a single visible dissenter from the group's position emboldens others to resist conformity (Morris & Miller, 1975). Why should that be? One reason is that dissenters reduce confidence that the group has *the* right answer (Allen & Levine, 1969; Gordijn, DeVries, & DeDreu, 2002); therefore, people seeking to select accurately begin looking beyond the group's choice to other possibilities.

Similarity If people follow the lead of others to make good choices for themselves, it stands to reason that most of the time they would want to follow the actions of individuals similar to themselves. Suppose you were trying to decide which of two classes to take next term. Wouldn't you be more likely to seek out and accept the advice of individuals like you, who match your background, interests, and goals? If they think one class is better than the other, the chances are good that you would too (Suls, Martin, & Wheeler, 2000).

Heightened sensitivity to the responses of similar others appears in a wide variety of situations. For example, in one study, New Yorkers were strongly influenced to return a lost wallet after learning that a similar other had first tried to do so. But evidence that a dissimilar other—a foreigner—had tried to return the wallet had no effect on the New Yorkers' decisions (Hornstein, Fisch, & Holmes, 1968). In a different study, children watched a film depicting another child's positive visit to the dentist. Did watching this film reduce the children's dentist office anxieties? Yes, but that was so principally when the child in the movie was the same age as those viewing it (Melamed et al., 1978).

Although similar others can take us in positive directions, they can lead us down dark, deadly paths as well. Take the phenomenon of copycat suicides. After highly publicized suicide stories appear in the media, the suicide rate jumps in those areas that have been exposed to the stories (Phillips, 1989). Apparently, certain troubled individuals imitate the actions of other troubled individuals in the act of suicide. What's the evidence that this increase in self-inflicted deaths comes from the tendency to look to similar others for direction? Copycat suicides are more prevalent among people who are similar in age and sex to the victim in the previously publicized suicide story. For instance, following a German television story of a young man who killed himself by leaping in front of a train, railway suicides increased dramatically, but only among other young German men (Schmidtke & Hafner, 1988).

In sum, we are more likely to match our actions to those of others when those others are in agreement with one another and akin to us. Both of these factors—consensus and similarity—stimulate conformity because they give us confidence that the others' choices represent good choices for us, too.

Uncertainty and the Desire for Accuracy

Now that it seems clear that one reason people conform to the majority is to choose accurately, wouldn't you agree that the more someone wants to be accurate, the more he or she will conform to what everyone else has decided? If you do agree, you would be right. But, sometimes, you would be wrong because another factor interacts with one's desire for accuracy, and it can change everything. It is a factor we have already discussed—uncertainty.

To examine how uncertainty and the desire for accuracy can interact, Robert S. Baron, Joseph Vandello, and Bethany Brunsman (1996) created a variation of the Asch line-judging procedure. Instead of choosing correct line lengths, University of Iowa undergraduates had to choose the correct suspect in criminal lineups. First, they saw a picture of a single criminal suspect. Then, they saw a picture of a lineup containing four suspects, including the one they had previously seen. Their task was to pick out of the lineup the previously seen suspect. This was repeated 13 times with 13 different pairs of pictures. To make accuracy especially important for one group of students, the researchers promised a $20 prize to those who made the most correct choices. But, for some students, there was an added complication—the pictures were flashed on a screen so quickly (half a second each) that they couldn't be very certain of their judgments. Other students did not encounter this uncertainty because, for them, the pictures were left on the screen for five seconds each.

How did the students choose when, on seven separate occasions, they heard confederates unanimously identifying the wrong suspects in the lineups? Did they conform to the majority or stay with their own judgments? That depended on how uncertain they were of their private judgments and on how important accuracy was for them on the task. Those who were unsure of their judgments became more likely to conform to the majority when accuracy was important; but those who were sure of their judgments became less likely to conform when accuracy was important (see Figure 12.5). Although the sure and unsure individuals moved in opposite directions, their movement was motivated by the same goal: to choose correctly. The critical difference between them was whether they felt that relying on themselves or on others offered the best route to choosing correctly. The motivation to be accurate pushes us toward conformity only when we are unsure of our own judgments.

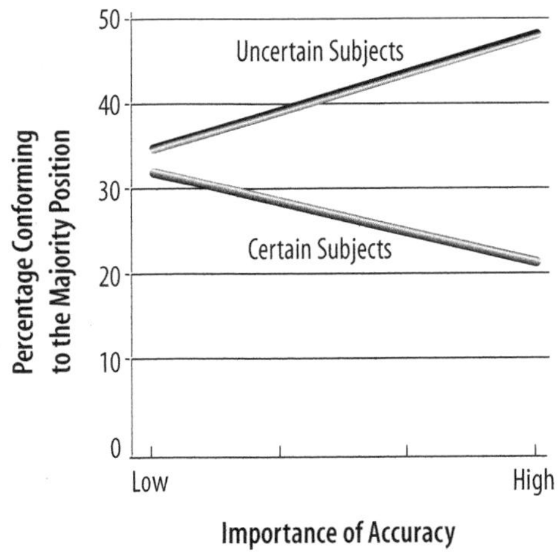

FIGURE 12.5 **Conformity and uncertainty**
Subjects who were uncertain of their judgments on a face-identification task (because the faces were presented very rapidly on a screen) conformed to the unanimous majority position more often when being accurate was especially important to them. However, those who were certain of their judgments (because the faces were left on the screen for five full seconds) conformed less often when accuracy was especially important. Thus, only the uncertain individuals chose conformity as the best route to accuracy.
Source: Adapted from Baron, Vandello, & Brunsman, 1996.

Gaining Social Approval

Most everyone wants to be correct. But it's not easy. Part of the difficulty comes from the fact that the term *correct* can have two different and sometimes opposing meanings. So far in this chapter, we've emphasized just one of these meanings—accuracy. We've focused on the willingness to be influenced in order to be *right*. But the second meaning of being correct—being socially appropriate or approved—can also leave people open to influence (Insko, Drenan, Solomon, Smith, & Wade, 1983). For example, after being ignored and excluded in an Internet game, participants (from 14 different countries) conformed more to the group opinion on a subsequent task (Williams, Cheung, & Choi, 2000). Thus, people frequently change to be more accepted in their group or culture—in other words; to belong (Baumeister & Leary, 1995; Williams & Zadro, 2001).

Take, for example, the account by Irving Janis (1997) of what happened in a group of heavy smokers who came to a clinic for treatment. During the group's second meeting, nearly everyone took the position that, because tobacco is so addicting, no one could be expected to quit all at once. But one man disputed the group's view, announcing that he had stopped smoking completely since joining the group the week before and that others could do the same. In response, the other group members banded against him, delivering a series of angry attacks on his position. At the following meeting, the dissenter reported that, after careful thought, he had come to an important decision: "I have gone back to smoking two packs a day; and won't make any effort to stop again until after the last meeting" (p. 334). The other group members immediately welcomed him back into the fold, greeting his decision with applause.

This account illustrates the old dictum that "it's easier to get along if you go along." In a classic set of studies, Stanley Schachter (1951) observed how groups pressure members who deviate from the consensus. In newly formed discussion teams, Schachter planted a male confederate who asserted an opinion different from the other members'. The group's reaction typically followed a three-step sequence. First, the others directed a large number of comments to the deviate, arguing heatedly with him. Next, when he failed to come into line with the group mind, the other members began to ignore him and to treat him with disdain. Finally, when he held firm through the shift from hot attack to cold shoulder, he was rejected outright with a vote to expel him from the group.

However, Schachter found that groups can respond with affection to opinion deviates, provided the dissenters admit the error of their ways and adopt the group's view. In some discussion groups, the confederate was programmed to be a "slider"—someone who began by disagreeing, but who gradually yielded to group pressure. What happened to the slider? He, too, received an initial barrage of comments designed to convert him to the group position. But, because he yielded, he never experienced the disdain and rejection that the unbending deviate did. In fact, the slider was embraced as fully into the group as any other member. For a deviate in a group, then, the unforgivable sin is not to be different; it is to *stay* different. As a result, many dissenting individuals shift toward group consensus to be accepted and to avoid rejection.

▣ Social Norms: Codes of Conduct

descriptive norms
Norms that define what behaviors are typically performed.

injunctive norms
Norms that define what behaviors are typically approved or disapproved.

How can people know which behaviors will lead to social acceptance? The message is carried in the social norms of the group or culture. Cialdini, Kallgren, and Reno (1991) have differentiated two kinds of social norms: **descriptive norms,** which define what is typically done; and **injunctive norms,** which define what is typically approved and disapproved. Although what is usually done and what is usually approved are frequently the same, this is not always so. For instance, the great majority of holiday shoppers may pass by a Salvation Army charity kettle without giving a donation, but that same majority may still approve of giving to the organization.

Descriptive norms can inform people of what is likely to be effective action for them. Thus, these norms connect to the first goal we discussed in this chapter, the goal of choosing correctly (accurately). By following what most people do in a setting, one can usually make an accurate choice. Injunctive norms, on the other hand, inform people of what is likely to be acceptable to others. These norms connect to the second goal of social influence, the goal of social approval (Crandall, Eshleman, & O'Brien, 2002). If you want to enhance the extent to which you are appreciated and wanted in a group, you would be best advised to pay special attention to injunctive norms.

One particular injunctive norm that is renowned for its favorable effect on social relationships is the norm for reciprocity. It produces potent forms of social influence. According to the sociologist Alvin Gouldner (1960), every human society abides by the **norm of reciprocity**, which obligates people to give back the type of behavior they have received.

norm of reciprocity
The norm that requires that we repay others with the form of behavior they have given us.

The norm of reciprocity creates one of the great benefits of social life. If you do me a favor today, you have the right to expect a favor from me tomorrow. Those traded favors allow us to accomplish tasks we could not do alone (moving a heavy dresser, for example) and help us all survive through uneven times (buy me lunch today when I'm broke, and I'll buy you lunch when my paycheck comes in). Through the exchange and repayment of gifts, favors, and services, people become connected to one another in ongoing relationships. Anyone who violates the norm by taking without giving in return invites social disapproval and risks the relationship (Cotterell, Eisenberger, & Speicher, 1992; Meleshko & Alden, 1993). Most people feel uncomfortable receiving without giving in return because they don't want to be labeled as "takers" or "moochers."

▣ What Personal Factors Affect the Impact of Social Approval?

Imagine that before going to dinner with friends, there is divided opinion about whether to eat Mexican or Italian food. At the restaurant, opinions diverge in a discussion of a hot political topic. After dinner, there is another difference of opinion, this time over whether to go to a crowded bar for a drink or to a quiet coffee shop for intellectual conversation. Do you have a friend who would be especially likely to go along with the group in each instance to keep things operating smoothly? Can you think of another friend who would be willing to resist to the bitter end? What might be the psychological differences between the two people? In other words, what factors inside the person affect the tendency to "go along to get along," the willingness to be influenced in order to be socially approved? Let's explore three person factors that affect whether an individual is likely to accommodate to the group position—approval, collectivism versus individualism, and resistance—beginning with approval.

Desire for Approval   Certain individuals are very concerned with social approval and seem highly motivated to gain the respect of those around them. In an early study of personality and conformity, researchers measured people's need for social approval before observing how these same people responded to group pressure to make incorrect choices (as in the Asch line-judging experiments we described earlier). Just as would be expected if need for social approval motivates people to yield to others, those whose personality test scores indicated a high need for approval were more likely to go along with the group (Strickland & Crowne, 1962). Other researchers found a similar effect when measuring voice patterns among people having a discussion. High-need-for-approval speakers were especially likely to adopt their partner's vocal intensity and pause lengths (Giles & Coupland, 1991).

Treating the desire for approval as a need frames it in a somewhat negative way, implying that going along with others is based in some personality weakness. However, there is another way to view it. The desire for approval is at the center of the "nicest" of the major personality factors—agreeableness. Agreeableness is made up of a host of positive characteristics, including warmth, trust, and helpfulness. In addition, agreeable people are described as accommodating and compliant. They are inclined to go along with others in their groups to avoid conflict (Suls, Martin, & David, 1998). Psychologists who have studied personality and social behavior have suggested that agreeableness may have been vitally important to our ancestors' survival in groups (Graziano & Eisenberg, 1997; Hogan, 1993). According to this perspective, yielding in order to be agreeable should be regarded positively, as a valued personal trait. After all, it would be impossible for groups to function efficiently without a substantial amount of member conformity (Tyler & Degoey, 1995).

Collective Sense of Self   Earlier, we said that the injunctive norms of a group or culture tell people which of their behaviors will be met with social approval. However, some individuals in these groups and cultures are more likely than others to live up to these norms. What determines this tendency to respond to social norms rather than to personal preferences? One cause is a person's definition of self. Some people characterize themselves in personal and individualized terms, focusing on features that distinguish them from others: "I am an avid outdoors person with a strong spiritual nature." Other people characterize themselves in collective terms, identifying themselves by the groups to which they belong: "I am a member of the Sierra Club and am active in the Campus Interfaith Council." David Trafimow and Krystina Finlay (1996) found that people who defined themselves in individualistic ways made their decisions on the basis of their personal attitudes rather than group norms. However, those who defined themselves through their groups were more affected by what they thought others felt than by what they felt. Cultures that differ in the extent to which they are individualistic or collectivistic also produce this effect. In the Asch line-judging procedure, citizens of the more collectivistic societies of the East conform to a greater extent than do citizens of the more individualistic societies of the West (Bond & Smith, 1996).

Resistance   Perhaps you've noticed that almost all of the processes and tactics covered in this chapter—for example, authority, social validation, the foot-in-the-door technique—cause people to *yield* to social influence. Eric Knowles and his colleagues (Davis & Knowles, 1999; Knowles & Linn, 2003) have argued that just as important as these influence-enhancing factors (which they have termed *Alpha forces*) are factors that lead people to resist social influence (which they have termed *Omega forces*). Thus, a relatively underappreciated way to get people to say yes is to reduce the power of the (Omega) forces causing them to resist your influence attempt. One such tactic is the **disrupt-then-reframe technique**. For instance, consider the problem facing Charlie, a door-to-door solicitor selling greeting cards at an excellent price. Part of his difficulty is that most customers feel resistant when asked to buy anything by someone who appears uninvited at their door, because they view the event as a potential scam. If Charlie could somehow disrupt the customers' perception of his offer as a scam and replace it with a more favorable conception of the offer, that should increase purchases by decreasing customers' resistance. To see if this was the case, researchers posing as salespeople went door-to-door offering a packet of eight high-quality greeting cards for an attractive price ("They're $3"); with this wording, only 35% of the prospects bought any cards. Adding a favorable label to the deal ("They're $3. It's a bargain"), didn't help the salespeople at all, as once again only 35% of the prospects bought cards. However, wording designed to confuse and disrupt customers' initial representation of the event and then quickly to reframe the event in favorable terms ("These cards sell for 300 pennies . . . that's $3. It's a bargain"), pushed the success rate to 65% (Davis & Knowles, 1999). Apparently, saying something unexpected ("These cards sell for 300 pennies") temporarily disrupted customers' typical, resistance-laden thinking about door-to-door sales, which allowed the salespeople to strike swiftly and reframe the exchange as a bargain. Perhaps the most instructive point in all this is that, besides human tendencies to say yes to social pressure, there are equally

disrupt-then-reframe technique
A tactic that operates to increase compliance by disrupting one's initial, resistance-laden view of a request and quickly reframing the request in more favorable terms.

important tendencies to say no. To fully understand the social influence process, we must consider processes that affect each type.

Various tendencies to resist social influence exist to some degree in most people. For example, according to **reactance theory** (Brehm, 1966; Brehm & Brehm, 1981), we all value our freedom to decide how to act. When something (such as social pressure) threatens to take away that freedom, we often respond by doing the opposite of what we are being pressured to do. For instance, one study found that drivers who returned to their parked cars were slower at leaving their parking spaces if another driver was waiting to take the space. In addition, they moved even more slowly if the waiting driver honked to pressure them to leave faster (Ruback & Jwieng, 1997).

Of course, some people respond against threats to their freedoms more strongly than do others (Nail & VanLeeuvan, 1993; Nail, McDonald, & Levy, 2000). These reactant individuals can be identified by a personality scale that includes items such as "If I am told what to do, I often do the opposite" (Bushman & Stack, 1996; Dowd, Milne, & Wise, 1991). Studies have found that highly reactant individuals are more likely to defy the advice of even their therapists and physicians (Dowd et al., 1988; Graybar, Antonuccio, Boutilier, & Varble, 1989).

reactance theory

Brehm's theory that we react against threats to our freedoms by reasserting those freedoms, often by doing the opposite of what we are being pressured to do.

🔲 What Situational Factors Affect the Impact of Social Approval?

Others' Appeal   Which features of a person's social situation are likely to alter the motivation to go along to get along? One factor is the appeal of the group or individual pressuring for change. For example, if you found yourself among people you didn't much care for, you would be unlikely to try to dress like them, comply with their requests, or obey their directives. In contrast, you would be much more receptive to the influence efforts of people you liked or valued (Hackman, 1992).

Would you choose a political decision maker simply because he or she was good-looking? Although you might think not, candidates' looks have a deceptively strong impact on elections (Budesheim & DePaola, 1994; Zebrowitz, 1994). For example, voters in a Canadian federal election gave physically attractive candidates several times as many votes as they gave unattractive ones—while insisting that their choices would never be influenced by something as superficial as appearance (Efran & Patterson, 1974, 1976). Looks are influential in other domains as well. Good-looking fundraisers for the American Heart Association generated nearly twice as many donations (42% versus 23%) as other requesters (Reingen & Kernan, 1993). Likewise, physically attractive salespeople are more effective at getting customers to part with their money (Reingen & Kernan, 1993).

In addition, we are more attracted to—and more influenced by—those with whom we share connections and group memberships, especially when these similarities have been made prominent (Burn, 1991; Turner, 1991). Thus, salespeople often search for (or fabricate) a connection between themselves and their customers: "Well, no kidding, you're from Minneapolis? My wife's from Minnesota!" Fundraisers do the same, with good results. In one study (Aune & Basil, 1994), donations to charity more than doubled when the requester claimed a shared group identity with the target person by saying, "I'm a student, too" (see Figure 12.6).

Public Observability   Just as we would expect, if social influence is sometimes based on the desire for acceptance and approval, conformity is less prevalent in private. When people can keep their decisions secret, they don't have to worry about the loss of connection and respect that an independent opinion might create.

FIGURE 12.6 Hat trick Influence professionals of all sorts recognize the compliance-producing power of common group membership.

Source: Drawing by Levin © 1978. The New Yorker Magazine, Inc.

Chester Insko and his colleagues (1985) demonstrated this point by presenting groups of University of North Carolina students with an ambiguous problem: judging whether a blue-green color was more blue or more green. When the students had to announce their judgments aloud and in public (rather than writing them down privately), they conformed more to what the other group members had said. Other studies have shown similar effects with judgments as trivial as evaluations of the taste of coffee and as serious as decisions about how to handle racist propaganda on campus (Blanchard, Lilly, & Vaughn, 1991; Cohen & Golden, 1972). After learning what others have said, people are especially likely to go along if their own responses are observable to the group (Campbell & Fairey, 1989).

In sum, people are more likely to go along with the influence attempts of appealing individuals because they are more motivated to gain the approval of those individuals. Two important situational sources of personal appeal are physical attractiveness and common group membership. Because the increased yielding comes from a desire to get along with these others, their influence is most pronounced when they can see whether yielding occurred.

Who's Strong Enough to Resist Strong Group Norms?

Norms don't always steer people in beneficial directions. What the people in one's group typically do and approve can be unhealthy. For example, among certain subgroups of young people, peer norms may support such dangers as alcohol and tobacco use. When these potentially harmful norms are strong, is there any psychological factor that will help resist them? Alan Stacy and his coworkers (1992) investigated several possible factors that might reduce high school students' vulnerability to peer norms for cigarette smoking. Only one proved effective: the students' belief that they possessed the ability to resist their peers' influence. A student who held this belief was significantly more likely to withstand even strong group norms—for example, when most of the student's small group of friends smoked and approved of smoking. Other research has found similar results among students in every ethnic group examined: white, black, Hispanic, and Asian (Sussman, Dent, Flay, Hansen, & Johnson, 1986). Thus, even strong group norms don't sway everyone.

These findings may offer a way to reduce negative social influence in schools. If the belief in one's own capacity to resist peer pressure can protect a person from such pressure, instilling this belief in schoolchildren should safeguard them from dangerous peer norms, right? Right, but research suggests that the way in which this belief is instilled is crucial to the success of the strategy, as the Focus on Application feature shows.

A second factor interacts with norms to affect their impact on group members' behavior: the degree to which the member identifies with the group. Chances are, if you are reading this book, you are a college student. But not everyone who is taking

Doing Wrong by Trying to Do Right

In many schools, it has become common to give students resistance training intended to equip them with the skills necessary to reject the influence efforts of peers who try to tempt them into unhealthy habits. The resistance-skills education often takes the form of "just say no" training, in which students repeatedly practice how to deflect the negative influence of classmates. These resistance-skills-only programs have produced an entirely unexpected result: Despite coming to see themselves as more able to resist peer influence, the students in the programs often become more likely to engage in the unhealthy habits!

How could this be? A study done in the Los Angeles and San Diego County public school systems offers an answer. It examined the impact of junior high school programs for limiting adolescent alcohol use. After participating in multiple "just say no" skits and exercises intended to bolster their resistance to peer pressure to drink, students came to believe that drinking was more common among their peers than they had previously thought (Donaldson, Graham, Piccinin, & Hansen, 1995). By giving students resistance skills through repeated "just say no" trials, the program inadvertently conveyed an unintended message "A lot of your peers do this and want you to do this." Thus, although these students became more able to resist peer influence, they became less motivated to do so because they perceived that drinking was the norm for people their age.

Alcohol reduction programs are not the only ones that have backfired in this way. After participating in an eating disorder program at Stanford University, college women exhibited more eating disorder symptoms than before. Why? A key feature of the program was the testimony of classmates about their own harmful eating behaviors, which made such behaviors seem more prevalent to participants (Mann et al., 1997). Similarly, a suicide prevention program administered to New Jersey teenagers informed participants of the alarmingly high number of teenage suicides. As a consequence, participants became more likely to see suicide as a possible solution to their problems (Shaffer, Garland, Vieland, Underwood, & Busner, 1991).

In all, there seems to be an understandable but misguided tendency of health educators to call attention to a problem by depicting it as regrettably frequent. It is easy to forget that the statement "Look at all the people like you who are doing this *unhealthy* thing" contains the powerful and potentially undercutting message "Look at all the people like you who *are* doing it" (see Figure 12.7).

What can program designers do to avoid these boomerang effects? Health educators must structure their programs so participants see the unwanted behavior as the exception rather than the rule. That way, the power of norms will work for the program rather than against it. Indeed, when resistance-skills training is included as part of a program that shows participants that healthy behavior is the norm, the resistance-skills training no longer reduces program effectiveness but instead enhances it (Donaldson et al., 1995). Under these circumstances, young people acquire both the ability to resist a peer's unhealthy influence and the desire to do so, because they recognize that *most* of their peers prefer the healthier route. As a result, the program is more likely to be successful.

Gross National Product.

This year Americans will produce more litter and pollution than ever before.

If you don't do something about it, who will?

Give A Hoot. Don't Pollute.

Figure 12.7 Message pollution
In an attempt to dramatize the problem of littering, the developers of this public service announcement have contaminated their message with a potentially harmful countermessage: "Littering is what we Americans do."

college classes identifies him- or herself primarily in that way. If asked "Who are you?" many college students would describe themselves first in terms of religious, family, or ethnic group memberships. For these individuals, college student norms may not be especially influential because they don't identify strongly with the group, even though they are members of it.

Deborah Terry and Michael Hogg (1996) found good support for this idea in a study of Australian university students. The researchers measured subjects' views of the strength of the student norm on campus for regular exercise by asking them to estimate the amount of approval for regular exercise among their peers at the university. The students also indicated how much they identified themselves with their university peer group. When asked about their own intentions to exercise regularly during the upcoming weeks, only those individuals who identified themselves strongly as university students planned to follow the norms of the group. Those who held little identification with the group didn't let the approval of other group members affect their exercise plans at all. In sum, even strong group norms won't guide the behavior of members of the group who don't identify themselves psychologically as group members.

Being Consistent with Commitments

Restaurant owners typically face a big problem with callers who make reservations but fail to appear. Tables that could have been filled by paying customers stand empty, causing substantial economic loss. However, Gordon Sinclair, who was the proprietor of Gordon's restaurant in Chicago, hit on a highly effective tactic. He instructed his receptionists to stop saying, "Please call us if you change your plans," and to start asking, "Will you call us if you change your plans?" and to wait for a response. As a result, his no-show rate dropped from 30% to 10% (Grimes, 1997).

What is it about this subtle shift that leads to such a dramatic difference? The receptionist specifically asks for and waits for the customer's affirmative response. By inducing customers to make a personal commitment to a behavior, this approach increases the chance that they will perform the behavior.

A **personal commitment** ties an individual's identity to a position or course of action, making it more likely that he or she will follow through. This is so because most individuals prefer to be consistent and have a strong desire to see themselves as the kind of person who lives up to promises and commitments (Baumeister, Stillwell, & Heatherton, 1994; Kerr, Garst, Lewandowski, & Harris, 1997). Indeed, students at Boston University behaved almost as consistently with a commitment they made to a computer as to another person (Kiesler, Sproull, & Watters, 1996). As a consequence, even seemingly insignificant commitments can lead to large behavior changes. For instance, getting people to answer a five-question survey about organ donation increases their willingness to become organ donors (Carducci, Deuser, Bauer, Large, & Ramaekers, 1989).

personal commitment
Anything that connects an individual's identity more closely to a position or course of action.

Men, Women, and Public Conformity

Because public commitments have the ability to change not just social image but also self-image, people may try to protect their self-concepts by being careful about when they publicly admit that they have been influenced. But which aspects of self-concept people choose to protect in this way can differ for men and women.

The Deutsch and Gerard (1955) experiment demonstrated that, in the face of conformity pressures, people are more loyal to their public decisions than to their private decisions. However, one study showed that men may be especially reluctant to conform under public conditions (Eagly, Wood, & Fishbaugh, 1981). In that study, male and female participants conformed to the group opinion to about the same extent when their responses were privately made, but males conformed less than females to the group opinion when they had to do so in public.

Why would men resist public conformity more than women? The researchers suggest that the males' nonconformity may have represented conformity at a higher level—with an image of independence that is socialized into the identity of most men (Eagly, 1987). Men prefer to see themselves as independent, unique, and self-sufficient. Election surveys over the last 40 years have found that men are even more likely than women to announce their political category as Independent (Norrander, 1997). A man who expresses nonconformity communicates a picture of himself as self-reliant, as a leader rather than a follower. To whom is he communicating this picture? It appears that he is sending the message as much to himself as to others. One series of studies found that men base self-esteem on factors that make them unique and independent, whereas women are more likely to base self-esteem on factors that connect them to members of their groups (Josephs, Markus, & Tarafodi, 1992). Thus, because of the potent impact of public pronouncements on private image, men may resist public conformity in an effort to stay true to a view of themselves as possessing independence.

Roy Baumeister and Kristin Sommer (1997) have suggested a further twist to the plot: men's public nonconformity might be motivated not by a desire to be independent of the group but by a desire to belong. They contend that men want to be accepted by their groups as much as women do; however, women seek acceptance from close cooperative relationships, whereas men aim to be accepted by demonstrating a unique ability or by showing the potential for leadership. After all, a leader is importantly interconnected with group members. In all, it appears that women and men don't differ much in their basic social influence goals—for example, to be accepted and to validate their self-images—but that they do differ in the routes they take to reach those goals.

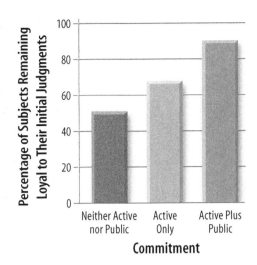

FIGURE 12.8 **The staying power of different types of commitments** Individuals who made active and public commitments to an initial set of judgments were most likely to stay loyal to those judgments when they were later attacked. Those who made neither active nor public commitments were least loyal.

Source: Adapted from Deutsch & Gerard, 1955.

Summary

1. Social influence is defined as a change in behavior caused by real or imagined pressure from others. It is different from persuasion in that it refers to shifts in overt actions rather than in private attitudes and beliefs.

Categories of Social Influence: Conformity, Compliance, and Obedience

1. Social psychologists have investigated three major types of social influence: conformity, compliance, and obedience.
2. Conformity refers to behavior change designed to match the actions of others.
3. Compliance refers to behavior change that occurs as a result of a direct request.
4. Obedience is a special type of compliance that occurs as a result of a directive from an authority figure.

Choosing Correctly

1. People often rely on two powerful psychological principles to help them choose correctly: authority and social validation. Thus, they are more willing to be influenced by authority figures, on the one hand, and similar peers on the other.
2. One reason authorities are influential is that they are often expert, and, by following an authority's directives, people can usually choose correctly without having to think hard about the issue themselves.

3. Just as following an authority is normally a shortcut to choosing correctly, so is following the lead of most of one's peers. The choices of these others provide social validation for the correctness of that choice.

4. People are most likely to allow themselves to be influenced by others when they are uncertain about how to respond in the situation—because when uncertainty and ambiguity reign, people lose confidence in their own ability to choose well.

5. When others share a consensus about the correct way to act, they are especially influential to observers.

6. In addition, observers are more likely to be influenced by others who are similar to them and who, therefore, provide better evidence about what the observers should do.

7. When choosing accurately is important, only uncertain individuals are more likely to follow the crowd; those who are already sure of the validity of their judgments are less willing to conform.

Gaining Social Approval

1. Frequently, people change in order to be more accepted and approved by their groups and to avoid the social rejection that often comes from resisting group pressure for change.

2. Injunctive norms of a group or culture inform people as to the behaviors that are likely to get them accepted or rejected there.

3. One such norm is that of reciprocity, which obligates people to give back to those who have given first. Anyone who violates this norm risks social disapproval and rejection, which makes people more willing to comply with requests of those who have provided an initial favor or concession.

4. The desire for social approval and a collective self-definition both increase one's willingness to submit to social influence in order to gain acceptance. But a tendency for reactance decreases one's susceptibility to social influence, especially when the influence is seen as threatening one's freedom to decide.

5. Two features of a person's social situation increase the motivation to go along to get along: the appeal of the group or individual pressing for change and the public observability of the person's actions.

6. Even strong group norms can be resisted when members feel that they have the ability to withstand group influence or when members don't feel highly identified with the group.

Questions for review:

1. For what reasons did the individuals in Solomon Asch's experiment knowingly give the incorrect answer when asked in a group setting?

2. What factors led the participants in Milgram's study to exhibit actions contrary to their normal behavior?

3. Is *captainitis* all about the captain? How can leaders promote an atmosphere where *captainitis* is unlikely to be observed?

13 *Group Dynamics*

Learning Objectives:

- Classify the stages of group development.
- Explain how the following factors affect group performance:
  - Presence of others (social facilitation and social inhibition)
  - Group size (social loafing)
  - Group diversity (homogeneous and heterogeneous)
  - Roles (role conflict and role ambiguity)
  - Status (status incongruence)
  - Norms (written and unwritten)
  - Cohesiveness (6 factors that induce and sustain group cohesiveness)

Reprinted from Vecchio, R. (2003). *Organizational Behavior: Core Concepts* (fifth ed.). South-Western College Publishing.

Group Dynamics

If your school experience has been like most you have probably fallen victim to the group project gone bad. Oftentimes we would rather just get the task done ourselves so that we know it is done right. Or perhaps you just cannot get along with the folks you have been teamed up with. Maybe you like the team members, they are even your friends, but it seems there are just too many people trying to accomplish one small task.

In the Navy and Marine Corps "group projects" are what we do. We put folks from every corner of the country into a unit and task them with accomplishing the mission. As officer candidates it is time to start recognizing your role as the leader of these groups. Soon it will be your responsibility to recognize the naturally occurring dynamics that exist in a group setting and utilize them to effectively accomplish the mission. From designing company bulletin boards to Saturday morning training to Sea Trials in May, much of the Plebe training program forces you into a team setting to accomplish a task. This next module in your *Preparing to Lead* course will help you to learn more about how team players interact and work together. As you work through the learning objectives ask yourself where you have seen this theory in real life. Then make the leap to start thinking about how you can use this theory to better your group during future evolutions.

The Nature of Groups

People are social animals—they seek the company of others both to satisfy social needs and to pool resources for improved effectiveness. Hence, people participate in groups. We can define a **group** as two or more people who interact with each other, share

---

*Note that our definition of a group also includes "virtual groups" wherein members may never actually meet face to face but only interact via technology (for example, videoconferencing, Internet chat rooms, e-mail, wireless communication, etc.). It is widely believed that the frequency of virtual groups will increase until all individuals can reasonably expect to participate in one at some point during their worklife.

certain common beliefs, and view themselves as being members of a group. At a minimum, to be considered a group, at least two people must deal with one another on a continuing basis. Before they interact with each other, they are likely to share common beliefs that impel them to band together. Over time, other shared values may emerge and be solidified. As a consequence of continuing interaction and awareness of shared beliefs, the individuals will come to see themselves as belonging to a distinct entity—the group.*

How much of your professional military career do you suppose will be accomplished either in a group or leading a group?

Formal Versus Informal Groups

In organizations, people are frequently assigned to work groups. These teams, which are essentially task-oriented, are classified as **formal groups.** For example, employees are typically assigned to departments or work crews. A committee is another example of a formal group. It can be said that every organizational member must belong to at least one formal organizational group—that is, every employee must have at least one formal role. Some organizational members may hold two or more formal group memberships (for example, by being on several committees). Such multiple members can serve as "linking pins" within the organization who can enhance integration by sharing information across groups and passing on directives to lower levels.

Informal groups arise from social interaction among organizational members. Membership in such groups is voluntary and more heavily based on interpersonal attraction. Sometimes the activities or goals of an informal group are attractive to prospective members. For example, department softball and bowling teams are informal groups whose activities attract interested individuals. Not all informal groups, however, have a specific set of activities. Often, they are simply comprised of co-workers who share common concerns. For example, a department head may informally meet with other managers to share information (or rumors) about an impending merger.

Informal groups are not inherently good or bad for an organization. When the informal group's goals are congruent with the organization's—such as when both seek to maximize customer satisfaction and produce a high-quality product—then all is well and good. In other instances, however, an informal group may oppose the organization's goals, as when employees decide to restrict daily output. In fact, informal groups are often sources of resistance to organizational change. They sometimes oppose approaches to job redesign and organizational restructuring. Because of the status and personal satisfaction they derive from their affiliation, members of informal groups can be counted on to resist attempts to disrupt or disband their social arrangement.

Open Versus Closed Groups

Groups in organizational settings can also be classified in terms of whether they are open or closed. An **open group** frequently changes its membership, with people constantly moving in and out of the group. In contrast, a **closed group** has a relatively stable membership. In addition, most closed groups have well-established status relationships among their members, whereas open groups tend to fluctuate on dimensions of individual power and status. Open groups are also more subject to disruption because of their changing membership and are less able to focus on long-term issues because of their relative instability. Nonetheless, open groups have certain advantages. For example, their high rate of turnover permits the infusion of "new blood," and therefore new ideas and talents. They are also more adaptable to changes in their surrounding circumstances.

Certain types of activities are better performed by each type of group. For example, for long-range planning, a closed group is likely to be more effective because it has a stronger commitment to dealing with the future. For developing new ideas or new products, an open group is likely to be more effective because of its more fluid and change-oriented atmosphere. Closed groups possess a stronger historical perspective, while open groups are more tolerant of developing and implementing new perspectives.

Reasons for Forming Groups

How might "Needs Theory" and "Maslow's Need Hierarchy" apply to reasons that people join groups or reasons why groups form?

By and large, people join groups for two reasons to accomplish a task or goal and to satisfy their social needs. These two reasons are not perfectly distinct, however, because many group activities satisfy both task and social needs. In fact, a review of the various needs that were considered in Chapter 8, such as those in Maslow's hierarchy, would reveal that, to some extent, nearly all needs can be satisfied by joining a group.

Security and Protection. Group membership can give an individual a sense of security and a real degree of protection. Being a member of a large organization can generate feelings of insecurity and anxiety, but belonging to a small group can reduce such fears by providing a sense of unity with others. During times of stress, such as when an organization is changing direction or leadership, belonging to a stable and supportive work unit can reduce individual anxieties.

By virtue of sheer numbers, groups afford a degree of protection that an individual might not otherwise enjoy. This principle is embodied in the union movement, which attempts to give members a sense of protection through highly organized collective strength.

Affiliation An individual's need for affiliation and emotional support can be directly satisfied by membership in a group. Acceptance by others is an important social need. Feeling accepted by others at work can help to enhance one's feeling of self-worth.

Esteem and Identity Groups also provide opportunities for an individual to feel important. They can give a person status and provide opportunities for praise and recognition. Many work-related achievements may not be appreciated or understood by people unfamiliar with the nature of the job. But in joining a group that does understand the job (either within organizations or through professional associations), people gain opportunities to receive recognition and esteem for their accomplishments.

Membership in a group also helps people to define who they are in the social scheme of things. Seeing oneself as a salesperson, an economist, or a teamster helps foster a feeling of identification with a larger purpose. Through membership in a work group, a person gains a formal title and a sense of purpose.

*It has been suggested that early in their history, humans recognized that group members benefited from cooperative effort. For example, members of a primitive tribe would work together in relays to wear out a game animal that the tribe would then share as a meal. No individual alone could defeat the animal, but together it was easy (and even something of a sport).

Task Accomplishment A primary reason that groups are created is to facilitate task accomplishment. A group can often accomplish more through joint effort than can an equal number of individuals working separately. In fact, many goals are attainable only through cooperative group effort. By sharing ideas, pooling resources, and providing feedback to members, a group can be an effective mechanism for attaining otherwise difficult goals.*

Stages in Group Development

Groups are not static, but change and develop over time. In the earliest stage of a group's development, members are concerned with testing each other's reaction to determine which actions are acceptable and which are unacceptable. In addition, the members depend on each other for cues about what is expected in the way of contribution and personal conduct. Problems associated with starting a group (for example, scheduling, finding a location, and obtaining resources) are also a significant part of this stage. This initial stage is called **forming.**

Might there be any positives to a "Storming" phase in group development? And if so, want might they be? Would you as a leader ever induce or encourage a little bit of artificial "Storming"? How would you do this?

The second stage, **storming,** involves intragroup conflict. Hostility and disagreement arise as the group's members wrestle with how power and status will be divided. Members may resist the formation of a group structure and ignore the desires of the group's leader.

During the third stage, **norming,** feelings of cohesiveness develop. New standards and roles are adopted, and opinions about task accomplishment are freely voiced. The members' attraction to the group is strengthened, and job satisfaction grows as the level of cohesiveness increases. Cooperation and a sense of shared responsibility are primary themes of this stage.

In the final stage, **performing,** the group has established a flexible network of relationships that aids task accomplishment. Internal hostility is at a low point as the group directs its energies toward the successful performance of valued tasks.

Of course, not every group goes through these four stages in a fixed sequence. For more formal groups, for example, in which the division of power may be less subject to debate, storming may be virtually eliminated. Also, as a group experiences change, it may return to an earlier stage. For example, if an established group receives a new leader, it may temporarily give up performing and return to storming or norming. Figure 13.1 outlines the sequence of group development.

Impact of Group Properties on Performance

▣ The Mere Presence of Others

Perhaps the most fundamental feature of groups is the presence of other people. Some interesting research has focused on the effects of the mere presence of others on an individual's task performance. In these studies, an individual is asked to perform a task without interacting with others who are present. Results of such studies indicate that having others nearby tends to facilitate performance on relatively simple and

Stages	Concerns
Forming	Testing and Dependency
Storming	Division of Power
Norming	Rule Making
Performing	Accomplishing Goals

FIGURE 13.1 Stages of Group Formation and Development

well-rehearsed tasks. However, for fairly complex tasks, the presence of others can have a detrimental effect. The positive effect of others being present is called the **social facilitation effect,** while the detrimental effect is termed the **social inhibition effect.**

You may have noticed that such effects are greatly magnified if you have ever been asked to perform in front of an audience. If your assigned task was relatively simple, such as spelling your name or reciting other well-rehearsed information, you probably had little difficulty. But if you were asked to solve a problem that you had never encountered before, you probably did poorly.* The reasons for these effects are twofold. First, when we expect others to evaluate us, we feel apprehensive (regardless of whether we are actually being judged). Second, the presence of others can increase arousal because of greater self-evaluation of performance. Such self-evaluation can aid performance of a simple task, but impair performance of a difficult task. The implications of this line of research are fairly direct. For tasks that are simple and repetitive, the presence of co-workers can have positive effects, while for complex and novel tasks, working in isolation is preferable.

🔲 Size

Group size has detectable effects on group performance. In larger groups, the potential impact and contribution of each individual are somewhat diminished, but the total resources of the group are increased. Overseeing a larger group also creates unique problems for managers.

Although most organizations settle on groups of five to seven persons to handle most problem-solving tasks, some organizations use much larger "spans of control" for simple tasks. Hard evidence about an ideal size for groups is sparse, yet several conclusions seem possible.

First, members appear to become more tolerant of authoritarian and directive leadership as group size increases. Apparently, group members recognize and concede the administrative difficulties that can arise in a larger work unit. In addition, as unit size increases, it becomes more difficult for a handful of subordinates to be influential, and members may feel inhibited about participating in group activities.

Second, larger groups are more likely to have formalized rules and set procedures for dealing with problems. Despite this greater formality, larger groups require more

*An illustration of the facilitation effect is reported by people who jog. Most joggers report feeling energized when running with another person, even though they are not truly competing with one another. Perhaps one of the more intriguing aspects of the social facilitation effect has been the pervasiveness of the phenomenon across species. It appears that even ants, cockroaches, and chickens demonstrate a social facilitation effect with well-rehearsed behaviors when in the presence of other members of their species!

time to reach decisions than smaller groups. Additionally, subgroups are not committed to the full group's formal goals and prefer instead to pursue the more selfish interests of a few members.

Third, a review of research on group size suggests that job satisfaction is lower in larger groups. This probably occurs because people receive less personal attention and fewer opportunities to participate. It is also likely that employees in smaller work units feel that their presence is more crucial to the group and therefore are inclined to be more involved. For blue-collar workers, absenteeism and turnover increase in larger work units. Cohesion and communication diminish with increased group size, making a job inherently less attractive and lessening the worker's desire to attend. In white-collar jobs, on the other hand, employees may have other sources of satisfaction to draw on.

Fourth, as group size increases, productivity reaches a point of diminishing returns because of the rising difficulties of coordination and member involvement. This may be a primary reason that five-member groups are so popular. Groups of five have several advantages. The group size is not intimidating, so that a member who disagrees with the majority is less inclined to remain silent. Having an odd number of members means that a tie or split decision can be avoided when voting. Members of such a group also have less difficulty in shifting roles within the group.

An interesting problem that tends to arise in larger groups is social loafing. In a famous study of this phenomenon, Ringelmann, a German psychologist, had workers pull as hard as they could on a rope. Each subject performed this task first alone and then with others in groups of varying sizes while a meter measured the strength of each pull. Although the total amount of force tended to increase as the size of the work group increased, the amount of effort exerted by each person actually decreased. In other words, the average productivity per group member decreased as the size of the work group increased. Researchers who later replicated Ringlemann's finding have argued that such social loafing occurs because each individual feels that the needed effort will be shared by the group's members and that he or she can count on others to take up necessary slack. The social loafing phenomenon suggests that under some circumstances, a group's effort may actually be less than the expected sum of individual contributions.

Group Diversity

How well a group performs a task depends in large part on the task-relevant resources of its members. The diversity versus redundancy of members' traits and abilities, then, is an important factor in explaining group performance. Groups comprised of highly similar individuals who hold common beliefs and have much the same abilities are likely to view a task from a single perspective. Such solidarity can be productive, but it may also mean that members will lack a critical ingredient for unraveling certain kinds of problems. As we saw in our discussion of individual versus group problem solving (Chapter 2), one of a group's greatest assets in comparison to individuals acting alone is the likelihood of achieving higher-quality solutions. Carrying this logic a step further, we can reasonably expect that diversified groups tend to do better on many problem-solving tasks than do homogeneous groups of highly similar individuals.

The diverse abilities and experiences of the members of a heterogeneous group offer an advantage for generating innovative solutions, provided the skills and experiences are relevant to the task. Thus, merely adding more people to a problem-solving group to broaden the pool of skills and experience will not guarantee a better job. Attention must be paid to the relevance of the members' attributes and the mix of these attributes within the group. Additionally, the more competent members of a work group must also be the most influential members. If the people who are the least informed are the most influential group members, the quality of the decision will be diminished.

One interesting finding about group composition is that members are more socially conforming in mixed-sex groups than in same-sex groups. This suggests that members of mixed-sex groups focus more on interpersonal relations and, therefore, conform more than members of same-sex groups. Members of same-sex groups tend to be more concerned with accomplishing the task at hand.*

ⓤ Roles

Every member of a group has a differentiated set of activities to perform. The set of expected behaviors relating to an individual's position within a group is called a **role.** Although the term *role* seems familiar enough (we can each easily define the roles of schoolteachers, managers, students, and others), it can be viewed in several different ways.

A person's **expected role** is the formal role that is defined in a job description or manual. This role may be conveyed through both a written job description and the signals that other members of a work unit send as they teach newcomers how to perform their jobs. An individual's expected role, however, may differ from his or her perceived role. A **perceived role** is the set of activities that an individual believes he or she is expected to perform. The perceived role may or may not greatly overlap with the expected role that originates with other members of the organization. Finally, an **enacted role** is a person's actual conduct in his or her position. It is more likely to reflect the individual's perceived role than the expected role.

Figure 13.2 illustrates how individuals receive information about their role and adjust their behavior accordingly. The process generally begins with the standards that are held by evaluators, such as managers, supervisors, peers, and subordinates. These standards or expectations are then communicated to the individual. Because communication is often imprecise, the expected (or sent) role may not be identical to the perceived (or received) role. Furthermore, due to constraints on actual behavior, the enacted role is observed by the evaluators, who then compare it to the standards they have set. This feedback then completes a single **role episode.** If the individual's behavior does not come sufficiently close to the standards, another role episode may be initiated.

The figure also suggests that many things can go wrong in a role episode. Sometimes the evaluators do not send consistent signals. For example, your superior may assign you a task, while his or her superior, in turn, may later tell you that you should not perform that duty, perhaps because it is not your responsibility or is not included in your job description. Different groups sometimes send different signals, as when a supervisor's subordinates indicate that they would like less pressure for production, while his or her superiors simultaneously insist on higher levels of output. Differing signals from evaluating groups and individuals result in **role conflict.** On occasion, the messages that evaluators send are not clear, or they give incomplete information, which leads to **role ambiguity.** At each step in the role episode depicted in Figure 13.3, poor communication and other obstacles may interfere with the process.

---

*Although this finding suggests that managers should segregate the sexes or mix them depending on whether task accomplishment or social conformity is a major goal, it is difficult to defend any contention that espouses segregating the sexes within work settings.

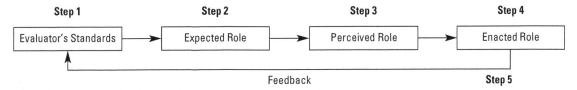

FIGURE 13.2 A Representation of a Role Episode

Although role conflict and role ambiguity seem to be undesirable, there are some indications that in modest amounts and under the right conditions, they may actually have positive effects. In fact, a work setting that is totally devoid of conflict and ambiguity can be dull and uninspiring. Thus, in order to avoid stagnation and encourage innovation, managers should perhaps seek to create a productive level of conflict and ambiguity.

There are a variety of roles that employees can assume in a work group. Although these categories do not fit into a workable model of role episodes, they do provide an insightful view of the ways in which individual group members tend to behave:

- *Task-oriented employees:* Those who can be counted on to get the job done and deliver the goods

- *People-oriented employees:* Those who are the Good Samaritans and social leaders

- *Nay-sayers:* Those who oppose most proposals, have thick skins, and find fault with nearly everything

- *Yea-sayers:* Those who counter the nay-sayers and help to circumvent the opposition

- *Regulars:* Those who are "in," accept the group's values, and are accepted by the group

- *Deviants:* Those who depart from the group's values—the mavericks

- *Isolates:* The lone wolves who depart even farther from the group than the deviants

- *Newcomers:* Those who know little and need to be taken care of by others; people who are expected to be seen but not heard

- *Old-timers:* Those who have been around a long time and know the ropes

- *Climbers:* Those who are expected to get ahead, often on the basis of potential rather than ability

- *Cosmopolitans:* Those who view themselves as members of a larger professional or cultural community

- *Locals:* Those who are firmly rooted in the organization and the local community

Status

Status is the social ranking or social worth accorded an individual because of the position he or she occupies in a group. Although we typically speak of status as a single notion, it is in fact made up of numerous factors, including salary, title, seniority, and power. However, a difference on only one of these dimensions is often sufficient to confer status. For example, a group of tool-and-die makers may all have equivalent job titles, but the oldest member of the department, due to seniority, may enjoy higher status and, as a result, greater deference. Of course, status must exist in the eyes of those who confer it. If the other tool-and-die makers in the work unit do not respect seniority, then the oldest individual will not in fact enjoy high status (even though he may feel that he deserves it).

Although status is often conferred on the basis of achievement, personal characteristics, and the ability to administer rewards, it is perhaps most frequently associated with formal authority. Symbols of status, such as titles and perquisites, are designed to communicate difference and distinction, and serve several purposes. Status symbols provide stability to the social order, which helps to reduce uncertainty about the appropriateness of conduct and role expectations. In addition, they can provide incentives for people to strive for superior performance. Finally, status symbols provide a sense of identification by giving individuals information about group membership and reminding them of the group's values.

If all attributes of a high-status individual are greater than those of low-status individuals, the high-status individual is said to be *congruent* on all dimensions of status. For example, if the highest-level executive is also the oldest, most expert, most experienced, best educated, and best paid member of that organization, then he is similar, or congruent, on all aspects of status. If, however, that executive holds the highest level on all attributes except pay (that is, if another member of the organization is highest paid but lacks equal standing on the other dimensions), the executive would experience **status incongruence.**

Status incongruence can have an unsettling effect on group relations. In progressive organizations, people are more likely to be promoted for personal achievement than for length of service. In such organizations, status incongruence can be prevalent as younger, talented managers are promoted over their more senior colleagues. A situation in which a subordinate is substantially older than his or her superiors can be uncomfortable for both an older person and a fast-track manager. As a consequence, some amount of jealousy and hostility can be expected in group situations involving status incongruence.*

Status differences may also have undue influence on group decision making. In one well-known study, bomber crews were assigned a task that could not be easily completed. After struggling with the task for some time; the men took a break during which one member of each crew (either the pilot or the tail gunner) was given a clue to the problem's solution. In crews where the clue was planted with the pilot, the suggestion was frequently adopted. But in crews where the tail gunner offered the new approach, the suggestion was adopted much more rarely. Pilots and tail gunners differ sharply on a number of status-related dimensions: pilots are older, more highly educated, hold higher military rank, have greater responsibility, and have more flying time than tail gunners. Thus, it is safe to conclude that the crew showed a bias toward favoring high-status members, rather than objectively assessing the quality of the proposal.

🔲 Norms

Norms are rules of conduct that are established to maintain the behavioral consistency of group members. They may be written (as in a code of professional ethics) or unwritten. Deviation from norms is frequently punished by ostracism and verbal

---

*In order to appreciate how uncomfortable a person can be in situations involving status incongruence, imagine taking a high-level math course that is taught by a professor who is 17 years old.

attacks. Other more formal sanctions may also be used, as when an unethical lawyer is disbarred. Work-group norms can be a powerful determinant of output.

Norms have two primary purposes (1) they give members a useful frame of reference for explaining and comprehending their group, and (2) they identify appropriate and inappropriate conduct. In addition, norms ensure that group members will focus their efforts in a common direction. This uniformity of purpose improves the group's chances of attaining its goals. J.R. Hackman has identified five major characteristics of norms:

1. They represent the structural characteristics of the group. Group norms are analogous to individual personalities in that they reveal the underlying processes that regulate behavior.
2. They apply strictly to behavior and not to private thoughts and feelings. Private acceptance of group norms is not necessary. What really matters is public compliance.
3. They are developed only for behaviors that are judged to be important by the majority of group members.
4. Although they usually develop slowly, norms can be developed rapidly if the need arises.
5. Not all norms apply to all members. High-status individuals may be exempted from certain norms, but new group members may be expected to comply closely with all norms. Often it is expected that distasteful tasks will be handled by initiates.

As is true of many social phenomena in isolation, group norms are neither good nor bad. Their value to an organization depends on whether they are directed to enhancing, rather than restricting, productivity. If norms lead a work group to produce a high-quality product or to be the best in its industry, they are highly desirable. But norms that encourage workers to reduce productivity are clearly undesirable because they undercut management's goals.

▣ Cohesiveness

Cohesiveness is the extent to which members are attracted to a group and desire to remain in it. Cohesiveness is sometimes described as the sum of all forces acting on individuals to remain in the group. As the term implies, cohesiveness pertains to how group members "stick together." Listed below are the factors that induce and sustain cohesiveness in groups, and the effects of cohesiveness on group members and the organization.

Factors That Induce and Sustain Group Cohesiveness

1. *Similarity of attitudes and goals.* As mentioned in the discussion of interpersonal attraction, when group members have similar attitudes, they find each other's company pleasurable. So, too, individual members will be attracted to a group whose goals and ambitions are similar to their own.
2. *Threats.* The presence of external threats can help to increase group cohesion in that sharing a mutual fate can lead to greater awareness of interdependence. Competition from sources outside the group can also enhance cohesiveness, whereas competition among group members will tend to decrease cohesion.
3. *Unit size.* Smaller groups tend to be more cohesive than larger groups because smaller groups offer greater opportunities for all members to inter-

act. Since diversity (and, therefore, dissimilarity of attitudes and values) tends to increase with group size, larger groups are likely to be less cohesive. In addition, in large units, the need for more rigid work rules and procedures reduces the informal nature of relations and communication among group members.

4. *Reward systems.* Cohesiveness can also be enhanced by offering rewards on a group, rather than an individual, basis. Group incentives, such as bonuses based on team performance, encourage a perception of a common goal and enhance cooperation. In contrast, reward schemes that encourage competition among group members—such as a winner-take-all bonus system for the single best performer in a unit—tend to diminish group cohesiveness.

5. *Work unit assignments.* The deliberate composition of work units based on interpersonal attraction, similarity of values, and common goals can facilitate cohesion. In a classic study, carpenters and bricklayers were assigned to teams based on a prior secret balloting of preferred workmates. The work teams that were formed on the basis of personal preferences had higher levels of job satisfaction than did the randomly assigned work units that served as a control group.

6. *Isolation.* Generally, groups that are isolated from others are more likely to be cohesive. Groups in isolation come to view themselves as unique and different. Isolation also helps to foster group members' sense of a common fate and need for defense against outside threats.

The Effects of Cohesiveness

1. *Satisfaction.* Members of highly cohesive groups are generally much more satisfied than members of less cohesive groups. This is, of course, to be expected, since the very definition of group cohesion implies a strong attraction among group members.

2. *Communication.* Communication among group members is significantly greater in highly cohesive groups than in less cohesive groups. Because members of cohesive groups are likely to share common values and goals and to find their own company satisfying, they are inclined to greater communicativeness. This communication in turn tends to foster greater personal revelation and depth of understanding, which cements positive social relations.

3. *Hostility.* Hostile and aggressive acts are more frequent in highly cohesive groups, but such hostility is usually directed toward people who are not members of the group. Cohesion apparently creates a sense of superiority among group members, which can result in hostility toward, and rejection of, outsiders.

4. *Productivity.* Some researchers have found cohesive groups to be very productive, while others have found that highly cohesive groups are not as productive as less cohesive groups. Still other researchers have reported no relationship between productivity and group cohesion. It appears that a primary determinant of the effect of cohesion on productivity is whether the group's goals are congruent with those of the organization. If the goals of a cohesive group include high performance, then high performance can be reasonably expected. Conversely, if a highly cohesive group values reduced productivity, then a relatively low level of productivity can be expected. In short, cohesive groups are

more likely to attain their goals than are less cohesive groups. In a study of over 200 small work groups in a manufacturing setting, cohesive groups were found to be less variable in their performance regardless of their absolute level of output. This occurred because cohesive groups tend to emphasize compliance with work norms. Whether its norms endorse high or low productivity, a group will probably produce within its own relatively narrow but prescribed range of output. Despite evidence of less variance for highly cohesive groups, one recent review of the relationship between cohesiveness and performance did find that, on average, highly cohesive groups outperformed less cohesive groups.

5. *Resistance to change.* Although it is less well documented, highly cohesive groups are believed to be more resistant to change than are less cohesive groups. Changes that disrupt the status quo threaten a group's networks and social supports and are, therefore, likely to be resisted. Attempts at job redesign that ignore the existing social relations among employees run a greater risk of failing.

Summary

1. **Contrast formal and informal groups and open and closed groups.** Formal groups are task-oriented groups to which people are assigned; informal groups arise from voluntary social interaction among members of the organization. Open groups frequently change their membership; closed groups have a relatively stable membership.

2. **List some reasons people form groups.** People join groups for security and protection, for affiliation and emotional support, for esteem and a sense of identity, and to accomplish tasks.

3. **Describe influences on the degree to which group members are attracted to one another.** The less the distance between people, the greater their interpersonal attraction. Distance can be either physical or psychological. People with similar attitudes or complementary needs and abilities feel greater attraction.

4. **Describe stages of work-group formation and development.** A popular view is that groups pass through four stages as they develop: (1) forming, during which group members look to each other for clues about what actions are acceptable and expected; (2) storming, a stage of intragroup conflict during which power and status are allocated; (3) norming, the development of feelings of cohesiveness; and (4) performing, the accomplishment of valued tasks.

5. **List some important group properties that affect performance.** Performance is affected by the mere presence of others, the size and composition of the group, the roles and status of group members, the norms of the group, and the degree of cohesiveness of the group.

6. **List factors that induce and sustain cohesiveness in a work group.** These factors include similarity of attitudes and goals, the presence of external threats, small group size, reward systems based on group performance, work unit assignments based on personal preferences, and isolation from other groups.

Group Assessment

This worksheet is designed to help you understand the Group Dynamics presented in this chapter. Answer these questions based on the group exercise that was done in class.

1. Did your group go through all *four stages of group development* throughout this exercise? Please list, define, and elaborate on each stage._____

_____

_____

_____

_____

2. How did tackling this task as a group facilitate or hinder its completion? Would it have been easier to do it alone? When does the presence of others provide a *social facilitation effect* as opposed to a *social inhibition effect*? _____

_____

_____

_____

_____

3. Did *social loafing* emerge? What factors may have contributed to this phenomenon? Consider whether or not your *group's size* had an impact on this. Is there an optimum number of participants for your project?

_____

_____

_____

_____

_____

4. Did you observe any of the roles identified on page 145? Did you observe *role conflict* and/or *role ambiguity* within your groups? What is the difference between these two dilemmas and what is their cause?

_____

_____

_____

_____

_____

5. Was any kind of pecking order or *status* established, implicitly or explicitly, within the group? Did anyone experience *status incongruence* as the task progressed? What causes status incongruence? _____

_____

_____

_____

_____

_____

6. Did the incentive proposed for this exercise spark *cohesiveness* within the group? Why or why not? If not, what factors did affect group cohesion?_____

_____

_____

_____

_____

14 *Brigade Leader Seminar: Peer Leadership*

⊘ Describe the personal attributes required for a successful peer leader.

⊘ Identify and apply stratagies to solve the problem of a friend that challenges your authority in a peer leadership situation.

Leading Friends

by Colonel Arthur J. Athens, USMCR (Retired)
Director, VADM Stockdale Center for Ethical Leadership
United States Naval Academy

So what does it take to lead friends, particularly in an Academy or ROTC setting? Should we love them, direct them, or ignore them? Every midshipman and cadet who has been placed in a leadership position and required to lead friends has struggled with this question. These young leaders wonder whether the basic tenets of leadership apply in this setting or whether there is a different set of personal attributes and strategies required for leading friends.

The theme of this essay is that leading friends in an Academy or ROTC setting requires personal character traits and strategies common to other more traditional leadership situations, but adapted and emphasized for the unique dynamics associated with friend leadership. I will address: (1) a definition of friend leadership, (2) the unique characteristics of friend leadership, (3) the personal attributes required for successful friend leadership, (4) the strategies required for successful friend leadership, and (5) the way ahead to study and address this issue.

A Definition of Friend Leadership

Friend leadership occurs when a peer, within a predominantly homogeneous group, is selected by someone outside the group to oversee, guide, and care for his group and accomplish objectives that are imposed externally, as well as developed internally. This homogeneous group is similar in age, experience, and expertise. Typically, the group has been together for an extended period of time and interacted as peers, without any senior-subordinate relationship. The peer who has been raised to a leadership position also has a number of close personal relationships with individuals within the group. Friend leadership is a distinct subset of peer leadership, differentiated by the group's homogeneity and intimate social ties. When a West Point cadet becomes a Platoon Commander, when an Air Force Academy cadet becomes the Wing Commander, when a Naval ROTC midshipman becomes a Battalion Commander, these individuals will, by definition, be leading friends.

The Unique Characteristics of Friend Leadership

Friend leadership has a unique set of characteristics that cause this type of leadership to be particularly demanding. Though some of these attributes can be found in more traditional leadership settings, they have a tendency to dominate in friend leadership. These characteristics are:

How do external and internal values conflicts play out in friend leadership?

- The friend leader is trying to find the balance between leading and maintaining friendships.
- The friend leader typically has limited leadership experience at the level to which appointed. This results in a crisis of confidence.
- The leader is experiencing loyalty tensions—the tension among loyalty to the organization, loyalty to the group, loyalty to individuals, and loyalty to himself.
- The friend leader has limited authority to punish or reward his subordinates.
- Some members of the group feel jealousy towards the appointed friend leader.
- Some members of the group question the selection process that elevated the peer to a leadership position.
- Conflict resolution between the friend leader and group members is particularly challenging.

Because of these unique attributes, friend leaders need to develop and demonstrate certain personal attributes and implement specific strategies to become successful. These attributes and strategies are outlined in the following sections.

The Personal Attributes Required for Successful Friend Leadership

The attributes presented are not unique to friend leadership, but take on an added importance when leading friends.

Humility: A humble friend leader has a much greater chance of connecting with his group and achieving mission and interpersonal success. Humility tends to diffuse conflict, make the leader approachable, and portray a picture of a peer who is more interested in the group and organization than personal glory or achievement. The description of Level 5 leaders in Jim Collins' book, *Good to Great,* captures the essence of this attribute. Collins describes Level 5 leaders, the ones who successfully transformed their organizations from mediocrity to sustained success, as those characterized by "professional humility and professional will." Collins observes that these leaders "channel their ego needs away from themselves and into the larger goal of building a great company."

The friend leader needs to credit his group for successes and take responsibility for group failures. Assuming responsibility for failure goes a long way in gaining the respect and loyalty of the group. The friend leader also needs to communicate by words and actions that he is not enamored with the trappings associated with the leadership position—whether those trappings are visible rank or special perks.

Moral Courage: A friend leader must be a man or woman of integrity. A breach in this area, even with a seemingly minor compromise, will cause irreparable damage. This moral courage must translate into a willingness to always place others' needs before the leader's own comfort, prestige, or advancement. This moral courage needs to be consistent both downwards and upwards. For example, the friend leader must be equally faithful in confronting his superiors on behalf of the group, relaying an unpopular order or policy from his superior without criticism or complaint, or choosing a particularly close friend for an important job because that friend is best qualified. This takes moral courage and a willingness to "take the heat," either from those above or those below. Ultimately, the friend leader needs to be willing to risk temporary social rejection to retain an unblemished character.

Professionalism and Competency: The friend leader needs to set a professional example in appearance, speech, priorities, and actions. The leader must do this without becoming a "brown nose," "butt shark," or "joe." The motivation for professionalism should not be for show or to impress one's superiors, but instead for the good of the unit. Friends will quickly pick up duplicity or hypocrisy and reject a friend leader who has been "co-opted" by the establishment. Coupled with professionalism must be competency. The friend leader needs to demonstrate the ability to plan, decide, and act. If an important competency is lacking, the friend leader must take the initiative to address the deficiency.

Why is competency important in peer leadership? Think back to where an authority figure's power comes from.

Realistic Mindset: The friend leader must remain cognizant that he must lead by nurturing, supporting, listening, helping, and serving. The friend leader is in a position of authority, but must be ever aware of his roots and the temporary nature of his position. Warren Bennis' image of herding cats is apropos for friend leaders. Bennis, in *Managing People is Like Herding Cats,* writes:

> Cats, of course, won't allow themselves to be herded. They may, however, be coaxed, cajoled, persuaded, adored, and gently led . . . Be humble. Stop trying to "herd cats" and start building trust and mutual respect. Your "cats" will respond. They will sense your purpose, keep your business purring, and even kill your rats.

Friend leaders must be mindful that their role is to build trust, not herd cats.

The Strategies Required for Successful Friend Leadership

Friend leaders must not only demonstrate certain attributes, they must be armed with strategies that can facilitate their work. Like the attributes, these strategies are important in most leadership situations, but they are critical when leading friends.

Develop a compelling vision: People are hungry to become part of a movement larger than themselves. If the friend leader can develop a simple and compelling vision for the group, combined with a few achievable goals, he can gain buy-in from the group on the authority of the mission itself. The leader can continue to return to this vision to unify the group, generate excitement, and address deviations. Max DePree in *Leading Without Power* captures this thought when addressing leadership of volunteers:

Leadership among volunteers is rather dependent in beautiful ways on shared values and commitment, on understood visions expressed in workable mission statements, and on moral purpose.

Similar comments could be made about the unity found in many athletic teams where the team's goal supplants the individual goals of the athletes.

The vision and goals should be developed with the full participation of the group, though the friend leader will ultimately need to narrow down the possibilities and articulate the direction.

Communicate: A friend leader must constantly communicate with his group. This communication must be less directive and more participative. The friend leader should spend time with people one-on-one and meet with sub-groups. For the friend leader, listening is much more important than talking. The group members want to know that the friend leader has a genuine interest in their lives, hears and understands their problems, and is willing to take action to address these problems. This will only occur through active listening.

Win over the group's informal leaders: There are always members of the group who do not hold an official position, but hold significant sway over others. The friend leader must be aware of these informal leaders, develop rapport with them and creatively win them to his side. The objective is to continue to develop a "critical mass of influence," where the peer pressure presses in a direction that supports the friend leader. Informal leaders are instrumental in achieving this critical mass.

Confront swiftly and with a consistent approach: When a member of the group is out-of-line, the friend leader cannot afford to look the other way. Ignoring a challenge to authority will undermine the leader and permit a rebellious cancer to spread. A method that works in the friend environment is the "4 step confrontation ladder." First, the friend leader approaches the offender one-on-one. The friend leader, in an informal setting, gently, but firmly explains the behavioral or attitudinal problem and asks the individual's support to correct the deficiency. Often, the offender will not realize the offense is a problem and correct it without any further mention. If the behavior or attitude continues, the friend leader should then enlist another member of the group who is well respected to go with him or her to confront the offender. The additional person helps the offender realize that this is not just a conflict between him and the friend leader; the offender now sees that others disapprove of his behavior or attitude. If this method does not work, the friend leader should return with his partner, sit down with the offender in a more formal setting and explain the specific consequences of a failure to conform. The last step is to use formal punishment. Often friend leaders are hesitant to use any type of formal punishment, even when it is warranted. The ladder, however, allows the friend leader to ratchet up the pressure on the group member in a logical and fair manner.

In addition to these four primary strategies, there are a number of other tactical actions that can assist the friend leader in his day-to-day leadership responsibilities:

@ Recognize accomplishments in both public and private forums. Making the effort to arrange for a more senior individual to say words of congratulations to your group or present awards has a powerful effect.

@ Say thank you to group members. A hand-written note, even to someone you see every day, makes a positive impression.

"Handling problems at the lowest level" is easy to say, but is it easy to do? What does it require of you as a leader?

- Solve a friend's problem.
- Use the unique talents of your friends—give them responsibility and authority.
- Organize team building events like ultimate frisbee games, bowling tournaments, or golf outings.
- Celebrate birthdays and special events as a group.
- Attend events where a member of the group participates. Your presence says a lot and means a lot.

Coupling humility, moral courage, professional competence, and level-headedness with specific strategies and tactics, gives the friend leader a fighting chance to not only survive, but thrive in his position.

The Way Ahead

This essay is only an initial thought piece on friend leadership. The ideas presented are based on years of personal experience and observation. The next step is to develop a sound theoretical foundation derived from experimentation and field study. We should ask questions like:

- What is the relationship between successful friend leadership and personality type?
- What is the relationship between successful friend leadership and emotional intelligence?
- How do various management and leadership theories, such as power-influence, expectancy, and equity, apply to friend leadership?
- Are there other attributes and strategies that facilitate success in the friend leadership environment?
- How can a friend leader's superior best support the friend leader in the execution of his duties?
- How can a friend leader best support his friends in the execution of their duties?
- What is the relationship between successful friend leadership and successful leadership in other settings?
- Is there an optimal methodology to select and prepare friend leaders?

The study of friend leadership is a worthwhile endeavor. It is a dimension of leadership that requires more discussion and debate. Our midshipman and cadet leaders have the potential to influence their peers profoundly and increase the professional excellence of our Brigade, Corp, Wing, Regiments, Squadrons and Battalions; and by extrapolation, our operational units. These midshipman and cadet leaders need and deserve some principles and techniques to help them execute their responsibilities.

Additionally, friend leadership doesn't cease when we trade our academy and college brass for Ensign boards and 2nd Lieutenant bars. As a very junior Marine Corps 1st Lieutenant, my Battalion Commander selected me to command a Firing

Battery where a friend of mine, with the same date of rank and career progression, became my Executive Officer. We were friends, but he felt strongly that he should have been the new Battery Commander Officer. The personal attributes that had been honed at the Naval Academy and the strategies I practiced while Brigade Commander provided the tools I needed to make the Battery a success and retain my XO's friendship.

Friend leadership doesn't start and stop with the military either—just ask the Rotary Club President, the Chairman of the Deacon Board, the coordinator for the American Heart Association event, or the captain of the high school football team. Friend leaders have a significant challenge, but also a significant opportunity. We can successfully lead our friends, but only if our attitude is right and our strategies are sound. With those two foundational elements in place, we will find our friends not only following, but following enthusiastically and energetically.

Note: For ease of reading and continuity, he, his, and him have been used throughout the article, but all concepts presented apply equally to men and women.

• • •

Questions for review:

1. Why is critical thinking vital to peer leadership?
2. How can you use your individual talents to improve yourself in the attributes required for a successful peer leader?

15 *Ownership*

- Identify and describe the three most significant problems with the "Damn Exec" approach to leadership.
- Demonstrate ownership in a given leadership scenario.

Damn Exec[1]

The Norfolk wind was streaking the water of Hampton Roads as Commander Martin K. Speaks, U.S. Navy, Commanding Officer of the USS Bowens (DD-891), stepped from his car, slammed the door, and straightened his cap. As he approached the pier head, a Sailor stepped from the sentry hut and saluted.

"Good morning, Captain."

"Good morning, Kowalski," answered Commander Speaks. He took pleasure in the fact that he knew the Sailor's name. Kowalski was a good Sailor. He had served his entire first cruise in the *Bowens* and did his work well.

The Captain noticed that, over his blues, Kowalski wore a deck force foul weather jacket, faded, frayed, dirty, and spotted with red lead. "Little chilly this morning," said the Captain as he walked by. "Yes sir, sure is," replied the Sailor with his usual grin.

As the Captain approached his quarterdeck, there was the usual scurrying of people, and four gongs sounded. "Bowens arriving," spoke the loudspeaker system, and Lieutenant (j.g.) Henry Graven, U.S. Naval Reserve, gunnery officer and the day's command duty officer, came running to the quarterdeck. Salutes and cheerful "Good mornings" were exchanged, and the Captain continued to his cabin.

Lieutenant Graven looked over the quarterdeck and frowned. "Let's get this brightwork polished, chief."

"It's already been done once this morning, sir," replied the OD.

"Well, better do it again. The Exec will have a fit if he sees it this way," said Graven.

"Yes sir," answered the OD.

As soon as Graven had left, the OD turned to his messenger, "Go tell the duty boatswain's mate that Mr. Graven wants the brightwork done over again on the quarterdeck."

Later that morning, Captain Speaks was going over some charts with the ship's executive officer, Lieutenant Commander Steven A. Lassiter, U.S. Navy. The Captain had just finished his coffee and lighted a cigarette. "Steve, I noticed our pier sentry in an odd outfit this morning. He had a foul weather jacket on over his blues; it looked pretty bad."

"Yes sir. Well, it gets cold out there, and these deck force boys have mighty bad-looking jackets," the Exec said.

[1] Landersman, S. D. (1965). Damn Exec. *Proceedings of the U.S. Naval Institute.*

The Captain felt the Exec had missed his point and said, "Oh, I realize they have to wear a jacket, but for a military watch like that, I'd like to see them wear pea coats when it's cold."

Lieutenant Graven was talking with a third-class boatswain's mate on the fantail when the quarterdeck messenger found him. When told that the executive officer wanted to see him, Graven ended his discussion with, "There, hear that? He probably wants to see me about the brightwork. I don't care how many men it takes to do it, the Exec told me to be sure to get that brightwork polished every morning."

The executive officer indicated a chair to Graven and asked: "How's it going these days?"

Lassiter had always liked Graven, but in the past few months, since he had taken over as senior watch officer, Graven seemed to have more problems than usual.

"Okay, I guess," Graven replied with a forced grin. He knew that things were not as they used to be. It seemed strange, too, because everyone on the ship had been so glad to be rid of the previous senior watch officer, that "damn" Lieutenant Dumphy. The junior officers even had a special little beer bust at the club to celebrate Dumphy's leaving and Graven's "fleeting up" to senior watch officer. Now the Exec was always after him. The junior officers didn't help much either, always complaining about the Exec. Maybe the Exec was taking over as "the heel" now that Dumphy was gone.

"That's good," said the Exec. "Here's a little thing that you might look into. These men who stand pier watches have to wear a jacket, but the foul weather jacket doesn't look good for a military watch. I'd like to see them wear their pea coats when it's cold." Graven had expected something like this, more of the Exec's picking on him. He responded properly, got up, and left.

Graven told his first lieutenant. "The Exec says the pier head sentries can't wear foul weather jackets anymore. If it's cold they can wear pea coats," he added.

"But the pea coats will get dirty, and then what about personnel inspections?" asked the first lieutenant.

"I don't know," Graven shook his head, "but if the Exec wants pea coats, we give him pea coats!"

"Pea coats!" said the chief boatswain's mate, "Who says so?"

"That's what the Exec wants," said the first lieutenant, "so let's give him pea coats."

"The Exec says pea coats for the pier sentries when it's cold," announced the chief to his boatswain's mates.

A third-class boatswain's mate walked away from the group with a buddy, turned and said, "That Damn Exec. First I got to have all my men polish brightwork on the quarterdeck, now they got to wear pea coats on sentry duty 'stead of foul weather jackets!"

Seaman Kowalski's relief showed up at the sentry booth at 1150. "Roast beef today," constituted the relieving ceremony.

"Good, I like roast beef," was the reply. "Hey, how come the pea coat?"

"Damn Exec's idea," said the relief. "We can't wear foul weather gear no more out here, only pea coats."

"Damn Exec," agreed Kowalski. "Captain didn't say nothin' when he came by."

"The Captain's okay, it's just that Damn Exec. He's the guy who fouls up everything," complained the new sentry.

Seaman Kowalski had just gone aboard the ship when Captain Speaks stepped out on deck to look over his ship. The quarterdeck awning shielded the Captain from the view of those on the quarterdeck, but he could clearly hear the conversation.

"Roast beef today, Ski."

"Yeah, I know, and we wear pea coats from now on."

For what reasons does the first lieutenant tell his chief the order came from the XO?

"Whaddaya mean, pea coats?"

"Yeah, pea coats on the pier, Damn Exec says no more foul weather jackets."

"Well that ain't all, we got to polish this here brightwork 'til it shines every morning before quarters. Damn Exec says that too."

"Damn Exec."

Captain Speaks was shocked. "Why 'Damn Exec' from these seamen?" he thought. It was easy to see that the executive officer had passed the order along in proper military manner. It was easy to see that the junior officers, leading petty officers, and lower petty officers were passing it along saying "The Exec wants. . . ." That's the way orders are passed along. Why? Because "it is easy."

"All ship's officers assemble in the wardroom," the boatswain's mate announced on the loudspeaker system. Lieutenant Commander Lassiter escorted in the Captain. The junior officers took their seats when the Captain was seated. The executive officer remained standing. "Gentlemen, the Captain has a few words to say to us today."

The Captain rose and looked around slowly. "Gentlemen, we are continually exposed to words like administration, leadership, management, capabilities, organization, responsibilities, authority, discipline, and cooperation. You use these words every day. You give lectures to your men and use them, but if I were to ask each of you for a definition of any of these words I would get such a wide variety of answers that an expert couldn't tell what word we were defining. Some we probably couldn't define at all. We still use them, and will continue to use them as they are used in the continually mounting number of articles, instructions, and books we must read.

"If I were to ask any of you how can we improve leadership I would get answers filled with these words—undefined and meaningless.

"If we listed all of the nicely worded theories of leadership, studied them, memorized them, and took a test on them, we would all pass. But this would not improve our ability as leaders one bit. I can tell a story, containing none of these meaningless words, that *will* improve your leadership.

"In 1943, I was secondary battery officer in a cruiser in the South Pacific. In my second battle, gun control was hit and I lost communications with everyone except my 5-inch mounts. I could see that the after main battery turret was badly damaged and two enemy destroyers were closing us from astern. At the time my 5-inch mounts were shooting at airplanes. I ordered my two after 5-inch mounts to use high capacity ammunition and shift targets to the two destroyers closing from astern. 'But Mr. Speaks, we're supposed to handle the air targets; who said to shift targets?' my mount captain asked.

"There were noise and smoke and explosions that day, but the explosion that I heard and felt was not from a shell, but from those words of the mount captain.

"Those attacking destroyers got a few shots in at us before we beat them off. Maybe those shots found a target and some of my shipmates died. I never found out. There was too much other damage.

"I thought over the battle afterward and realized that this entire situation was my fault, not the mount captain's. I may have been responsible for the death of some of my shipmates because up to that day I always gave orders to my subordinates by attaching the originator's name to it.

"What does that mean? It means that it was the easy thing to do, to say, 'the gunnery officer wants us to shift targets.'

"In this peacetime world you may say that we no longer have this struggle on a life or death basis. Quick response does not mean life or death now, but it might tomorrow, or sometime after we've all been transferred elsewhere and this ship is being fought by people we don't know.

USS San Jacinto (CG 56) (left) takes on fuel from USNS Big Horn (T-AO 198) during replenishment at sea operations in the Central Mediterranean.

Official U.S. Navy photo.

"Whether you're cleaning boilers, standing bridge watch, or administering your training program, it's easy to say 'The Exec wants' or 'Mr. Jones says.' It's the easy, lazy way: not the right way. You can sometimes discuss or even argue with an order, but when you give it to a subordinate, make him think it is coming from you.

"Giving orders the lazy way is like a drug. Once you start saying 'The ops officer wants' you will find yourself doing it more and more until you can't get a thing done any other way. Your men will pass along orders that way, too, and it will become a part of your organization right down to the lowest level. When some problem arises and you want action, you'll get 'Who wants this?' or 'Why should we?'

"Each of you ask yourself if you have given an order today or yesterday in the lazy manner. I think almost all of us have. Now ask yourself if that order really originated

Why does the Captain feel this type of management is the "lazy way"?

with the person who gave it to you, or did he receive it from a higher level? We never really know, do we, but why should we even care?

"In almost every unit the 'lazy' ordering starts on a particular level. From personal experience I can tell you that this can be an exact measure of the unit's effectiveness. If it starts at the department head level or higher it's a relatively bad outfit, and if it starts at the chief's level it's a relatively good outfit. You can find the level below which it starts by hearing a new title preceding a primary billet. 'Damn Exec' means that the executive officer is the lowest level giving orders properly. 'Damn division officer' means that the division officers are taking responsibility for the order.

"Here I am using some of those words, responsibility and authority, those undefined terms we want to avoid, but perhaps we have helped define them.

"To be more specific, every officer does some 'lazy' ordering, but we need to do it less and less. We must try to push the 'damn' title down as far as it will go.

"Let's push the 'damn officer' down all the way to the chiefs and below, then we will have a Damn Good Ship."

Ownership

LT Allen Murphy, USN

"Damn Exec" is one of those military parables like the often retold "Message to Garcia" that possesses a great moral for midshipmen and junior officers. The fable-like sea story stresses the importance of ownership for the military leader. Why is ownership so important?

Ownership, like many other attributes of a good leader, is not always easy. Passing down a difficult task or an unpopular order will not help to make any friends among one's subordinates. This is significantly compounded when an individual does not agree with the decision that he or she is passing down. Officers, however, are not in the business of making friends but are instead in the business of supporting the chain of command and enhancing the readiness of their unit at the lowest level. It is easy to "damn" the XO or the Company Officer and pass blame up the chain of command but in time this habit may prove detrimental to one's functionality as a junior officer.

Provide examples of when midshipmen utilize the "damn exec" approach to leadership.

The three most significant problems with the "Damn Exec" approach to leadership are:

1. It demonstrates a lack of ownership or " buy-in" to the organizational goals

A wardroom or company staff must always present a united front to the command. The desires of the Commanding Officer are the desires of the command and must be promoted by every officer in the command down to the most junior Ensign or Second Lieutenant. If there is grumbling among the officers, the rest of the command will pick up on it and the dissatisfaction and morale will only worsen. Let's think about the following scenario:

Your ship is two weeks away from a major inspection and the Commanding Officer is very concerned with the status of the preparations. On Wednesday, the CO makes the decision that Saturday will be a mandatory workday for the ship in order to continue the final preps. You have tickets to a big football game on Saturday and have some friends coming into town to join you. You are disappointed and not looking forward to working until 1800 on a Saturday but how will you break this news to your division? If you complain to them and "damn the exec" in the process, how will their morale be affected? How much effort and enthusiasm will they display for the rest of the week and on Saturday if they know that you want to be there less than they do?

By claiming ownership of the CO's decision and displaying a high level of command buy-in, you may still get some grumbles among your sailors but your positive attitude and support of the decision will make it easier for them to justify the sacrifice of their Saturday for the needs of the command.

2. Subordinates may begin to view you as merely a puppet of the " Exec"

By consistently pushing the blame of unpopular decisions up the chain of command, an officer is essentially passing off his or her role in any decisions. Sailors and Marines will see this kind of officer as nothing more than a middle manager as opposed to a leader.

3. Subordinates may question the validity of any decisions you make for yourself

This truth was best illustrated in "Damn Exec" when the Mount Captain questioned the decision of the Gunnery Officer at a pivotal moment during combat. By deferring ownership of unpopular decisions to superiors, an officer's credibility is damaged to the point that when he or she does have to make a tough decision, it is second guessed by the subordinates if there is no evidence of validation from above. Let's reexamine the scenario in section one. What if it was you who desired your division to come in on a Saturday because of an unproductive work week or an upcoming assessment? If you were a "Damn Exec" leader, your sailors may seriously question your authority to give that level of order and may even seek verification from another officer.

Role play: How would you present this directive to your sailors or marines at morning quarters formation?

In closing, be an officer that demonstrates ownership. Although not always easy, it is fundamental to being a commissioned officer. Supporting your chain of command and command level decisions is an important part of being a military officer. If you are constantly damning the exec, your subordinates may begin damning you through a loss of respect and support.

Questions for review:

1. Why is it important for junior officers to buy in to organizational decisions, even when they disagree?
2. Why would subordinates be more likely to challenge a leader that damns the exec than one that demonstrates ownership of unpopular decisions?

16 *Moral Leadership*

- List Dr. Albert Pierces' four steps of Moral Leadership.
- Describe how VADM Stockdale personified this moral leadership with specific examples and be able to apply the model to your life as a career military officer.

Vice Admiral
James Bond Stockdale
1923-2005

An American Hero

Vice Admiral James Bond Stockdale, Naval aviator, senior Navy Prisoner of War in Vietnam, Medal of Honor recipient, hero, author and academic, has died at the age of 81 after a lengthy battle with Alzheimer's disease.

Admiral Stockdale was born on December 23, 1923 in Abingon, Illinois. After graduating from the Naval Academy in 1946, he attended flight training in Pensacola, FL and in 1954 was accepted to the Navy Test Pilot School where he quickly became a standout and served as an instructor for a brief time. Stockdale's flying career took him west, and in 1962 he earned a Master's Degree in International Relations from Stanford University. He was the first to amass more than one thousand hours in the F-8U Crusader, then the Navy's hottest fighter, and by the early 1960's Stockdale was at the very pinnacle of his profession when he commanded a Navy fighter squadron.

In August 1964, Stockdale played a key role in the Gulf of Tonkin incident, which the Johnson Administration used to justify large-scale military action in Vietnam. Stockdale always maintained that he had not seen enemy vessels during the event, but the next morning, August 6, 1964, he was ordered to lead the first raid of the war on North Vietnamese oil refineries.

On September 9, 1965 at the age of 40, Stockdale, Commanding Officer, VF51 and Carrier Air Group Commander (CAG-16) was catapulted from the deck of the USS Oriskany for what would be the final mission. While returning from the target area, his A-4 Skyhawk was hit by anti-aircraft fire. Stockdale ejected, breaking a bone in his back. Upon landing in a small village he badly dislocated his knee, which subsequently went untreated and eventually left him with a fused knee joint and a very distinctive gait.

Stockdale wound up in Hoa Lo Prison, the infamous "Hanoi Hilton", where he spent the next seven years as the highest ranking naval officer and leader of American resistance against Vietnamese attempts to use prisoners for propaganda purposes. Despite being kept in solitary confinement for four years, in leg irons for two years, physically tortured more than 15 times, denied medical care and malnourished, Stockdale organized a system of communication and developed a cohesive set of rules governing prisoner behavior. Codified in the acronym BACK

U.S. (Unity over Self), these rules gave prisoners a sense of hope and empowerment, which many credited with giving them the strength to endure their lengthy ordeal. Drawing largely from principles of stoic philosophy, notably Epictetus' The Enchiridion, Stockdale's courage and decisive leadership was an inspiration to POWs.

The climax of the struggle of wills between American POWs and their captors came in the spring of 1969. Told he was to be taken "downtown" and paraded in front of foreign journalists, Stockdale slashed his scalp with a razor and beat himself in the face with a wooden stool knowing that his captors would not display a prisoner who was disfigured. Later, after discovering that some prisoners had died during torture, he slashed his wrists to demonstrate to his captors that he preferred death to submission. This act so convinced the Vietnamese of his determination to die rather than to cooperate that the Communists ceased the torture of American prisoners and gradually improved their treatment of POWs. Upon his release from prison in 1973, Stockdale's extraordinary heroism became widely known, and he was awarded the Congressional Medal of Honor by President Gerald Ford in 1976.

He was one of the most highly decorated officers in the history of the Navy, wearing twenty six personal combat decorations, including two Distinguished Flying Crosses, three Distinguished Service Medals, two Purple Hearts, and four Silver Star medals in addition to the Medal of Honor. He was the only three star Admiral in the history of the Navy to wear both aviator wings and the Medal of Honor.

When asked what experiences he thought were essential to his survival and ultimate success in the prison, Admiral Stockdale referred to events early in his life: his childhood experiences in his mother's local drama productions which encouraged spontaneity, humor, and theatrical timing; the lessons of how to endure physical pain as a football player in high school and college; and his determination to live up to the promise he made to his father upon entering the Naval Academy that he would be the best midshipmen he could be. It was the uniquely American ability to improvise in tight situations, Stockdale believed, which gave him the confidence that the POWs could outwit their captors and return home with honor despite their dire situation.

In 1984, Admiral Stockdale and his wife Sybil co-authored *In Love and War*, detailing his experiences in Vietnam as well as her experiences founding the League of American Families of POWs and MIAs at the same time she raised their four sons. After serving as the President of the Naval War College, Stockdale retired from the Navy in 1978 and embarked on a distinguished academic career including 15 years as a Senior Research Fellow at the Hoover Institute of War, Revolution and Peace where he wrote numerous articles, published *A Vietnam Experience: Ten Years of Reflection, Thoughts of a Philosophical Fighter Pilot*, was awarded eleven honorary doctoral degrees, and lectured extensively on the stoicism of Epictetus and on those character traits which serve one best when faced with adversity. In 1992 he graciously agreed to the request from his old friend H. Ross Perot to stand in as the vice presidential candidate of the Reform Party. Stockdale disliked the glare of publicity and partisan politics, but throughout the campaign he comported himself with the same integrity and dignity that marked his entire career.

Upon his retirement in 1979, the Secretary of the Navy established the Vice Admiral Stockdale Award for the Inspirational Leadership presented annually in both the Pacific and Atlantic fleet. Admiral Stockdale was a member of the Navy's Carrier Hall of Fame and The National Aviation Hall of Fame, and he was an Honorary Fellow in the Society of Experimental Test Pilots.

Can you see any connection with Stockdales' behavior while in captivity at the "Hanoi Hilton" and our lesson on "Staying on Track"?

▣ Moral Leadership—The Stockdale Model[1]
Dr. Albert Pierce

I was invited to be the principal speaker at the fourth annual James Bond Stockdale Symposium on Leadership and Ethics at the University of San Diego, which was held in April of 2001. My topic was moral leadership, a challenge that was simultaneously fitting and intimidating with Admiral Stockdale sitting in the room! What encouraged me to press on was that I had developed my model from Admiral Stockdale himself—not only from what he had written, but more so from what he had done. This is the model I will use here.

As I studied his career and life, especially those years in the Hanoi prison, and read his works, I came to believe that one can derive a simple, workable model for moral leadership from him. Moral leadership, Stockdale-style, involves:

(1) setting noble goals of great moral worth;

(2) taking active steps to pursue those goals;

(3) being willing, in pursuit of those noble goals, to accept costs and to pay a price personally; and

(4) being willing to ask, even order, those subordinate to you, those close to you, to accept similar costs and to pay a similar price.

It's a package deal—you have to do all four to practice true moral leadership.

Though simple, this model is more complex and certainly more demanding than some you read or hear about. There are those who would have us believe that moral leadership is merely a matter of having noble goals, or of declaring or preaching noble goals. They are the ones who think, or even say in effect, "I must be a moral leader. Look at how inspiring my goals are! Look at the lofty speech I just gave! Look at the vision I've laid out! Look at the dreams I've articulated!"

Then, too, there are those who set and actively pursue their goals, willing to pay even severe prices. But, if their goals are self-serving, or perverted, or evil, that is hardly moral leadership. Think of Stalin, Pol Pot, Saddam Hussein, or Osama Bin Laden.

And there are those who set noble goals, pursue them, but draw back when it starts to cost them or theirs something tangible and dear. They draw the line at paying a price. Not a new phenomenon, to be sure, but one I think is all too common in the American experience over the past couple of decades. I'll return to this later and more specifically.

Back to the model and the man it is derived from. In his POW years, James B. Stockdale first set himself two noble goals: to remain loyal to his country and to remain loyal to his troops, those other POWs under his command. There were endless ways he could have violated those loyalties, and the North Vietnamese were experts in trying to get him to do so!

Second, Stockdale set out from the very beginning to pursue those noble goals by his deeds, not just his words tapped out in code on prison walls. As he had from the cockpit of his combat aircraft, he continued to fight the war, now by other means, behind bars. His fellow prisoners and he set up clandestine communications networks. They sought out new prisoners to inculcate them into this new society, to make sure no one of them had reason to feel he was alone. In a phrase, he took command!

---

[1]Pierce, A. C. (2003). "A Model for Moral Leadership: Contemporary Applications," *Occasional Paper 15*. The Maguire Center for Ethics and Public Responsibility.

Third, he demonstrated early on that he was willing to suffer great personal costs. "The good," he later wrote, "became individual self-sacrifice in defying our jailers." And sacrifice he did—brutal beatings, painful leg irons, years of isolation and solitary confinement, and inhuman torture. Here's his own description of the torture: "knocked down and then sat up to be bound with tourniquet-tight ropes, with care, by a professional, hands cuffed behind, jack-knifed forward, head pushed down between your ankles held secure in lugs attached to a heavy iron bar . . . knowing your upper-body circulation had been stopped, and feeling the ever-growing pain and the ever-closing-in of claustrophobia as the man standing on your back gives your head one last shove down with his heel and you start to gasp and vomit. . . ." They called that "being put through the ropes."

Fourth, in addition to all that, Stockdale also asked, even ordered, his subordinates to suffer the same punishments and to pay the same price at a certain point in order to remain loyal to their country. Among the most poignant aspects of his POW story are the times, several times, in fact, when he tried to be compassionate with his troops and tell them to "just do what you think is right" in the face of intense interrogation and perhaps torture. And repeatedly they came back to him and said, as he put it, "We are in a spot like we've never been in before. But we deserve to maintain our self-respect, to have the feeling we are fighting back. We can't refuse to do every degrading thing they demand of us, but it's up to you, boss, to pick out the things we must all refuse to do, unless and until they put us through the ropes again. We deserve to sleep at night. We at least deserve to have the satisfaction that we are hewing to our leader's orders. Give us the list: What are we to demand to take torture for?" And he did. And they did.

That's moral leadership, Stockdale-style, his deeds and his words:

(1) Set noble goals.
(2) Take active steps to pursue them.
(3) Pay a price yourself, if necessary, for them.
(4) And also, if necessary, ask or order others near and dear to you to pay a price as well.

This model of moral leadership reflects values long exemplified in history and literature, the stories, factual and fictional, of our moral heroes and saints. Take, for example, Thomas More. Determined to remain faithful to his religious beliefs and to his God, More takes deliberate, though carefully modulated, steps to remain faithful to his beliefs and to his God, and—for as long as he can—to his king. But when the oath is drawn up and he can no longer avoid and evade the confrontation of conscience, he resigns as lord chancellor, then is imprisoned in the Tower of London, a punishment he stoically accepts.

But the price is paid not just by Thomas More himself: When he loses his position, he loses his income, and his family is impoverished while he is imprisoned. In one of the most emotionally powerful scenes in Robert Bolt's play *A Man For All Seasons*, More's wife Alice, daughter Meg, and son-in-law Roper visit him in his damp, dank Tower cell. They do not agree with his stand. Indeed, they have all signed the oath he in conscience could not, yet *they* are suffering because of *his* choices. When his beloved Meg starts to taunt him about what life is like at home, he recoils, "Don't, Meg. . . . Meg, have done! . . . The King's more merciful than you. He doesn't use the rack."

The Tower is easier for him to take than being confronted with the harsh reality of his family's deprivation and pain. With the stroke of a pen he could free himself from the Tower and his family from their suffering, but he asks *them* to pay a price

How might you prepare yourself now to be able to withstand the kinds of challenges and pressures that VADM Stockdale endured, to "return with honor" as well?

for *his* principled pursuit of *his* noble goal. It's a package—the noble goal, the active pursuit of it, the personal price willingly paid, and the willingness to have his nearest and dearest pay as well. That's moral leadership!

Questions for review:

1. Why is the Stockdale Model of Leadership a "Moral Leadership"?
2. How might popularity and subordinate regard for leadership come into conflict when following the Stockdale Model of Moral Leadership?
3. Would the Stockdale Model of Moral Leadership be a good fit for you given your values, personality and talents?

17 *Leadership Case Study*

Interdiction in Afghanistan

Written by CAPT Bob Schoultz

*The below case study is a fictionalized account based on an incident that
actually happened. Some details have been modified, but the key portions
of the incident happened as described.*

It was 2000 hours, March 2002 in the Joint Special Operations Task Force (JSOTF)
headquarters in Afghanistan, and LCDR Reynolds had just returned from the chow
tent where he had lingered talking with some of the other officers on the JSOTF
staff. LCDR Reynolds was a SEAL officer in charge of the SEALs assigned to JSOTF
conducting Special Operations during Operation Enduring Freedom. Upon returning to the headquarters building to catch up on paper work and review intelligence
reports, he was summoned by the JSOTF Operations Officer, LTC Thompson, who
wanted to talk to him about a mission they had just received.

LTC Thompson handed LCDR Reynolds an intelligence report and a copy of an
email that had just arrived from the Operations Officer of the Land Forces Component Commander (LFCC). The email directed the JSOTF Commander to provide a
concept of operations for interdicting a vehicle convoy of Al Qaeda and Taliban terrorists that was expected to be moving down a road about 70 miles to the south the
next morning sometime after 0730, apparently trying to escape Afghanistan into
Pakistan. It was believed that the convoy might include some key Taliban or Al
Qaeda leadership. The LFCC wanted the mission concept in two hours. This meant
essentially that the staff wanted to know if the JSOTF thought they could undertake
the mission, what support they would need, and whether their plan could be decon-
flicted with other ongoing missions. LTC Thompson had already contacted MAJ
Mark Wyatt, the XO of the Army H47 Helicopter squadron who would be over
momentarily to look at the mission with LCDR Reynolds and his men. The mission
was to interdict the convoy, and to capture if possible, kill if necessary, any suspected members of Al Qaeda or Taliban who they might encounter.

LCDR Reynolds knew he had limited time to plan, rehearse, and go over contingencies with his team. Tight time-lines had become standard, but they were all fully

aware of the increased risk they assumed when they had less time to prepare. A tight time line meant less time to consider and plan for the numerous 'what ifs,' to carefully check the intelligence, and make sure that everyone knew the plan and its various 'branches and sequels.' A recent tragedy could at least in part be attributed to a very abbreviated planning and rehearsal timeline. In a high risk, high stakes operation, a SEAL reconnaissance team had been ambushed on insertion by Al Qaeda forces who had been undetected during the pre-mission reconnaissance. The team had been surprised, and two of their friends and teammates had been killed as well as a number of Rangers, under the relentless fire of the enemy. The deaths of these teammates were fresh in the minds of his men, and had only steeled their resolve to do whatever it took to find and kill these terrorists. But the enemy was not to be underestimated—LCDR Reynolds and his men knew that their planning must be thorough, and in quick reaction, emergent missions, they always had to weigh the trade off between the opportunities presented by late breaking intelligence, and the increased risk of a short planning cycle.

The risks to rapid and short fused planning however had taken an ugly twist two days earlier, when LCDR Reynolds and his team had seen first hand the tragic, but unintended consequences that can come from fast paced operations and decisions made with incomplete or inadequate intelligence. Several days earlier overhead surveillance had seen armed men around a walled compound and corroborating intelligence had indicated that this compound would be used for a meeting of high level Taliban officials. A precision guided missile was launched and struck the main building of the compound during the window when the meeting was scheduled to take place. LCDR Reynolds and his men had been staged to go into the compound minutes after the missile struck to gather any intelligence that remained, capture and treat any wounded, and to determine whether any of the dead or wounded were key Taliban or Al Quada leaders. When they arrived, they found the dead on target had been non-combatants—farmers and their families who were living in the compound. The weapons that were found were personal fire arms that virtually all rural Afghanis possessed and carried for self protection. LCDR Reynolds and his men were shaken by the gruesome results of this miscalculation: elderly people, farmers, women, children, with no apparent connection to the enemy. After determining that there was no exploitable intelligence on the target, he and his men returned to base and reported to his superiors what had happened including his dismay at the mistake. He then refocused his efforts on being ready for his next mission. Part of preparing for the next mission involved dealing with the psychic effects of this one; he contacted the chaplain, told him what had happened, and asked him to talk to the men. Afterward, he knew that having the chaplain meet with them had made a difference, to some of the men more than others, but it felt like the right thing to have done after witnessing, and in a sense participating in the tragic consequences of a mistake in war.

After receiving the mission to interdict the convoy from LTC Thompson, LCDR Reynolds knew what to do and started going into his mission planning routine, which had become almost automatic. He was the mission commander, and MAJ Wyatt and the H47s would be under his tactical command. This was just like the seemingly hundreds of exercises he'd conducted, and similar to many of the missions he'd recently conducted during this war. The years of training were paying off. His team was gelling into the type of unit he and every other military officer wants to lead: they only needed to be pointed in the right direction, with a good mission concept and clear commander's intent, and then the plan and preparation just seemed to come together. If everything went as planned and as rehearsed, his role in the execution of the operation would be minimal—communicate with higher headquarters and keep the squad leaders informed about any new developments, and let the squad leaders execute the plan. But of course, nothing ever goes exactly as planned, and it would be his job to make immediate adjustments to whatever unforeseen circumstances they would find, and understand the ripple effect that changes to the plan inevitably caused. That was what he got paid for.

Intelligence indicated that ongoing allied operations were putting significant pressure on Al Qaeda and Taliban forces in Southeast Afghanistan. This increasing pressure was making local Al Qaeda and Taliban movement and operations more and more difficult. Allied forces had received an intelligence tip that some senior leaders, with a group of their armed supporters, would be attempting to escape into Pakistan by vehicle soon after first light the following day. The enemy had already realized that allied aircraft routinely and easily targeted vehicles moving at night; consequently, the terrorists were now seeking to blend in with the normal daylight traffic on the roads. It appeared that Taliban and Al Qaeda were having some success in escaping into Pakistan blending in with the stream of refugees coming out of Afghanistan.

The intelligence indicated that a convoy of three vehicles would be leaving a particular village the next morning and moving toward Pakistan. The vehicles would be SUV's of the Toyota Land Cruiser type and/or compact pick up trucks full of people traveling south on the one road leading to Pakistan. Intelligence sources indicated that normally, the terrorists put their heavily armed men in lead vehicles as an armed reconnaissance element, while the leadership with their personal armed guards would follow some distance behind, maintaining communications with the lead vehicles about any difficulties encountered. Also, and particularly worrisome, were the indicators that the terrorists were probably carrying "Man-portable Air Defense Systems" (MANPADS), specifically, Soviet-era SA-7 shoulder-fired missiles, which are particularly effective against helicopters, especially during daylight when helicopters can easily be seen.

In short order, his men had worked out a plan with MAJ Wyatt and his team. Also the intelligence planners had coordinated with the assigned overhead surveillance; Navy P-3 aircraft would be watching the road and it would be their mission to find and track the targeted vehicles. A very difficult part of the mission was to 'interdict' the convoy in such a way as to achieve complete surprise, while still offering the opportunity for the occupants of the vehicles to surrender without putting his own men at risk. "Capture if possible, kill if necessary" is always tricky, and frequently requires a split second decision, some clear indicator of hostile intent, but also an intuitive sense of threat. But capturing the occupants would be a great coup; he and his men knew that the key to unraveling the terrorist network in Afghanistan was intelligence, and the people in this convoy represented a potential gold mine of intelligence. The SEALs would capture them if they could, but if the terrorists resisted with lethal force, as they usually seemed to do, then the SEALs were to shoot to kill.

LCDR Reynolds went to see COL Smith, the JSOTF commander to discuss his perspective or any limitations he might have for this mission. With the tragedy of the mission a couple of days previously still on his mind, LCDR Reynolds also wanted to know how certain they were of the intelligence, and whether the rules of engagement had changed. The rules of engagement define the circumstances under which lethal force can be used, and what are the restrictions in the use of that force. COL Smith replied that he understood the intelligence to be quite reliable and the rules of engagement hadn't changed. If the vehicles they encounter demonstrate hostile intent, by displaying or firing weapons, they are legitimate targets. COL Smith believed that the reason higher headquarters wanted the JSOTF to send helos and SEALs to do this mission, rather than targeting them from a distance, was because of the desire not to repeat the mistake of two days ago, with which LCDR Reynolds was only too familiar. That said, he reminded LCDR Reynolds that his tactics had to take into account the desire to bring back prisoners if at all possible, while not taking undue risk. In other words, bring back prisoners if you can, but not if it means taking significant risks with the lives of any of your men. COL Smith reiterated to LCDR Reynolds that the rules of engagement gave him all the guidance he needed.

That was what LCDR Reynolds wanted to hear. He felt the rules of engagement as they stood made sense, and gave him and his team the latitude to exercise their professional judgment to complete the mission and stay alive. Rapid assessment of hostile intent in a fast moving tactical environment is a standing requirement, and they had rehearsed and talked through a wide variety of situations many times. He and his men knew the value of prisoners, but they also knew the value of aggressiveness and firepower to staying alive in a gunfight. Their tactics, their survival, and their mission success depended on "Surprise, Speed, and Violence of Action"—there was no room for timidity. Yet they had recently witnessed the tragic results of "Surprise, Speed and Violence of Action" exercised without good judgment—in other words, aggressiveness and firepower misapplied.

V

The plan came together quickly—it had to. MAJ Wyatt would be the lead helo pilot for this mission; LCDR Reynolds would be in his helo. There would be a total of three helos, referred to as Chalk One (with MAJ Wyatt and LCDR Reynolds), and Chalks Two and Three which would carry the rest of the SEALs, led by LCDR Reynolds' Assistant Officer in Charge and Platoon Chief respectively. They talked through the contingencies with the pilots and went over the map, and had the intel guys coordinate with the P3's doing the overhead surveillance.

The plan was submitted and quickly approved. The plan was simple and made sense, and at any rate, there was little time to debate it. Their plan had them taking off at 0645 the next morning and flying to a point near the road where they would loiter at a low altitude, visually and audibly sheltered from the road by the mountains, and wait for a cue from the P3 watching the road. When the P3 saw what appeared to be the convoy, it would notify the helos, and vector them to the vehicles on the road. The helos would then move in under the cover of the mountains and surprise the convoy, quickly determine whether to take the vehicles under fire, or if in doubt, land and put the SEALs on the ground, and let the SEALs make the final determination. The helos would be available to provide cover fire or extraction, as required.

Everyone was very aware of the threat of shoulder fired SA-7's, to which the helos were very vulnerable. An SA-7 missile, in the hands of a reasonably proficient operator, could spell disaster. In daylight however, helos are also easy prey and vulnerable to small arms fire, and bullets from an AK47 can puncture the skin of their aircraft killing and wounding pilots and passengers. A couple of lucky shots from an AK47 can also bring down a helo and kill everyone on board. As the events in Mogadishu and "Black Hawk Down" had made clear, being in a low-flying helo, near the enemy in daylight is very risky business.

Early the next morning, all went as planned. LCDR Reynolds even got a couple of hours of sleep prior to his meeting at 0530 with his squad leaders and the helo pilots, to go over the plan and review details, one final time prior to launch. The SEALs embarked the three H47's, and after all systems checked out and the pilots had established communications with the P3, they took off and headed for the designated loiter point. After about 40 minutes of flight time, they arrived at the loiter point, again checked in with the P3 and began flying in low slow circles, far enough away from the road so as not to be heard, yet close enough to respond quickly when called by the P3.

LCDR Reynolds had been through this drill many times before. Sitting in the helo, with the headset on, partially listening to the relaxed banter of the pilots, he was lost in his own thoughts with the muffled hum and shake of the helo in the background of his awareness. Waiting for the call he mentally walked through the plan for the operation and its various contingencies; how they would make their approach to the convoy, how quickly they would have to determine threat level and response. How far back would the trail vehicle be with the so-called leaders? Would they stumble upon one of the key leaders of the Taliban or Al Qaeda? Did they really have SA-7's?

He pushed from his mind what would happen if the bad guys could get off a shot at the helos with an SA-7 before they could be neutralized. Worrying about it wouldn't do anything. He knew the pilots were very concerned as well; they had discussed it during the planning. But LCDR Reynolds also knew they had a lot going for them on this op—the confidence and skill that comes from extensive training and lots of experience. Surprise, Speed, Violence of Action—their keys to survival, the keys to success.

Approximately 20 minutes after arriving at the loitering point, LCDR Reynolds heard on the head set that the P3 had spotted what appeared to be the target convoy: two pickup trucks traveling together, followed about a mile back by another pick up truck. It would be about 20 minutes before the vehicles reached that section of the road where LCDR Reynolds and the helo pilots had determined that the terrain gave them the greatest advantage for surprise, and the bad guys the least opportunities for escape, on vehicle or on foot. After discussing it briefly with MAJ Wyatt, LCDR Reynolds advised the SEAL Leading Petty Officer (LPO) in his helo what he had just heard, and the LPO alerted the rest of the SEALs. The SEALs then seemed to come alive. Up to that point, they had been sitting in the back with their eyes closed, some probably dozing lightly, some probably rehearsing the mission in their heads, some probably thinking of things completely unrelated to this operation. But now all the men were alert and focused, checking their gear one more time, adjusting their position to be better prepared to exit the helo in a hurry.

MAJ Wyatt continued to get information from the P3. The convoy was continuing down the road toward the interdiction point. After about 10 minutes, the P3 crew advised MAJ Wyatt that it was time to leave the loiter position and begin moving toward the road. LCDR Reynolds advised his LPO and the LPO passed it on to the men in the helo.

As the helos approached the interdiction point, they stayed very low to the ground, flying at about 50 feet, to minimize the chances that the 'wop, wop, wop' of their approach would get over the mountains and alert the convoy. At about 2 minutes out, the P3 passed on some disturbing news. "We've lost the trail vehicle. We haven't seen it for several minutes—last we saw it was about 3 miles back. It might be masked by the mountains between us and them. But two vehicles are on final into your target zone and will be there in a couple of minutes."

"Damn!" LCDR Reynolds thought. Quick decision time. The plan had been for him and MAJ Wyatt to break off from Chalks Two and Three in the last twenty seconds, and to go to the trail vehicle, to permit a simultaneous hit on the lead and trail vehicles. He was going to the trail vehicle, because that was where the real valuable targets would be—the leaders. LCDR Reynolds quickly considered the possibility of his helo flying thru the mountains searching for the trail vehicle while Chalks Two and Three were taking care of the lead vehicles. There was no telling where that vehicle could be or what it could be doing. Even though the primary target was the leadership in the trail vehicle, with this new uncertainty, LCDR Reynolds did not want to take off on a potential wild goose chase, splitting his force, now that the plan may be coming unraveled at the last minute.

He told MAJ Wyatt he wanted to keep all three helos together until they had a better idea what they were up against, or at least until the P3 found the third vehicle. MAJ Wyatt concurred and told the Chalks two and three that the plan had changed and they would stay together and all hit the lead vehicles. They then started their climb up and over the final hill that lay between them and the road, and presumably the two lead vehicles. LCDR Reynolds ensured that the word was passed to the SEALs in Chalks Two and Three. Everyone in the helos was on full alert, the pilots and crew calmly passing information back and forth, the SEALs on their feet, looking out the windows, weapons at the ready, on safe.

 # VII

As they popped over the summit of the hill, they saw at five hundred feet below them and to the left, two pick up trucks approaching from the north. LCDR Reynolds suddenly experienced that familiar jolt of adrenaline, a combination of stress, excitement, responsibility and complete focus. The helos came over the crest of the hill and headed down low and fast, directly toward the vehicles, approaching at full speed, circling from left to right, counter-clockwise. LCDR Reynolds stared intently at the occupants in the back of the pick up truck, looking for any sign of hostile intent. First the front vehicle, and then the rear vehicle stopped when they saw and heard the helos, and he saw men get out and begin running. Then LCDR Reynolds thought he saw weapons and muzzle flashes. LCDR Reynolds was looking over the shoulder of the left door gunner, who also saw the weapons and muzzle flashes, and immediately opened up on the lead vehicle with his mini gun, shifting to the second vehicle as soon as he could get a good shot at it. At about that time, the second helo picked up the lead vehicle and started cutting it to pieces. LCDR Reynolds saw more muzzle flashes and then saw men fall. No sign of anyone setting up to fire an SA-7. The helos passed the vehicles flying fast and low and putting out a huge volume of fire. The two pick up trucks were being cut to pieces, and men who had not been able to get out of the vehicles in time were being chewed up as well. Those who had left the trucks were scrambling in chaos and disorder, some firing at the helos, several of them falling victim to the withering fire coming from the door gunners. LCDR Reynolds saw that this part was going well. Now, where was the trail vehicle with the leadership?

As his helo was turning to circle the vehicles and make an approach from the other side, LCDR Reynolds felt that Chalks Two and Three could handle this. He said to MAJ Wyatt on the headset, "Mark, I think they've got this under control. Let's go find the trail vehicle. What do you think?" "Roger," he responded. "I'll advise Chalk Two to take control here." (At which point he pulled up out of the pattern and told the pilot of Chalk Two that he and LCDR Reynolds were detaching to go look for the other vehicle.) The P3 had just called to tell them that they still had no sign of the third vehicle. MAJ Wyatt told the P3 what he was doing, and then he turned and headed up the road down which they had seen the two vehicles coming.

 **VIII**

LCDR Reynolds called his LPO up to him, took off his head set, and yelled over noise of the helo to tell him what they were doing. The LPO nodded and then went to the back of the helo to tell the other SEALs who, still very tense and focused, were looking toward him with some anticipation. They knew that something was up. LCDR Reynolds then moved to the door gunner on the right side of the aircraft, since the helo was flying with the road on the right side. The longer it took to find the vehicle, the greater the risk. They had to assume that the trail vehicle had heard the helos and the gunfire, and perhaps even had radio communication from the lead vehicles. That gave the bad guys plenty of time to set up on the helo—they would certainly be expecting them. These were the leaders, and they would have the most devoted soldiers with them as bodyguards, and probably the best weapons, possibly to include SA-7's. Helos are big, easy targets in daylight, especially if you know that they are coming. The right door gunner had not expended any ammunition on the assault on the other two vehicles—he was keyed up, ready, and had a full load of ammo.

As the H47 flew down the narrow valley that hugged the road, there was an intense and anxious silence on the headsets. The pilots, crew and LCDR Reynolds knew that this was where they were most vulnerable. Though they may not achieve complete surprise, they hoped to overwhelm the bad guys by hitting them suddenly and with overwhelming firepower. But they had to be lucky and good.

As the H47 turned a corner in the valley, they looked up a narrow canyon. LCDR Reynolds saw the pick up truck just as he heard MAJ Wyatt calmly say, "There they are." What looked like a truck full of people was stopped on the side of the road about 200 yards ahead to the right. The door gunner had a clear shot, and he quickly swung his mini-gun and took aim.

 IX

LCDR Reynolds suddenly sensed something wasn't right. Just as the truck came into view, just as the door gunner swung his weapon in the direction of the truck, just as MAJ Wyatt said, "There they are," LCDR Reynolds in an instant realized that no one was running from the vehicle, and he thought he saw someone in the truck (a woman?) hold something up high as if to display it to the helo. He grabbed the door gunner and yelled "NO!" and held his fist in front of the door gunner's face in the signal for "Stop what you're doing!" The door gunner was confused, but he followed the order and didn't shoot. The helo continued toward the truck, low and fast as LCDR Reynolds looked hard at the truck, looking for signs of hostile intent. In the two long seconds it took to get to and pass the truck, they noticed that this was different from the other vehicles. No one left the truck. No one ran for cover. It was hard to tell whether these people were armed or not, given the speed and approach angle of the helo. The helo sped past the truck so close that the people in the bed of the truck were ducking from the rotor wash, and LCDR Reynolds saw that he had been right—it had been a woman he'd seen, and what she was holding up appeared to be a baby. He didn't see any weapons yet or anyone displaying hostile intent. That didn't mean they weren't bad guys, and that they weren't a threat. LCDR Reynolds told MAJ Wyatt to circle around and land in front of the vehicle, far enough away to be safe, but close enough for the SEALs to quickly envelope the vehicles, clarify the situation, and take appropriate action.

After speeding by the vehicle, MAJ Wyatt exhaled. When he didn't hear the door gunner firing, he thought the weapon had jammed and that they were 'done for'. He flew the H47 at full throttle farther down the road, banked around a bend in the road, and then ascended to fly over a hill to come back to a position several hundred yards in front of the vehicle. He was ever mindful of the possibility that an SA-7 was being prepared for the first clear shot. LCDR Reynolds dashed back to his LPO and told him that the SEALs would debark and move in to observe the vehicle—it wasn't clear if these were hostiles. He then moved back to the front of the helo so that he could get oriented prior to landing.

The helo flared and landed fast. The SEALs quickly debarked out the rear ramp and moved to outside the rotor-wash to set up a hasty perimeter in the nearest cover. The H47 lifted off the ground, turned 180 degrees away from the direction of the vehicle, and took off. The SEALs patrolled to the vicinity of the pick up truck and observed the passengers not moving, sensing their danger. The LCDR Reynolds was able to signal to the passengers to move away from the pick up truck. He then had his team search the pickup truck and its passengers, and determined that they were neither Taliban nor Al Qaeda leadership, nor was there any evidence that they had any connection to them. Either the intel had been wrong about the three-vehicle convoy, or the situation had changed since the source had reported it. It didn't matter. These people did not fit the profile of Taliban or Al Qaeda and happened to be in the wrong place at the wrong time.

LCDR Reynolds realized that he had narrowly avoided making a tragic mistake. He was still worried about a possible trail vehicle, and called MAJ Wyatt to ask him if he had any other information. MAJ Wyatt had been in touch with the P3, and had gone to altitude himself to see if he could see any other vehicles, and there was nothing. LCDR Reynolds then got on the radio with the SEALs who were on the ground at the site of the two lead vehicles. They had already debarked from the helos, taken control of the site with no resistance, and they were inspecting the dead and wounded. All were males and had been carrying arms. Eight were dead, the three wounded were being treated, and they had taken two unscathed prisoners, who had survived the initial assault, and had stood with their hands raised when the SEALs approached. This was all good news.

LCDR Reynolds then had his LPO direct the civilians to sit down and to remain where they were. They were still sitting on the ground away from their pick up truck when the SEALs were picked up by the helo and flown to join their teammates at the site of the two lead vehicles.

COL Smith, the JSOTF Commander had heard that his helo pilots believed that LCDR Reynolds had taken undue risk during an operation from which they had just returned, and that this was causing some tension between the SEALs and Army helo crews. COL Smith had heard what had happened and was familiar with the events of the operation, but knew he needed to get the story directly from his two commanders. He called MAJ Wyatt and LCDR Reynolds into his office to get the issues out on the table.

LCDR Reynolds and MAJ Wyatt walked into his office, and after COL Smith indicated that he understood that there was some disagreement about how the operation had been conducted, MAJ Wyatt, clearly emotional, addressed the issue right up front:

"Sir, we could have all been killed, and lost the bird. We were a sitting duck. We're real lucky Tom was right, because if he'd been wrong, we would have a lot of dead Americans and this war would look a lot different right now." MAJ Wyatt stepped back and exhaled slowly.

COL Smith looked at LCDR Reynolds and indicated it was his turn to speak.

"Sir, he's right—we could have all been killed—if I'd been wrong. But I wasn't. I was in charge. And I was right. I made the call based on what I saw, and what I sensed, and I stand by it. It was clearly the right thing to do. We knew we were at risk, but we still have to do the right thing."

MAJ Wyatt jumped on him. "Right Tom, but all the indicators were there that these were bad guys, and you didn't KNOW, and my guys and yours were sitting ducks for several seconds, and that put not only all of us, but potentially the whole focus of everything we're doing here at risk. Can you imagine what this task force would be doing right now if those had been bad guys we had taken an SA-7 right down the throat? I don't want to kill innocent people either, but if you had been wrong, nobody, I mean NOBODY, would forgive you. And we'd all be dead."

"Mark—it just didn't feel right—and, we saw no hostile intent."

"We didn't have time to see hostile intent, Tom! When we took off after that third vehicle, my understanding was that we were going hunting. We knew we had flushed the bad guys, and at that point, we were in a gunfight. When we came around that bend in the road, it was either them, or us. When you stopped my gunner, and I didn't hear the guns, I figured it was us. I expected a flash and woosh and then lights out."

"You two calm down and come back and see me when you get your stuff squared away," interrupted COL Smith. He knew that he was the one who had to take responsibility for risk, and if there was something unclear about risk, he needed to resolve it. "I'm going to have to think about this, and talk to the lawyers. Now get out of here and get some rest. We've got a bunch of other things hopping and we'll need you to be focused."

MAJ Wyatt and LCDR Reynolds left the Colonel's office and agreed to get together in a couple of hours after they had taken care of their men and their gear, and sorted out the other details from their mission. MAJ Wyatt was clearly still upset as he walked away to rejoin the other pilots preparing their reports.

As LCDR Tom Reynolds walked back to where his men were working, he thought about what his friend MAJ Mark Wyatt had said. He had gambled and won, but he had bet the whole farm—not just his farm, but the lives of everyone else in the helo, as well as the future capability of the Special Operations Task Force.

Questions:

1. Who is the mission commander, thus the Officer in Tactical Command, in this case? _____

2. Who were the primary planners for this mission and how long did they have to determine whether or not the mission could be done? _____

3. What weapon poses the greatest threat to this mission? _____

4. How did LCDR Reynolds and his men feel following the following their intelligence gathering mission on the compound struck by a precision guided missile just days prior? _____

5. What are the Rules of Engagement for this mission, and how are they different from previous missions? _____

   _____

6. What were the callsigns of the helos? _____

7. Are the door gunners SEALs or members of the helo aircrew?

   _____

8. Who coordinated with the P3 PRIOR to the execution of the mission? _____

   _____

9. How many vehicles were expected to be in the convoy? Where was the leadership expected to be in that convoy? What type(s) of vehicles were expected to be in the convoy? How many and what type(s) were actually reported by the P3 initially once onstation? _____

   _____

10. What was the goal of the mission? _____

    _____